THE HOUSE OF NOMURA

THE HOUSE OF NOMURA

THE INSIDE STORY OF THE LEGENDARY JAPANESE FINANCIAL DYNASTY

ALBERT J. ALLETZHAUSER

Arcade Publishing • New York
Little, Brown and Company

FIRST U.S. EDITION

Alletzhauser, Albert J., 1950–
    The house of Nomura: the inside story of the legendary Japanese financial
dynasty / Albert J. Alletzhauser. — 1st US ed.
        p.   cm.
    ISBN 1-55970-089-0
    1. Nomura Shōken Kabushiki Kaisha — History.   2. Stockbrokers — Japan.
    3. Securities industry — Japan. I. Title.
HG5774.5.A45   1990
332.6'2'0952 — dc20
                                                                89-48502
                                                                CIP

Published in the United States by Arcade Publishing, Inc., New York,
                        a Little, Brown company

                    10 9 8 7 6 5 4 3 2 1
                            MV PA
                PRINTED IN THE UNITED STATES

This is dedicated to my friends in Hong Kong and to the magical years of 1984 and 1985. To Ann Lackey, Mark Lawrence, Hans Tiedemann, Doug Clayton, Dick Leonard, Danny Rustemeyer, Pam MacLeod, Jonathan Lowe, Jeremy King, Arthur Lai, Marcus Brauchli and Cindy Babski.

CONTENTS

CONTENTS

Preface

Japan was built by people not machines. The reams of literature about the greatness of Japan Inc. and the marvellous corporate environment that exists in Japan are misleading. Villains and heroes abound in Japan alongside the incorrigible and incorruptible, yet the only refrain we hear is the cold, far-off, metallic clinking of Japan Inc.

Japan's business history is filled with legends. Its financial moguls rival the American banking genius of J.P. Morgan and the aggressive trading acumen of Jesse Livermore, while its railway tycoons match the vision of Cornelius Vanderbilt and the cunning of Jay Gould. The story here is of one of Japan's greatest stockmarket operators: that of Tokushichi Nomura II, born in 1878, the year of the founding of the Tokyo Stock Exchange. This is also the tale of post-war influence peddling: of how Tsunao Okumura used his friendship with Japan's prime ministers to promote the stockmarket; and of how Minoru Segawa, known as the 'fixer' of corporate Japan, played upon his connections with gangsters and politicians to forge Nomura into a global powerhouse.

Scores of books have been written about the rise to power of the Rockefellers and the mighty European Jewish merchant banking houses of London – the Rothschilds and the Warburgs. This is the story of the Buddhist Tokushichi Nomura, who built an empire comparable to any Western pre-war financial house. By World War II the thriving Nomura enterprise had become the tenth largest *zaibatsu*, or family oligarchy, in Japan. Then it was torn apart. General MacArthur stripped the Nomura heirs of their banks and brokerage houses, their real estate, plantation and mining interests, selling everything off to Nomura employees, although, as we shall see, some Nomura family members secretly retained assets worth a fortune today. However, a major difference between the Japan of yesterday and today is that corporate ownership is now firmly in the hands of institutions.

The first half of this book was the result of listening for hours over the weeks and years to the Nomura family telling me their story. They provided me with the family papers of Tokushichi, which my research assistants then translated. Over the years I researched the book, I spent much enjoyable time with Kozo Nomura, Tokushichi's sprightly septuagenarian nephew, who was dispossessed of his wealth in 1945. Then there was Tomohide Nomura, a scholarly man who helped me untangle his grandfather's corporate labyrinth. I became quite close to these two gentlemen and purposely did not involve them in anything relating to the present-day Nomura Securities, the one remaining splinter of Tokushichi Nomura's empire.

How did a small Osaka moneychanging firm founded in 1872 come to be such a dominant force in world finance over a hundred years after its birth? Riding his bicycle around the Osaka streets before the turn of the century, Nomura pioneered retail stockbrokerage in Japan, the buying and selling of shares for a fee. After World War II, the formidable Nomura sales force, under commission quota pressure, knocked door-to-door persuading and pleading with housewives and shopkeepers to buy stock. Meanwhile, Nomura's leaders helped fund the rise of Japan's post-war prime ministers, ensuring to this day favourable tax treatment for capital gains.

Bold headlines may sensationalize Japanese purchases of Western art, real estate or corporations, but it is the retail brokerage network to which Japanese finance, and the stockbrokers, still owe their greatness. Nomura alone has over five million customers, of whom 96 per cent are individuals.

Nomura accounts for 15 per cent of all traded volume on the Tokyo Stock Exchange, the world's largest stockmarket. When in the early 1980s it found that it had problems attaining a daily market share over 15 per cent, it simply created a new brokerage firm. It was called Kokusai, meaning international, and it grew in a few short years into Japan's fifth largest firm, ranking larger than most American brokerage houses. Counting in Nomura's many stockbrokerage subsidiaries, such as Kokusai, and its many affiliates, such as Sanyo Securities, the Nomura group transacts more than one out of every five shares traded in Japan.

The list goes on: Nomura has more assets under custody than the Daiichi Kangyo Bank, the world's largest bank; makes more money than any financial firm in the world; controls 20 per cent of the Japanese bond market; and dominates the Eurobond underwriting tables. There is more. Most people who have heard of Nomura think of it as a brokerage house, but Nomura has applied its sales tactics to other fields and now has the nation's fifth largest real estate firm and its second largest software firm, while its research operation, the largest in Japan, was known by Japanese as 'the brain of Nakasone', the prime minister until 1987.

Although most of this book is about Nomura Securities, I have not ignored Nomura's three little sisters, Daiwa, Nikko and Yamaichi. Together they comprise the 'big four'.

In writing this book, however, my aim was to do more than simply examine a present-day financial giant. How did it fit in with the cycles that nations, companies and people go through? Nomura Securities is symbolic of something greater than one firm breaking away to the top. Throughout history the most powerful nations have been those with the most money, the investing nations of the world. Britain ruled the globe in the nineteenth century with railways, coal and the pound sterling, only to be overtaken by the United States with the advent of the automobile, oil and the dollar in the twentieth century. Then came Japanese post-war industrial dominance over everything from petrochemicals to steel, electronics to automobiles. Nippon Steel began to overtake US Steel, Fuji Photo to displace Eastman Kodak and Toyota to vie with General Motors. Then the Japanese simply began taking over American giants to increase their market share, as Firestone fell to Bridgestone.

Within Japan itself a revolution was taking place. Sometime in the late 1970s and early 1980s finance became more important than manufacturing – the Ministry of Finance surpassed the Ministry of International Trade and Industry as the government's most authoritative arm. In 1975 another phenomenon came into being. Corporate Japan stopped using its local banker to borrow money and began tapping the shoulder of its local broker, in most cases Nomura, to raise money in the stockmarket. As if to symbolize Japan's new-found financial strength, Nomura overtook the Toyota Motor Company in 1987 to become Japan's most profitable firm.

Nomura's prowess could no longer be ignored and in the summer of 1988 *Time* magazine ran a cover story entitled 'Yen Power', with a no-nonsense picture of a slightly suspicious-looking Yoshihisa Tabuchi, Nomura's president, on the cover. The photograph was taken by Greg Davis, a well-known photo-journalist, who was allowed the rare opportunity of penetrating Nomura's inner sanctum.

While staying at the serene, gardened confines of the Nomura villa in Kyoto, Davis found the rumours of Tabuchi's suspicious nature justified. When Tabuchi gave Davis a tour of the Nomura villa, past the Noh theatre and pre-war residence of Tokushichi Nomura, he pointed out some special rooms which, he explained, were for secret meetings; Nomura even had the rooms swept for electronic listening devices. Whenever Nomura wanted to hold discussions with high-level businessmen, but were afraid of the Nomura head office being watched, Tabuchi had the businessmen flown into Osaka airport and secretly whisked off to the Kyoto villa an hour away. Davis found all this amusing and pointed up to the hills surrounding Kyoto. 'Couldn't your competitors use a telescope to spy on you here?' he asked jokingly. Tabuchi, however, took the question in earnest, frowned and walked on with a worried expression on his face.

A word about the Tabuchis: Yoshihisa Tabuchi, Nomura Securities' president, is called 'little Tabuchi' by the Japanese to differentiate him from Setsuya Tabuchi, or 'big Tabuchi', the firm's chairman. They are not related. Setsuya Tabuchi was born in 1923 and became president of Nomura Securities in 1978, ascending to chairman in 1985 when Yoshihisa Tabuchi became president. Although both men headed Nomura in its race for supremacy, I do not pay them as much attention as I pay to two others. Both Tabuchis are tough men. Big Tabuchi fought his way up on the corporate finance side, while little Tabuchi was always closer to the troops, earning his respect on the sales side. But both Tabuchis are historical footnotes compared with Tsunao Okumura and Minoru Segawa, who shaped post-war Nomura and thereby Japanese financial history.

Nomura's corporate wariness would have made the second half of *The House of Nomura* impossible to write had I confronted Nomura formally through their public relations department. But I took a different approach and phoned the oldest surviving members of the Nomura group of companies, asking to discuss their personal histories. Over a three-year period, with two exceptions, I found every door open.

I interviewed the senior man before asking for an audience with his younger colleagues. For example, after gaining access to the friendly Shoshi Kawashima, Nomura class of 1934, and chairman of Kokusai Securities, the powerful Nomura subsidiary, I was then free to secure meetings with his *kohai* or juniors in age. 'Juniors' in this case included some of Japan's renowned men of finance: Yokio Aida, class of 1948, then chairman of Nomura Investment Management, and the amiable Yoshio 'Terry' Terasawa, class of 1954, the first Japanese member of the New York Stock Exchange and the man who brought Japan to Wall Street. The network grew and word got around so that by the end of my stay in Japan, in 1988, Nomura men felt slightly ruffled if I had *not* interviewed them.

In this manner I spent two years searching through the memories of Nomura men, some old, some young, some at the centre of power in Japan and others forgotten, enjoying a retired life. I was frequently asked, 'How did you manage to get the Japanese to talk?'. That was the easy part. Once in the door I found that they all liked to talk about their life. The Japanese are no exception to the general rule, and I enjoyed listening. This book is the result of hundreds of interviews with Nomura men, Nomura women and Nomura family members, about each of whom a book could have been written. Many of the men with whom I spent long nights talking go unheralded in my acknowledgements, for fear of their jobs and for the sake of friendships.

When I began researching the House of Nomura in 1986, I was fascinated by the conspiratorial aspect of the Japanese stockmarket: how gangsters extorted Nomura, other securities firms and the rest of corporate Japan into yearly hush-money payments. Then there was the somewhat romantic notion of going off to elegant geisha restaurants and discussing how stocks were manipulated. I became close to a few speculative groups and was let in on some of their secrets before I decided it had gone far enough. It was disconcerting to find myself beginning to live the stories of the gangsters and speculators about whom I was writing. During the day I was working for James Capel selling Japanese stocks and warrants. Lunchtimes were usually spent interviewing Nomura people or holed up in the library of the Foreign Correspondents Club in Tokyo, while the evenings were spent talking or writing.

Most readers, including myself, dislike the disruptive stutter of footnotes, and sources are therefore given at the back of the book. As a general rule, I have not included any information for which I do not have two sources, either written or verbal. I had to be careful since there are hundreds of scurrilous journalists, disgruntled investors and fierce competitors who are always keen to disparage Nomura Securities, accusing Nomura of everything from insider trading to murder.

The first accusation, as with most Japanese securities firms, is true, but the second most certainly is not.

Then there were small pieces of information I simply could not verify. I was told by one senior Nomura manager that Nomura Securities wanted to offer Merrill Lynch 25 per cent of its own stock during the prolonged market crisis leading up to the Yamaichi Securities collapse of 1965. Retired Merrill Lynch executives, such as Donald Regan, have no recollection of such an offer – a stake that would later be worth over $13 billion. How I would have loved to have woven that into my text.

Dramatis Personae

Descriptions of the following people relate only to their situations within Nomura or to the context of this book.

Aida, Yokio: Nomura class of 1946 who became head of Nomura's international department. He was best known as chairman of Nomura Investment Management.

Aono, Harunobu: well-liked manager of the Nomura New York baseball team in 1983.

Araki, Shoko: cultural adviser to Nomura foreign trainees.

Bains, Dhana Singh: An Indian resident of Tokyo who successfully sued Nomura for trading improprieties in 1984.

Doi, Toshitsura: Osaka samurai and reputed father of Tokushichi Nomura I.

Egashira, Keisuke: Nomura class of 1954 who opened Nomura's London office in 1964. He left Nomura in 1982 to become president of Seibu International.

Fukuhara, Ken'ichi: A Nomura salesman in the late 1970s who was put through difficulties to procure stockmarket orders.

Hashimoto, Kisaku: newspaper reporter and first Japanese stockmarket analyst. Hired by Tokushichi Nomura II in 1905, he later rose to become president of Osakaya Shoten.

Iida, Seizo (1894-1976): president of Nomura from 1941 to 1947 when he was forcibly removed from office by occupation authorities.

Ikeda, Hayato: prime minister of Japan from 1960 to 1964 and former minister of finance and minister of international trade and industry. Known as the 'architect of the Japanese miracle'. As best friend of Tsunao Okumura, he ensured securities transactions would never fall prey to capital gains.

Inagaki, Mariko: Yoshio Terasawa's wife.

Ishida, Tadashi: Nomura class of 1946 and salesman who went on to manage Nomura New York in 1956.

Ito, Masanori: nicknamed 'the Apache' and 'the Godfather', he tried to corner every major department at Nomura. After taking control of the international department in 1978, he applied high-pressure Japanese sales tactics to overseas offices.

Itoyama, Eitaro (1942-   ): young LDP member and billionaire who used stockmarket to make a fortune. Itoyama tried to corner Yomiuri Land shares during the late 1970s and early 1980s. He is married to niece of Ryoichi Sasakawa, 'the world's richest man'.

Iwamoto, Einosuke: son of wealthy Osaka moneychanger. A friend of Tokushichi Nomura II and a stock speculator, he lost everything in the market and committed suicide.

Kamata, Narajiro: auditor of Nomura *zaibatsu* in the 1930s. Kamata uncovered fraud within Nomura Life Insurance and was later promoted to secretary of the Nomura Partnership. He helped save family assets during the dissolution.

Kaneoka, Koji: head of eponymous, short-term financing company in Tokyo that cut credit in 1986 in return for stock quotation listing.

Kataoka, Otogo (1881-1948): first head of Osaka-Nomura

Bank (1918) and later first president of Nomura Securities (1925).

Kawada, Fujio: a manager of Nomura Shinjuku branch who died as a result of being beaten by clients.

Kawashima, Shoshi: Nomura class of 1935 and first post-war head of Nomura New York. In 1982 he formed Kokusai Securities, becoming its first president.

Kiku: Tokushichi Nomura II's wife.

Kitao, Yoshitaka: head of sales for Nomura's New York office during the mid-1980s.

Kitaura, Kiichiro (1911-1985): president of Nomura Securities from 1968 to 1978 and known for setting up the Nomura Research Institute in 1965.

Kodama, Fujio: salesman and director of Oi Securities during Yamaichi crisis in 1965. Later became chairman of Wako Securities.

Komoto, Toshio: powerful LDP member and erstwhile head of MITI and the Economic Planning Agency. Founder of Sanko Steamship, the go-go stock of Japan in the early 1970s which foundered in 1982.

Matsukata, Takashi: head of Ministry of Finance secondary markets division during the Great Crash of 1987.

Matsuo, Tsutomu: newspaper reporter at *Nishi-Nippon Shimbun* and man who broke story on the Yamaichi crisis.

Miyazawa, Akira: head of Bank of Japan's securities bureau in 1965 during Yamaichi crisis and man who aided brokers during time of plight.

Nagasawa, Masao: Nomura class of 1934 who as head of international department in 1960s purged Shoshi Kawashima.

Nagata, Shuzo: Nomura salesman in the go-go years of the late 1950s who later took over as president of Kokusai Europe.

Nakazawa, Nobuo: Nomura class of 1968 who became one of the firm's youngest main board directors.

Noda, Iwajiro: Mitsui man appointed as second chairman of Holding Company Dissolution Committee.

Noda, Yoichiro: general manager of Nomura trading desk during Great Crash of 1987.

Nomura, Fumihide (1934-   ): son of Yoshitaro Nomura and grandson of Tokushichi Nomura II. Briefly heir to Nomura empire in 1945 before dissolution. Chairman of Nomura Construction company and former main board member of Nomura Securities.

Nomura, Jitsusaburo (1880-1919): beloved brother of Tokushichi Nomura II who had been earmarked to run the Nomura Bank before his sudden death.

Nomura, Keiji (1911-   ): eldest nephew of Tokushichi Nomura II and head of the Nomura Life Insurance Company before the dissolution.

Nomura, Kozo (1911-   ): nephew of Tokushichi Nomura II who was put in charge of Nomura East Indies. Began Nomura Microscience in the post-war years.

Nomura, Motogoro (1887-1954): youngest brother of

DRAMATIS PERSONAE

Tokushichi Nomura II who studied at Birmingham University and later ran the Nomura Bank.

Nomura, Sae: widow of Yoshitaro Nomura.

Nomura, Tokushichi I (1850-1908): Osaka moneychanger and illegitimate son of samurai who founded Nomura Shoten in 1872 as a shop to change gold, silver and copper coins.

Nomura, Tokushichi II (1878-1945): founder of Nomura *zaibatsu* who formed Nomura Securities in 1925. Known in childhood as 'Shinnosuke' and in this book as 'Nomura' or 'Tokushichi'.

Nomura, Tomohide (1935-): grandson of Tokushichi Nomura II and auditor of the Nomura Construction Company.

Nomura, Yoshitaro (1905-1945) aka Tokushichi Nomura III: short-lived, humanistic scion of the Nomura *zaibatsu* and son of the founder of Nomura group.

Ohtaka, Norm: westernized trading manager who served as head of Nomura trading desk in New York when the troops rebelled in 1985.

Okinori, Kaya: pre-war finance minister and friend of Tokushichi Nomura II. He was thrown into prison for Class A war crimes and upon release was hired by Nomura Securities as a senior adviser.

Okumura, Masiko: wife of Tsunao Okumura.

Okumura, Tetsuo: nephew of former Nomura Securities president. Began as a salesman in the 1950s and worked his way up to become head of Nomura's Global Trading Team, but left Nomura after the Great Crash of 1987.

Okumura, Tsunao (1903-1972): president of Nomura Securities from 1948 to 1959 and through political connections and social amiability rebuilt the house of Nomura.

Rondan Doyukai: notorious *sokaiya* group which extorts money from public companies in Japan by threatening annual meetings.

Saito, Andy: power-hungry head of equity sales for Nomura in New York during 1985 revolt. Sent back to Tokyo by president Akira Shimizu.

Sakurai, Haruhiko: Tokyo journalist who covers financial news and who broke story on Nomura's involvement with Rondan Doyukai.

Sasakawa, Ryoichi: ex-blackmarketeer with underworld ties. Now turned philanthropist, he presides over the Japan Shipbuilding Foundation, from which he distributes his wealth. Appears in this book as supporter of Itoyama and Sasaki in their bid for Yomiuri Land.

Sasaki, Shintaro: slightly dubious business tycoon who made millions in real-estate and hotel businesses. Father of Eitaro Itoyama.

Sasayama, Tadao: first chairman of Holding Company Liquidation Commission.

Segawa, Minoru (1906-): hands-on president of Nomura Securities from 1959 to 1968 and one of Japan's most influential men.

Sekine, Chozaburo: president of Yomiuri Land during Itoyama's attempted takeover. Married to the daughter of Matsutaro Shoriki, the founder of Yomiuri Land.

DRAMATIS PERSONAE

Shibusawa, Keizo: finance minister during early dissolution, grandson of Meiji industrialist Eiichi Shibusawa.

Shibayama, Washio: banker who lent money to save Nomura Shoten in 1907 and later joined Nomura as head of finance.

Shimizu, Akira: genteel former president of Nomura in New York under Yoshio Terasawa during 1985 revolt.

Shoriki, Matsutaro: father of professional baseball and TV in Japan and founder of Yomiuri leisure group. Close friend of Nomura presidents.

Suzuki, Juniichi: stockmarket speculator who pulled off largest greenmail in Japanese history by accumulating shares in Fujii, a confectionery company.

Tabuchi, Setsuya (1923-): president of Nomura Securities from 1978 to 1985.

Tabuchi, Yoshihisa (1935-): selected president of Nomura Securities in 1985.

Takeyama, Shigeru: Nomura general manager responsible for foreign trainees in 1984.

Takeshita, Noboru: prime minister selected on day of Great Crash in 1987 only to fall in disgrace in 1989 as a result of improprieties in accepting Recruit Cosmos shares.

Terao, Takeo: ex-president of Daiwa Bank; anti-Nomura.

Terasawa, Yoshio: nicknamed 'Terry' and 'Mr America'; Nomura class of 1954, Terasawa was the man who brought Japan to Wall Street by becoming the first Japanese member of the New York Stock Exchange.

Tonamura, Hitoshi: Nomura general manager assigned to overseeing foreign trainee project in 1982. He later rose to the powerful post of chairman of Nomura Europe.

Tsuchiya, Yozaburo: son of a stockbroker, he took over his family firm Tsuchiya Shoten, renamed it Nitto Securities and later Sanyo Securities, Japan's sixth largest brokerage house. Nomura bailed out Nitto in the early 1950s and took a small stake in the firm.

Yamanouchi, Takiko: wife of Tokushichi Nomura I.

Yasuhiro, Yutaro: founder of stock-trading firm by same name and of Fukushima Boseki, the present-day textile firm called Shikibo. Brother-in-law of Tokushichi Nomura II.

Yasui, Kaishi: architect and post-war head of Nomura Construction, the firm that retained Nomura family assets after the war.

Yoshida, Shigeru: twice prime minister after the war, and friend of Nomura president Tsunao Okumura.

1
The Day Nomura Helped Save the World

For Tetsuo Okumura, Tuesday morning, 20 October, begins bleakly. He is awakened as usual at 5.30 am as he feels his wife climb gently from their bed to prepare his breakfast. That means he has another fifteen minutes to sleep. Although their early morning routine has hardly varied for twenty-five years, Okumura still treasures these few moments alone, drifting in and out of slumber until, instinctively, he jolts awake at 5.45.

This morning is different. Just as Okumura begins to doze off, the phone by his bed rings. His hand moves swiftly to pick it up before the second ring. He already senses who it is. 'Moshi, moshi.' It is the New York office, calling at 3.30 pm, Monday afternoon, their time. His adrenaline begins to flow. The trader gives a quick summary of the day's collapse on Wall Street, and a burning sensation hits Okumura in the chest. He slams the phone down without saying goodbye. His heart races as his feet momentarily hit the cold floor before finding their slippers. He shouts to his wife that he is in a hurry, rushes through his early morning ritual of shower and shave, then snaps on the television.

Okumura anxiously follows NHK television, the state-run broadcasting network, awaiting the six o'clock morning financial news round-up. He wants confirmation of how the Wall Street market closed in Monday trading half an hour earlier.

It is helpful to remember that time moves westward in the direction of the sun. The first major financial market to open is Tokyo, at 9.00 am, which begins trading while New Yorkers are sitting down to dinner at 8.00 pm the previous evening. As time moves on, London opens trading at 9.00 am,

1

just as the Japanese are preparing to leave work at 5.00 pm.
New York, where it is 4.00 am, is fast asleep. By the time the
US financiers are at their desks at 9.00 am, Londoners are just
coming back from lunch at 2.00 pm, while in Tokyo, where it
is 10.00 pm, the Japanese are preparing for bed.

His wife brings him coffee and toast. As he stares at the
television screen, Okumura does not bother to explain what
has happened. She knows almost nothing of his business life,
and has long since given up asking questions. He, of course,
already knows the bombshell the newsreader is about to
drop: that the Dow Jones Industrial Average, symbol of
corporate America, has collapsed, falling 508 points, *23
per cent*! He finishes breakfast, gives his teeth a cursory
once-over with the brush and heads for the door. Somewhere
in Okumura's morning ablutions, Wall Street has seemingly
been washed down the drain.

The salarymen — the prototypical office workers who comprise most of the Japanese middle class — just shake their
heads and mutter as they rush to work by train. Everyone feels
the world has somehow changed, but they are not certain how.
As citizens of an island nation, these men are much more
attuned to global developments than their American counterparts. The crash is now part of their lives. Okumura resists the
urge to lean over and talk to the man next to him. He must
remember his position: a Nomura Securities man does not
need to console himself with idle stockmarket chatter.
Nomura *is* the market.

On the surface everything appears normal, except for the
blank stares of disbelief on the travellers' faces. Okumura is
virtually indistinguishable from the salarymen in their navy-blue
suits. Of medium height and build, with a slight stockiness, he
might be called pudgy if he held a less exalted position. His hair
is black with occasional streaks of grey. The only distinctive
feature of his appearance is a tiny blue Nomura Securities pin
on his left lapel, setting him apart from other variously tagged
commuters.

As the train pulls into Tokyo Station – Tokyo's main terminal – Okumura is thankful for one thing: at least Wall Street had already fallen sharply in the week prior to the crash. As head of Nomura's Global Trading Team, risking Nomura's money buying and selling large blocks of stock for clients, he and his colleagues had gone sour on the markets. Since last Thursday they had been refusing to buy stock for the Nomura house account.

Not that Okumura is worried about being fired. He is too senior. Besides, Nomura seldom fires its traders the way American brokerage firms do. Incompetents are simply transferred to less risky departments, such as the computer division. The fifty-one-year-old Okumura has not come this far only to find himself suddenly deleted from Nomura's list of golden boys. Aggressive, hard-hitting and tough, Okumura is one of the few Nomura men to have made it to the status of *bucho*, one of the firm's imposing general managers.

He is just one step away from a main board directorship, the reward that should await the man who in 1985 created the Nomura Global Trading Team, cleverly imitating American houses such as Merrill Lynch and Morgan Stanley. Okumura's team helps salesmen to compete for large block trades of foreign clients. His specially trained men stand by in London, New York and Hong Kong, ready to use Nomura's money to trade large blocks of stock when they spot a chance of making a profit.

Alighting from the train, Okumura walks past the coffee shops, which are just beginning to open, and hops on to the Ginza subway line which takes him to Nihonbashi, Tokyo's financial district. He strides briskly to Nomura's ageing, brown, seven-storey headquarters on the brackish Kanda river. A ride in the lift to the third floor takes him on to Nomura's giant trading arena to prepare for the day's battle.

On the train Okumura was just another salaryman, but here he is king. Nomura and its broking affiliates account for a startling 20 per cent of all stock and bond transactions in Japan, and their actions have an overriding influence on the rest of the country's financial market.

It is now 7.15 am. The phones are already ringing while traders scurry about in readiness for the onslaught. But even in their rush, the traders and office ladies take time to bow to Okumura. He is, after all, the second most powerful figure on the trading floor. Office ladies are busy clipping mountainous rolls of telexes filled with foreign selling orders, carefully placing then on the traders' desks. Okumura organizes himself for the pre-opening calls from distressed institutions. At eight o'clock he breaks off to listen to the in-house briefing, prepared daily by Nomura headquarters and broadcast live to all domestic branch offices. He then meets with his small group of traders as the crescendo in the trading room mounts with the approach of the nine o'clock opening bell.

* * * * * * * * *

Although, like everyone else at Nomura, he is a self-made man, Tetsuo Okumura has one secret he has kept discreetly hidden over the years from all except the most senior management. He is the nephew of Tsunao Okumura himself, the man most responsible for transforming Nomura from post-war ruin as an indebted bucketshop into a world-influencing oligopoly. As the nephew of the firm's president from 1948 until 1959, a man who was close to Japan's prime ministers and corporate chieftains, Tetsuo Okumura commands respect from Nomura's top board members. Few of his associates, however, know of his pedigree, and for good reason. His modesty is a guard against potential accusations from underlings that he has risen to power through family connections.

Okumura the younger was born in 1936 in Otaru, a remote fishing village on Japan's northernmost island, Hokkaido. Otaru faces Vladivostok across the Japan Sea and for most of the year the cold winds of Siberia seem to make the village their first port of call as they head east towards the city of Sapporo. Most of Tetsuo Okumura's neighbours were poor

4

fishermen, though his own family were relatively prosperous *shoyu* merchants, who lived by selling soy sauce to the surrounding districts.

Growing up in a cold fishing port made him tough. By the time he could walk, his parents had put him on skis, and by the age of seven he had become an expert downhill skier. In the evenings he learned to play mah-jong with his friends, a skill that would serve him well in his later years as a stockbroker. Mah-jong games are well known as occasions for cementing friendships and exchanging invaluable bits of market information. In fact, every securities firm has its own mah-jong apartment.

He studied hard in high school, hoping to gain entrance to a college which would lead on to a well-paid job in Tokyo. Eventually he was accepted at St Paul's College in Tokyo, thereby clearing the biggest hurdle – for the difficulty in Japan is to get into a college in the first place. Once in, students are under no pressure to work. Okumura spent three years playing sports, drinking with friends and chasing women, secure in the knowledge that once his college days were over, his uncle would find him a job. Good jobs were hard to come by in post-war Japan, and he had a suspicion that his coming working years would be hard. Much later he was to look back and find he had been right: the carefree days of college were his happiest.

There had never been much doubt that Okumura would be guaranteed a post with Nomura Securities after finishing his education. He joined the firm in April 1958 as a domestic salesman in Tokyo. The elder Okumura took good care of his nephew and allowed him to live in his Hiroo home in Tokyo for the following two years. The flow of prestigious visitors at the house seemed never-ending: Nomura's chief was befriended by countless powerful politicians and businessmen, such as Hayato Ikeda, then Finance Minister, who in 1960 would be elected prime minister.

There was, however, to be no shortcut for the younger Okumura. For the next six years he barely had time to think about anything except work. Installed in the crowded, noisy trading room with other salesmen, he was given a phone, a desk and no clients. He was told to pound the streets of Tokyo looking for customers. Okumura worked alone, with no help or formal training. Each morning he would leave the home of the president of Nomura and walk into the head office, a salesman completely devoid of status, the lowest of the low.

He had two tasks: to peddle stocks and to persuade customers to put money into investment trusts – the Japanese equivalent of mutual funds – giant pools of money that Nomura invested in the stockmarket on clients' behalf. Okumura went knocking from door to door in his efforts to make a sale. Often he would be ridiculed by passers-by. When he did manage to get in the door he was often hastily shown out again, often abused.

Those six years were the toughest of Okumura's life and he hated them. After two years he decided to move out of his uncle's home into the company dormitory, in the belief that he would get to know a few of the other men, who might give him some tips on how to do better at his seemingly thankless task. In fact, most nights he returned home from work exhausted and barely able to hold a conversation before falling asleep. Looking back, he finds it difficult to remember anything of those years as a salesman. They are a hazy blur. He does, however, recall wearing out pair after pair of shoes as he scoured Tokyo for clients.

Things began to look up in 1964 when Okumura reached the age of twenty-eight. It was the year of the Tokyo Olympics, Japan's coming-out party for the world. Okumura was transferred to Osaka, where after a painless eighteen months he rotated into corporate finance, spending four years there before moving over to the investment department for a further four and a half years. By 1973 he had entered the stock-trading department, where he was to spend the next fifteen years. By 1987, having been a salesman and a trader since 1958, he thought he had seen everything in the way of peaks and troughs in the Japanese stockmarket. Until, that is, Tuesday 20 October 1987, the day of the Great Crash.

* * * * * * *

On the Nomura trading floor, Okumura tries to cope with his emotions and wonders silently what the day will bring. Only a week earlier, had not the mighty Nomura itself been wildly optimistic about domestic prospects in its Friday market forecast? The firm had been promoting steel, paper pulp, semiconductor and textiles stocks, and had had the temerity to declare that any fall on Wall Street would not hurt Japan. The Nomura Research Institute, the biggest commercially owned think-tank in the world, had been right to warn clients that Wall Street was poised for a tumble. They had pointed out that the Dow Jones Index had not fallen more than 10 per cent since July 1984. They had suggested investors switch to Japanese and European stockmarkets. And sure enough, Okumura now recalls, the Tokyo market had hit a new record high on the previous Wednesday, 14 October. The Dow Jones, in contrast, had puttered along, unable to break through to the high ground last seen on 25 August.

A week earlier, it had seemed nothing was out of place. Records in Japan had been there to be broken. Stocks had, after all, been going up since the war. The year 1987 was the Year of the Rabbit, and in bounding fashion the markets in Japanese bonds, stocks and currency had hit new peaks. And, as if to herald Japan's financial dominance, in the spring of that year the total value of the market in Tokyo had finally surpassed that of the New York Stock Exchange.

On 14 October, the Nikkei 225 stock average had hit new highs. But close observers of the Tokyo markets had already realized that the boom had become an unhealthy one. The broader market index of 1,100 stocks on the Tokyo exchange, a more accurate reflection of the real condition of the market, had peaked four months earlier, on 11 June. By 14 October it had fallen a tell-tale 3 per cent below that

7

peak. Most financial issues, including the stockmarket's great bellweather, Nomura Securities, had also dropped below their high point. Indeed, the Nomura share price had peaked in the spring at 5,990 and had been slipping ever since. The alarm bells had been going off, but nobody had been listening.

Perpetual optimists had abounded in Kabutocho, Tokyo's Wall Street. One voice that had been largely ignored in the bullish din had been that of Kozen Yoshida, a spindly septuagenarian chartist, well respected by the Japanese investment community and by Nomura itself. He had been telling everyone to sell the market, but even his most loyal patrons, who paid him for his technical predictions, had dismissed his warning sounds.

'Nomura Investment Trust kept calling before the crash,' Yoshida later crowed. 'They wanted to know if I was coming out as a bull, but I kept quiet.'

At that point it had seemed unreasonable for the brokers to sell stock. Moreover, selling stock was not considered a commercially wise decision by Japanese brokers. They rarely issued sell recommendations. Why lose a corporate client, they reasoned. To say 'Sell' was to blaspheme a company in the eyes of the Japanese. The most they would offer was 'Sell Wall Street and buy Japan', as the Nomura Research Institute had already urged. Japanese brokerage firms had in the past always prospered on buying, and no firm reflected that policy better than Nomura, who in autumn 1987 had not only surpassed Toyota as the most profitable company in Japan (with a net profit of more than $2 billion) but had outstripped even American giants such as Citibank, Merrill Lynch and American Express to become for the moment the most profitable financial institution in the world.

Perhaps, though, there had been just too much optimism. Some had seen the flaunting of opulence by Japanese women, among the best dressed in the world, as a warning sign of harsher times ahead. Shoppers had happily charged thousand-dollar designer dresses by Issey Miyake, Christian

Dior, Gucci and Chanel without a second thought. Sports-car sales had zoomed ahead as BMW became the biggest-selling luxury import car, spawning the phrase 'BMW poor' to denote men who had no other possession than their car.

The yuppies of Japan had arrived, and been nicknamed the *shinjinrui*, meaning the 'new generation'. In the evenings they flocked to Roppongi, the centre of Tokyo's Western-style glitz and fast-lane discos and bars, ignoring the more sedate and traditional Japanese night-life of Ginza and Akasaka. Decked in sunglasses, the coolest of the *shinjinrui* would drive their BMWs through the centre of Roppongi, playing just the right Madonna or Michael Jackson track as they paused at the main intersection. The *nouveaux riches* packed into French restaurants that charged a minimum of $150 a head. Their talk turned on recent art and real-estate acquisitions and, in the tradition of aspiring glitterati, they flaunted their baubles of wealth with abandon.

One quarter of all fine art coming under the auctioneer's hammer in America and Europe was destined for Japan, while the nation spent $2 *billion* on diamonds alone during 1987. Bubbles and champagne bars were in. Even creating bubbles became an art form, as solid gold swizzle-sticks put expensive effervescence into the lives of the elite. Other bars were a bit more practical, providing Quick machines to monitor stock-price quotations, the Japanese equivalent of Quotron or Reuters. The Japanese had reason to celebrate their newly acquired wealth. Their country's GNP now exceeded $19,500 a head, more than America's. Only two decades earlier America's output per person had been four times greater than Japan's.

There had been other signs of the coming crash. Many of the older, more affluent brokers held part of their wealth in golf-club memberships, which traded over the telephone in the secondary market and were quoted twice weekly in the *Nikkei Sangyo* newspaper. Golf in Japan is the ultimate status symbol, and as a result, prestigious club memberships soared into the hundreds of thousands of dollars. However, prices of membership had begun slipping as early as February 1987, although certainly not enough to cause panic. At the same time there had been signs that Tokyo property values were starting to boil over after an astronomical ascent. The share prices of the major, publicly listed realty companies had peaked earlier that spring.

It had been hard to spot signs of uncertainty in the general euphoria. Interest in finance had never been greater. The readership of the *Nikkei Shimbun*, Japan's financial daily, had reached four million, almost twice the circulation of the *Wall Street Journal*.

There had also been a massive shift of funds from savings accounts to the brokerage investment trusts. The Japanese post office, where deposit accounts were favoured by tax breaks, had a staggering $700 billion stashed away by compulsive savers. Each family had been allowed only one account, restricted in size, and when the post office discovered there were more accounts than people in Japan – some in the names of cats and dogs – the government had decided to clamp down. Money had poured out of post office accounts, where every family had been permitted to keep the equivalent of $25,000 dollars on deposit, tax free – at a miserly 4 per cent rate of interest. With the government looking to tax these deposits, investors had funnelled their money into the stockmarket.

There had been a more sinister source of new funds for the stockmarket: the so-called 'black money' from speculative stock and real estate gains. Closely linked with Japan's underworld, speculative groups on some days had constituted up to 10 per cent of Japanese trading volume. The stockmarket was an ideal place for black money to find a home, since Japanese shares paid derisory dividends and did not have to be registered.

The most dramatic source of capital, though, had been *zaitech*. Companies themselves had fuelled the market's rise in 1986 and 1987 by issuing new stocks and bonds and then

putting the proceeds back into the market rather than spending the money developing their businesses.

* * * * *

On Friday 16 October, three days before the crash, a hurricane in Britain forced the London market to close – the most
costly effect of a natural disaster in the City's history. British
financiers weighed the consequences of not going into the
office but decided, with a certain amount of cheer, to spend
Friday at home with their families.

The alert reader leafing through the British papers on
Friday or Saturday might have noticed a small item buried
under the avalanche of anecdotes about the storm. The Tate
Gallery had announced to the world that Nomura Securities
had donated $2.5 million for the construction of a new
gallery. Nomura had arrived in London society. The price
paid, Nomura executives reasoned, was one they could easily
afford on a profit of $2 billion, and was worth the prestige.
Prime Minister Margaret Thatcher swallowed her anti-
Japanese rhetoric in accepting the money: 'I am delighted
that Nomura Securities is giving this money to build a new
gallery and I hope other firms will follow that lead.'

Within a week, those other firms to which she referred
were to have other problems not remotely connected with
art galleries. Many of them would begin a fight for their very
survival.

In New York that Friday, trouble had already been brew-
ing. The Japanese were asleep when Wall Street tumbled
sharply in its final hour of trading to close down by 108
points, or 4.5 per cent. It was the biggest one-day point fall
of the Dow Jones average ever recorded in the history of the
New York Stock Exchange. (On Black Tuesday, 29 October
1929, the Dow Jones industrials fell thirty points, or 11 per
cent.) But the worst was yet to come.

On the eve of the crash, however, the Japanese nation had
other concerns about the stockmarket – for that Monday

night a new prime minister was to be selected. But the Japanese stockmarket itself was on edge all day Monday, and by the end of trading had fallen almost 2.5 per cent. The only signal that Wall Street might be in for a shock was emitted by other Asian markets: that Monday Hong Kong fell a staggering 11 per cent, while both Singapore and Australia dropped 12 per cent. Few would have guessed that a day later, on Tuesday 20 October, one would have to scrutinize the front pages of the world's newspapers to find a mention of Noboru Takeshita's selection as the nation's new ruling politician.

The global market clock ticked ominously on. As Japan closed on Monday, weatherbeaten Londoners returned to work for the first time since Thursday. Traders immediately unscrambled positions left unsold through the hurricane. Prices plummeted. By the day's end, the London market had fallen 10 per cent.

Meanwhile, Wall Street traders were going into work and succumbing to panic as the global bear market ricocheted back across the Atlantic from Europe. Prices that had cracked in New York on Friday collapsed on Monday. Before the 9.30 bell, investors had lined up half a billion dollars' worth of stock ready to be dumped on the New York Exchange's automatic transaction system. Floor dealers could not cope with the avalanche of sell orders. In the delay and confusion, artificially high stock quotations masked the reality of the crash. Index arbitrageurs added to the chaos by selling without realizing that stock prices were actually falling much faster than the screen quotes indicated. Then one institution began a wave of thirteen 'sell' programmes, each for a $100 million worth of stock, further pummelling the index.

By the New York Stock Exchange closing bell, the Dow Jones had fallen 508 points. For the moment, Japan was the last thing on the minds of members of the global financial community. They all were busy thinking about how they themselves would survive.

THE DAY NOMURA HELPED SAVE THE WORLD

* * * * *

Okumura gathers his thoughts, and, fighting down nausea, prepares for his pre-market morning meeting with his traders. Inevitably, with some Japanese stock positions on its books, Nomura faces large losses.

Tokyo is now the front line of battle. Foreign investors, terrorized by the global panic, are already deciding they must get out of Japan. Yet a strange calmness reigns over the Nomura trading room, where the only audible activity is the hum of conversation with clients enquiring anxiously about market conditions.

Japanese investors appear uncertain what to do. Okumura's nerve is not what it was and he demurs, breaking the one rule of the Nomura trading desk: always buy stocks that are being heavily sold. This time he just holds on. Though he remains a great bull of Tokyo and tells all his clients to buy, he is not himself in a position to buy stock for the firm's book, by decree of senior management. Nomura is uncertain at this point whether world markets can survive Wall Street's collapse. 'Japan is not the problem. The world is the problem,' he tells colleagues, in an attempt to reassure them.

Fortunately, damage to Nomura's house dealing accounts is limited. The rules restricting trading to no more than 20 per cent of capital reserves mean that Japanese houses are to avoid the losses of tens of millions of dollars already suffered on Wall Street. Unlike firms in New York, which are leveraged to the hilt, the Japanese carry little equity inventory.

The cavernous Tokyo Stock Exchange remains like the eye of a typhoon. Under stock-exchange regulations, traders cannot sell until buy orders materialize. But there are no buyers. Some clients begin to panic. They feel trapped, with no way out.

Averse to risk, the Japanese did not structure their exchanges with 'specialists' like those in New York whose job it was to make a market in a stock. The function of the traders on the Tokyo Stock Exchange floor was simply to match buyers and sellers. Technically there is nobody in Japan who can provide a liquid market, acting as market-maker. Prices can move up or down for days at a time with hardly any shares changing hands. By the end of Tuesday morning, although the bellwether of the Japanese market, the Nikkei 225 average, is theoretically down 7 per cent, only 5 per cent of Tokyo's 1,100 stocks have traded. Only ten million shares have changed hands – a hundredth of recent trading volume.

Then come placating remarks from the battered Kiichi Miyazawa, the Finance Minister, who has just lost his battle for the premiership to Noboru Takeshita. Beleaguered, he states that the Japanese markets will not follow New York down. Miyazawa is derided by the markets, and the urge to sell continues. The head of the Economic Planning Agency makes similar soothing noises, but everyone is in the throes of panic. Claims of innate Japanese superiority are momentarily dismissed.

The cascading Tokyo market bounds downward from price to price without trading, as stocks that have taken months to climb retrace their ascent within a matter of hours. The big insurance and savings institutions, managing billions of yen on behalf of ordinary Japanese, make a beeline for the relative safety of the bond market. Officials there are overwhelmed and forced to suspend trading.

Investors have been driven overnight from greed to fear. Dreams of owning one, two or even three houses are replaced by worry over paying the rent. Men with high hopes of leaping the corporate ladder begin praying that they may hold on to their jobs. Everyone is at first embarrassed about their losses and tries to cover up their shame. The Japanese house-wife in Yokohama feels the same fright, shame and anger over losing money as does the stockbroker in Hiroshima, the construction worker in Osaka or the hotel-owner in Tokyo.

Nomura's large clients remain inactive. They include the Nippon Life Insurance Company – or Nissei, as the Japanese call it – which, as Japan's largest shareholder on the Tokyo exchange, controls over 3 per cent of all publicly quoted shares. Nissei's senior managers reason that selling a few stocks will only devalue the overall worth of their portfolio. 'There was nothing we could do,' one Nippon Life fund manager is to say in retrospect. 'We just held on.'

But he is wrong. There *is* something Nippon Life can do. Although the fund managers, many of them under the age of thirty, seem resigned to a plunging market simply because there are no buyers in sight, men with a longer-term view are about to meet for lunch.

Even amid the fear and chaos in Nihonbashi – Tokyo's financial district – the two-hour lunch-break is dutifully observed. Tokyo is the only major global market to have retained a restful midday trading recess. Traders, salesmen, clerks and office ladies take time at eleven each morning to eat noodles or sushi, then chat in coffee-houses until work resumes at one o'clock.

This is the crucial pause in the unfolding drama. The powerful heads of stock trading at the 'big four' – the nation's four largest brokerage firms – are meeting for their regular Tuesday lunch at Japan's Ministry of Finance.

Visitors to the Ministry of Finance are surprised by its drab 1940s-style headquarters. The austere stone building looks more like a dungeon than a great nation's financial nerve-centre. The Ministry of Finance holds sway over Japanese finance with a mailed fist, empowered to rule everything vaguely associated with money.

Takashi Matsukata is the man responsible for the delicate task of market-support operations. He can be seen daily, dining, drinking or golfing with the stockmarket kings, but in his official capacity as director for secondary – or traded – markets, Matsukata also spends much time assiduously burrowing through papers on the fourth floor of the Ministry while, nearby, his minions hunch behind grey desks piled high with files and reports.

Routinely, Matsukata gathers the views of the big four's equity trading managers, the most powerful of whom is

Yoichiro Noda of Nomura. As head of domestic trading, he is responsible for the firm's equity sales and trading division, the backbone of Nomura's profit. Noda is effectively in charge of the firm's day-to-day market activity, and therefore effectively in control of the tempo of the Japanese stockmarket.

Matsukata turns the lunch into a crisis-control meeting. He seems calm, but underneath tension simmers. Less than a year ago this man organized the sale of 12.5 per cent of Japan's state-owned telecommunications company, Nippon Telephone and Telegraph (NTT). This is the most valuable company in the world in stockmarket terms, worth in excess of $200 billion, more than the entire stockmarket capitalization of West Germany. Success has propelled him into the crucial task of overseeing the Japanese stockmarket. Not least of his worries is the prospect of trying to sell another 12.5 per cent of NTT on to the market in less than three weeks' time. How can it be done with the market in its present state? Matsukata has to find a way to restore confidence quickly or the sale cannot go ahead.

He is aware of the importance of this meeting and later recalls: 'It was an emergency. In order to normalize the markets we listened to the opinions of the leaders of the securities industry and asked them to co-operate.'

Matsukata asks each man in turn what he thinks of the market. Together they calculate that the furthest the market can fall that day is 19 per cent. In the 1960s, limits had been placed on advances and declines, but few had ever considered the prospect of all stocks closing down at their limit.

Now comes the critical moment. Matsukata is asked whether it is the wish of the Japanese government that the big four support the market.

Matsukata leans forward and, almost imperceptibly, nods. Here, in a nod that is to give hope to the whole financial world, a tacit understanding is reached: the big four will return from lunch to begin their buying operations. Wall

Street has haemorrhaged; it is time for the Japanese single-mindedly to take over the controls of global finance. 'This is Japan Inc.,' market guru Keiji Yasuda of New Japan Securities is to explain later. 'We are a consensus society – a nation that likes to move in one direction.'

The Ministry of Finance has just given silent assent to an undertaking to save its own financial system. The main instrument of that policy is be Nomura Securities and its sales force. 'Nomura is the Ministry of Finance,' concedes one senior official. 'We consult them on our every move, and even let them draft legislation.'

Back on the trading floor Noda and Okumura confer, gather their trading managers together and give them the command. 'We are buyers of the Japanese market,' shouts Okumura. 'I want everyone to get on the phone to start preparing for tomorrow's rally.'

Mysteriously, if not miraculously, in the afternoon buy orders begin to appear in certain strategic shares. Government-owned stocks due for privatization, such as NTT, start to recover. NTT has been near its 'stop low' of 2.51 million yen per share, but now jumps to 2.65. Nomura's powerful hand hurls buy orders into the market. Its influence is seen on a number of the larger capital stocks. At the three o'clock closing bell, most stocks are resting on their downside limit. But Nomura has organized things so that when dealing resumes tomorrow any outstanding sell orders will be greedily snapped up. Although only seven stocks manage to end the day on the upside, the market has not fallen as far as it could have done under Japanese rules. It is down 3,836 points out of a possible 4,380 – a 15 per cent loss, the worst percentage fall since the death of Joseph Stalin in 1953, when prices fell 10 per cent.

The circuit-breaker system of stop losses has muted the fall. So too has the conservatively run Japanese unit-trust or mutual-trust industry. Only 35 per cent of the industry's funds are in the stockmarket, compared with 90 per cent of their American equivalents. The insurance and trust banking industry in Japan has the same cautious stance on the market; only 17 per cent of insurance assets and 11 per cent of trust banking assets are in stocks. Japanese individuals are also cushioned. They have only 11 per cent of their savings in the stockmarket. Their postal savings accounts are still clenched tightly in hand – out of the reach of smooth-talking brokers.

Nomura's market share on this historic day takes its rightful, but unenviable, place at 18 per cent. There is no joy in taking orders today. It is as if a giant finger has somehow pressed the wrong button on the Tokyo Stock Exchange's computer and erased an entire six months' manual input. Almost $400 billion (or fifty-seven trillion yen) of Japanese wealth have vanished. The index now stands where it did in the spring of 1986, a year and a half ago.

The carnage elsewhere in Asia on Tuesday is far worse than that in Japan. Australia loses 25 per cent. Angry Chinese investors swarm outside the closed doors of the Hong Kong exchange demanding the right to trade. But Hong Kong will not open for another six days – and will then dive 33 per cent. Later in the day the downward spiral moves to London, where prices fall an additional 12 per cent and dealers wish they had not stayed at home so willingly after the hurricane on Friday.

As the market closes in Tokyo on Tuesday, the public-relations machine of the Japanese establishment swings into action. Satoshi Sumita, head of the Bank of Japan, announces that all financial market trading procedures will be adhered to in spite of the crisis. He is followed by the chairman of the Tokyo Stock Exchange. The world economy is functioning well, he claims, and investors must not worry. In a gesture of faith in the market, he lowers the margin requirements for dealing in shares and relaxes the rules on collateral for securities, which were tightened up only the previous week.

The chief of the securities bureau at the Ministry of Finance assures investors that there will be no further decline in the market. Later, ordinary Japanese investors read his statement in their evening papers and believe him. They now wish they could have back the stock they had been panicked into selling earlier in the day.

Greed, so rapidly replaced by fear only hours earlier, once again becomes the dominant market emotion. The resilient Japanese, reduced to nothing more than speculators, are being lured back by the chance of a quick profit on Wednesday's market opening.

They do not realize, perhaps never will, that their greed has been collectively calculated. It is this psychological ingredient that will be systematically used to save the Japanese market. Individual investors will be brought back to the market *en masse* – by Nomura.

Fuelling dreams of profit has been the never-ending task of the *kabuya* – Japan's often maligned but crucially important stock salesman – whose very name smells of speculation and whose sales techniques have changed little from the days of Tokushichi Nomura. With nearly half of Japanese securities firms' revenues coming from commissions on retail sales, it is the *kabuya*'s efforts more than anything else that have been responsible through the years for the extraordinary growth in the fortune of Japan's investment houses. Moreover, a Nomura salesman is known to be hungrier and more driven than his competitors at Daiwa, Nikko and Yamaichi. The Japanese jokingly call Nomura Securities 'Seven Eleven' after the American quick-service food chain whose shops dot Japan and open their doors at seven and turn off the lights at eleven every evening.

* * * * *

The next morning, Wednesday, few at the opening bell in Tokyo realize how close, on Tuesday, the New York Stock Exchange came to shutting down completely. The Japanese see only the reading on the Dow Jones Index: up 102 points. A recovery, they think. 'Not that it mattered, since our path was set,' Okumura later boasted. Stock prices in New York have in fact become meaningless numbers. Tuesday,

20 October, was the day when stocks in America came to symbolize nothing but paper, the day when the Dow Jones fell a chilling 27 per cent between ten and noon – the worst decline in market history. A month later, two journalists will make the front page of the *Wall Street Journal* with a Pulitzer Prize-winning account of how America's stock exchanges faced total disintegration. Somehow amid all this chaos, on Tuesday, 20 October, a sharp, manipulated rally occurred in an obscure Chicago futures contract called the Major Market Index. This was enough to trigger buy-backs by major American corporations, keeping the patient alive until Japan could operate in Tokyo.

The idea of Japan's superiority is quick to catch on. Almost as if to underscore the nation's greatness and back up pronouncements made by the government, Nomura Securities has mobilized its troops. Some 2,500 salesmen (or *kabuya*, as they are known by the Japanese), 2,900 door-to-door saleswomen and 2,000 customer-service ladies have been commanded to start telephoning and knocking on doors, a process that actually began on Tuesday night. The message has been broadcast to Nomura's five million accounts: from the opening bell on Wednesday, the market is going up. And throughout the network of 131 branches, the army of salesmen have persuaded even the most timid and frightened investors to buy the market. Nomura salesmen have a distinct advantage over smaller brokerage houses – they *know* the market is headed north, and every sentence in their sales pitch has an edge, sharpened by conviction.

Sure enough, panic buying ensues. Into 1988 and 1989 the Japanese market will be the wonder of the world, rising virtually in a straight line, widening still further the gap between itself and a dazed and battered Wall Street.

* * * * *

By the time of the second Wall Street crash, on Friday 13 October 1989, the Japanese investor – and indeed the world

– had learned a lesson. Wall Street plummeted 7 per cent on Friday, but Japanese investors were convinced of the superiority of their market and refused to sell stock on the following Monday. While the world briefly fell apart a second time, Japan remained stable, faltering less than 2 per cent.

Less than a month later, on 6 November 1989, the Japanese had had enough. Trade officials, fed up with Japan-bashing on the part of the American media and government, issued a list of their criticisms of America. Among other things they cited America's low savings rate, short-term corporate outlook ('Americans look ahead ten minutes while Japanese look ahead ten years,' noted Akio Morita, chairman of Sony), high tax rate, anti-trust laws, lack of worker education, poor research and development and, perhaps most important, the excessive number of leverage buy-outs.

Leverage buy-outs were doubtless the most important difference between how America and Japan did business. While Americans were turning equity into debt, the Japanese turned debt into equity. While Americans tapped their bankers on the shoulder for capital, thus saddling their company with debt, the Japanese tapped their brokers for equity capital, which was virtually free since Japanese companies paid nominal dividends and cared little about dilution of earnings per share.

There were other major reasons for Japan's economic prowess. For one thing, what Americans consider conflict of interest, the Japanese believe to be vested interest. American banks, for instance, are prohibited from buying shares in companies to which they lend money. Japanese banks, on the other hand, will purposely take large-percentage, long-term shareholdings in their client companies. Moreover, as opposed to high capital-gains taxes in Britain and America, the Japanese had virtually none.

Finally, perhaps the most significant factor in Japan's rise to prominence had been its attitude towards what Westerners consider 'insider trading'. In the West, it is a crime to trade on privileged information. Until recently, Japan has had no such restraints, however surprising that seems.

These cultural and economic differences are important in tracing the rise of Nomura from its obscure origins in Osaka to world prominence.

PART I
THE RISE TO WEALTH

2
The Moneychanger

According to family legend, Tokushichi Nomura I, the father of the founder of Nomura Securities, was the misbegotten son of a samurai and his serving girl. He was born in 1850, towards the end of the Tokugawa era (1603-1867), the romantic age of feudal lords and samurai, in a Japan closed to the outside world. The era took its name from the Shogun Ieyasu Tokugawa, who by the year 1603 had united the battle-torn Japanese fiefdoms into a nation, moving the capital to Edo, the eastern city today called Tokyo. Although the ultimate source of political legitimacy was still the Emperor, in practice he was no more than a puppet of the Tokugawa shogunate and never left his palace in the ancient capital of Kyoto. Life was much harsher than the poems and woodblock prints suggest; the Shogun ruled the general populace with an iron hand.

Toshitsura Doi, Nomura's father, was thirteenth in an exalted line of samurai who served the Shogun. He was the keeper of the monumental Osaka Castle and one of the nation's richest men. He disavowed any blood relation to young Tokushichi and banned him from using his noble name. Tokushichi took his mother's name, Nomura, a fairly common Japanese surname, and a wealthy landowner was paid to rear him. At the age of ten he was apprenticed to a moneychanger named Yahei Osakaya.

Apprenticeship was the normal form of schooling for male Osaka children in the nineteenth century. Tokushichi's tasks in the Osakaya household included sweeping the street in front of his master's money-shop and sprinkling it with water from the communal well to keep the dust down. Any Japanese shopkeeper, then as now, who failed to maintain tidiness in his small area by watering it during the day was considered lazy by his neighbours and his shop destined to failure.

Later, Osakaya gave him the arduous work of wheeling copper coins around in a cart. These heavy coins were in constant use for daily transactions, and it was Tokushichi's duty to haul them around to customers who wanted to exchange them for silver or to break a silver coin into smaller change.

In the mid-nineteenth century Osaka was Japan's main entrepot centre, an intensely practical and entrepreneurial city. Not until the twentieth century would Tokyo become Japan's commercial centre. Even the greeting in Osaka reflected its singular focus. Instead of saying *konnichi wa*, 'good day', people hailed each other as they do to this day with *mokari makka*, 'how's business'. Practicality as a principle extended to the city's architecture, with houses carefully erected on the east-west streets to capture the full benefit of the cool sea winds during the hot summer months.

Known as the 'kitchen of Japan', Osaka derived its status as a hub of economic activity, and much of its character, from its central role in rice trading. Rice was then the key to the Japanese economy, the staple against which wealth was measured and through which power was maintained. The Dojima rice market, located on a small island at the delta of three main rivers in northern Osaka, supported more than 1,300 registered rice dealers. Established in 1688, it provided a clearing mechanism for surplus rice that enabled rice-growers to sell their crop ahead of a harvest if they felt an exceptionally good year would drag down prices. Or, if a poor harvest was anticipated, they could buy rice and sell it later at an inflated price.

The feudal lords saw an additional use for the rice exchange. When money became tight, as often happened during the costly annual pilgrimage to the Tokugawa shogunate in Tokyo, they could sell rice tickets, receipts for rice stored in warehouses or for crops not yet harvested. These tickets became a form of currency in which rice dealers were only too happy to trade and this secondary market at Dojima became the world's first futures market.

The Osaka rice brokers gained a well-deserved reputation for being a particularly passionate, underhand, slippery
crowd. Trading began each morning at eight on the signal
given by an exchange official: the ignition of a slow-burning
rope, which was suspended in a wooden box, away from
mischievous hands, on a central beam for all to see. Not
until the last wisp of smoke had wafted from the box did
trading close, the last price of the day becoming the opening
price for the next day as well as the official closing price by
which all the day's accounts were settled.

Generally this meant that trading ended some time in the
late afternoon. But in the heat of trade, brokers would often
go to great lengths to prolong the day's business. To shut
down the exchange when trading was still at a frenzied level,
officials would call on the services of the 'water men', who
would try to disperse the crowds by splashing water on them
or, when necessary, by heaving entire buckets of water over
their heads, the last traded price of the day becoming known
as the 'bucket price'. If there was no trading price when the
rope burned down, or if for some reason it was snuffed out
in advance, all transactions that day were cancelled. Needless
to say, this rule often encouraged riotous behaviour at closing
time. A trader who had suffered huge losses during the day
might charge through the market on horseback to break up
trading or try, by force or stealth, to reach the burning rope
in the box and extinguish the flame prematurely.

For almost 300 years the government tried to control
the price of rice, but without success; it remained in the
hands of the rice brokers. Not until the mid-twentieth
century were the first laws enacted to ban futures trading.

The status of merchants such as Tokushichi's employer,
Osakaya, was not dissimilar to that of the Jews as far back
as medieval Europe. They were envied for their commercial
skills, but assumed to be crooked. Moneychangers were the
most despised of the merchant class. They were the only
individuals allowed to amass wealth freely and were hated

since their wealth was generally acquired at the expense of others.

But the moneychangers played a vital role in the economy. They converted rice into money, at a rate they themselves set, to determine the official exchange rate between gold and silver. As the currency of Osaka was silver and that of Tokyo gold, all trade between these two key centres depended on the moneychangers. And as the financial agents of the feudal lords, supplying them with banking facilities and credit against future rice shipments, these merchants wielded an additional power that had far-reaching socio-economic implications.

Tokushichi Nomura was twenty-one in 1871 when Yahei Osakaya officially adopted him. Osakaya died the following year, leaving Tokushichi the heir to his estate and a modestly rich man. He renamed the family business Nomura Shoten (*shoten* meaning 'shop'), a common name for many merchant businesses of the day. Tokushichi's shop was a two-storey, wooden merchant home with a ceramic-tiled roof and balcony. The premises were simple but pleasant; he changed money on the ground floor and had his living quarters upstairs. Having opened his own shop at the age of twenty-two, Tokushichi considered himself lucky. Most of the hard work seemed to be over. He had no goals other than to find a wife, raise sons to take over his business and live out a comfortable existence as a prosperous merchant.

Tokushichi found a wife within his own small company. His bride, Takiko Yamanouchi, came from a samurai family who had become merchants after the restoration of the Meiji Emperor and the abolition of the warrior class in 1868. Tokushichi was lucky. Few men in the mid-nineteenth century became proprietors before the age of twenty-five and most waited until their early thirties before submitting to an arranged marriage. By his early twenties Tokushichi had these challenges well in hand. His wife knew the moneychanging business and could manage it while Tokushichi was away on errands. She also knew how to cook and look after a household, and Tokushichi was proud that he had found himself the ideal wife.

Meanwhile the Meiji Restoration had taken place. The samurai who had deposed the Shogun and taken power in the name of the Emperor had instituted some remarkable reforms. They created a strong central government and set the trend for private ownership where previously government had dominated. Land ownership now became negotiable, mortgages came into existence and ownership of business began to pass from the state to the individual. There had been private enterprises in Japan before the 1870s, but they had been, for the most part, small shops such as Tokushichi Nomura's. When industrial growth began to outpace the state's ability to finance the necessary technology, the government wholeheartedly supported the entry of private investment. Little by little, the Ministry of Finance sold off its fledgling industrial ventures to the highest bidder.

National wealth soared in the late nineteenth century, not only because of heavy industry or the building of Japan's naval and merchant fleets, but also as a result of the booming manufacture of simple products that improved the ordinary Japanese lifestyle: rickshaws and bicycles; chemicals to improve farm productivity; motorized fishing boats; and incandescent lamps. Finally, the formation of limited-liability companies ensured that an owner could separate his company assets and liabilities from his private wealth.

This dramatic economic growth was facilitated by the emergence of banks. The new laws converted samurai rice stipends into bonds and banks were initially formed to take in deposits. This money was then lent out to foster a rapid expansion of industry.

The Japanese lost little time in taking to capitalism. By 1872, banking companies had begun issuing shares in a country where only a decade earlier an entity such as a company had not even existed. These share issues were not for the purpose of capital formation, but rather served to divide ownership. Although joint stock companies existed, companies used bank loans and bonds, rather than stock offerings, as their primary source of capital. For the next hundred years banks, and not the stockmarkets, were to foster the growth of Japan's private sector.

Trading and speculative fever still had their place, but in a considerably less prestigious sphere of money-making. By 1878 exchanges had been established in Tokyo and Osaka to handle gold, silver and bonds. The moneychangers too had to be able to trade and hedge positions in silver and gold to meet their own daily business requirements and to this end the exchanges provided a valuable vehicle.

For the speculators of Osaka, though, it was only a short walk from the Dojima rice market to the Kitahama securities exchange, which was open for only two short periods each month. The proximity of these two markets ensured that Dojima rice-trading practices were carried over into the trading of company shares. By 1894 corporate shares began to trade actively, and a stock futures market emerged that mirrored the trading of these shares.

Though particularly conservative in his business practices, Tokushichi Nomura found that trading bullion and specie on an exchange was a development that he could not afford to ignore. In 1878 he joined the Osaka Securities Exchange – solely to meet his daily moneychanging needs. He had no intention of gambling on stocks. On 7 August of the same year, his first son, Tokushichi Nomura II, was born.

3
The Profligate Son

It was common in Tokugawa and Meiji (1868-1912) Japan for men to assume other names at various times during their lives. The young Nomura was known to family and friends simply as Shinnosuke, meaning 'trust' or 'sincerity', a name he kept until he took over his father's business in 1904, when he became known simply as Tokushichi. Shinnosuke was raised to be a moneychanger in the same house where his father had learned his trade from Osakaya. For a restless, stubborn youth it was a stifling existence.

The narrow, dusty street in which the family lived was slightly wider than a man's outstretched arms, obliging intimacy between neighbours. To the Nomura family, Osaka was a world that extended no further than a few houses to either side of their own, in a city where families considered themselves lucky not to be living next to a fighting couple, noisy children or wandering animals. Theirs was a busy household. Shinnosuke had a sister, Kiku, four years older than he, a brother two years his junior named Jitsusaburo (always his trusted second), a sister seven years younger named Tani and a brother, Motogoro, nine years younger.

The ground floor of the house, as in most Japanese homes, was used for business, with a small dark kitchen to one side and *tatami*-matted upstairs rooms for sleeping. The platforms in front of the shop were used for unloading goods during the day and for sitting and chatting with neighbours in the evening. One of the only areas of privacy was the cool balcony upstairs where sea breezes could sweep through; it was used by Takiko, the mother of the family, ostensibly to dry laundry, but more importantly to get away from the men's business talk.

Tokushichi the elder was a conservative businessman and

stayed clear of speculation that might threaten the family's security. But gradually, as his son later recalled in his autobiography, he began to drink heavily, which impeded his ability to look after the shop, and it was his wife who held the family together and raised Shinnosuke. 'My mother was tough,' Shinnosuke wrote. 'Not only did she show me all the things my father should have, but she also managed the store behind his back.'

As a merchant, the elder Tokushichi was naturally sceptical of classroom learning – the age-old custom of apprentice-ship made more sense to him – but the new education laws forced him to send his son to the Osaka Commercial School. Shinnosuke's grades at school were outstanding, but he was rebellious and was always getting into scrapes with other boys. Since he was not as physically strong as his school-mates, he took the huge family dog with him, but his mother mocked him, saying that for a descendant of a samurai it was shameful to fight with the aid of anything except bare hands. 'You must never behave like a girl,' she told him when he was eight years old. 'A true samurai is one who can commit hara-kiri at any place and any time.' She then took out one of her family's short ceremonial swords, with its finely curved blade, and showed him how to cut his stomach from left to right and from bottom to top.

One of Shinnosuke's best friends was Einosuke Iwamoto, the son of an important moneychanger who lived close to the Nomura family. They would walk to school together each day. Shinnosuke's first experience of wealth was not in his own impecunious household, although they were considered reasonably successful, but through the affluent Iwamoto, who always wore the finest silk clothes and whose house was full of servants. Shinnosuke worked for his father in his free time, but his friend never had to work. The embarrassed Shinnosuke would try to hide when he saw Iwamoto out for a Sunday walk, dressed in his grandest strolling attire, when he himself was only in his dirty work-clothes, usually pulling a cart with his brother. Shinnosuke was a year older than

Iwamoto and as a young boy he used to give his textbooks to his friend at the end of each school year to save Iwamoto's family the expense of buying new ones. But each autumn he noted that Iwamoto would appear with brand-new texts. Only later did he realize that the rich did not think of saving money if it meant using soiled goods. Any bitterness and jealousy that Shinnosuke felt quickly turned to ambition. He was going to become fabulously wealthy.

But Shinnosuke's health was weak. At the age of eighteen he contracted pneumonia and dropped out of his third year of high school with poor grades. He never went back, preferring instead to work full-time with his father, learning the moneychanging business. But he soon became restless and pleaded with his father to allow him to learn stock trading. He was the eldest son and marked out to inherit the small shop, but he asked his father to let his steady younger brother, Jitsusaburo, learn moneychanging.

Tokushichi turned down the request. With the advent of the industrial revolution, the Japanese financial industry was beginning to blossom: noblemen, former samurai and artisans were all interested in making money and moneychangers were gaining a new respect. Why take unnecessary risks with stock trading when the Nomura family was already doing well and stood to do a great deal better? But the younger Nomura, by incessant pleading, eventually exhausted his father into agreement. Reluctantly, Tokushichi apprenticed his son to Yasuhiro Shoten, an eponymous stock-trading firm owned by his son-in-law.

Stockmarket dealing has always been considered a form of gambling by the Japanese. A deep-rooted suspicion towards stock salesmen still lingers from the era of Shinnosuke's early apprenticeship, when the exchanges were seen as a profitable alternative to rice trading.

Although the stockmarket generated a lot of excitement among the merchants of Osaka, it was ignored by the general public. Respectable people did not associate with the exchanges of the Meiji period, and no decent father would

33

let his son embark on a career in stock trading. Banking was the proper financial profession. Even the wealthy who owned shares in the few listed companies did not use the exchange to buy or sell them. Most shares were held by banks and trust companies as expressions of 'mutual economic interest' in firms they were financing. For the most part these shares did not trade, but when they did, it was, by necessity, off the exchange. At that time there were no specific rules requiring shareholders to use the exchange – and there was little incentive, since brokers were notorious for front-running, trading in shares ahead of clients. Illiquidity on the exchanges made it difficult for accurate prices to be recorded. It was common even until the mid-twentieth century for brokers to purchase shares on behalf of clients at cheap prices and pass them on to their unsuspecting customers at the highest possible price, pocketing the balance.

Major shareholders such as banks and wealthy families saw little need to jeopardize their business plans by trading their shares on the open market. As the general public had yet to acquire a strong financial base, stock ownership remained the domain of the rich and stock trading the province of the hustling rice trader. Stock exchanges represented big business for the exchanges themselves – the more shares traded on the exchange, the more money the exchange members made. Although formed as joint stock companies, these exchanges were often the personal provinces of men like Tomoatsu Godai, the wealthy merchant who founded the Osaka Stock Exchange, and Eiichi Shibusawa, who created the Tokyo Stock Exchange.

Shibusawa, who started over 140 companies in his lifetime, epitomized the spirit of emerging capitalism that arose at the end of the feudal era. Born in 1840 into an Osaka peasant family, he had managed to purchase a samurai title, shortly before the samurai class was abolished, and to embark on a career in the new Meiji government. Eventually this government connection became an important base for his own industrial empire. He founded the Osaka Spinning Mill, which was the first large factory in Japan and had the technology to produce material competitive with Western manufactures. His success in cotton spinning ushered in an economic boom, beginning in Osaka in 1883. His lead gave the newly purchased private enterprises the financial foothold that enabled them to grow into large conglomerates, or *zaibatsu*, that would dominate the Japanese economy up until World War II. Shibusawa was also credited with founding the Bank of Japan and the First National Bank – Japan's first incorporated bank and the forerunner of the Daiichi Kangyo Bank, which by 1986 became the largest bank in the world.

Turnover brought about the financial success of these early Japanese exchanges. Although Shibusawa and other founders of exchanges had borrowed heavily from the rules of the London Stock Exchange and from the constitution of the San Francisco Stock Exchange, the Japanese exchanges were unlike their Western counterparts. In the West, stockmarkets provided a source of corporate funding and a vehicle for individuals to participate in future corporate growth. In Japan, however, the stock exchanges promoted churning and speculative trading much as the early rice-trading exchanges had. Business was so brisk that the boards of the Tokyo and Osaka stock exchanges paid out hefty annual dividends to themselves as shareholders, sometimes in excess of 40 per cent per annum.

When Shinnosuke joined Yasuhiro Shoten in 1896, just after the First Sino-Japanese War, the stockmarket was booming for the first time since its foundation in 1878. Shady pawnbrokers, pickle merchants, furniture dealers and moneychangers all tried their hand at trading. War brought a boom to the market as industries expanded at record pace to meet the increasing demands of the military.

The growth in corporate earnings of shipping companies, banks and textile companies sent share prices up as stock-exchange volume rocketed. Capitalization of the Tokyo Stock Exchange rose from 200,000 yen in 1878 to 600,000 yen by 1896. This proved to be a banner year and, as if to

35

point up Japan's new era of stocks and shares, the Tokyo Stock Exchange paid out a 100 per cent dividend to shareholders. As activity on the exchanges increased, a great many new exchanges were created. By 1897 there were, amazingly, 155 in Japan and one of the largest was the Osaka Securities Exchange.

Trading on the Osaka exchange began at nine in the morning as an official walked around the city sounding wooden clappers. The special rope used by the rice exchanges, the *hinawa*, was lit when the market opened, and not until it burned down towards mid-afternoon was trading halted. During the summer the exchange, seething with throngs of sweaty stock dealers, was ventilated by rope-operated ceiling fans, while traders on the sticky floor itself were cooled by attendants carrying huge fans. Stockmarket news became indispensable to merchants. Young 'singsong' boys ran through the streets of Osaka relaying market information obtained by peeking through the exchange windows and when street noise drowned out their voices, they resorted to basic body language to transmit market conditions.

Shinnosuke became entranced with the market. Although he was keen to trade stocks and stock futures, he was obliged by Yutaro Yasuhiro, his brother-in-law and now his boss, to perform the duties that every young apprentice had to endure: cleaning the street, fetching water, bowing to customers and serving them tea. When he was lucky he would be sent on an errand to Kitahama in the northern part of Osaka. Once there, he would prolong the visit, listening to stock traders tell him how to get rich quickly.

He discovered that stock dealers bought and sold shares and share futures on a short-term basis, not thinking of their holdings as ownership of a company. Shares went up and down as the stories behind each share changed. Shares in companies whose profits were good simply went up and in 1896 profits were at record levels, so traders bought stock.

For Shinnosuke, the urge to speculate became too great and one day, while his brother-in-law was out of the office, he opened the company safe where the firm's securities were kept and removed 500 yen (more than the average working man's annual salary) of government bonds. He took the bonds to the stock exchange as collateral to buy stock, in the hope of quickly doubling his money and returning the original 500 yen without getting caught. With dreams of becoming rich overnight, the eager young man put the entire 500 yen into the stockmarket, buying shares on the strength of a rumour he had heard from one of the reliable stock dealers. The shares plunged and he lost everything. His brother-in-law, furious, took him home to his father, who repaid the 500 yen to prevent a family scandal. At the age of twenty, Japan's future stockmarket king was penniless and jobless.

Embarrassed but not disheartened, Shinnosuke went back to work for his father, this time to sell stocks for Nomura Shoten. The official company history of Nomura Securities portrays Tokushichi Nomura II as a unique young man caught up in the spirit of the Meiji westernization: while most men wore a kimono, he wore a shirt and trousers. In his autobiography, Nomura admits to having been something of a dandy and relates how one day he went home with a new hat, which he proudly displayed to his mother. She threw it in the river, telling him he was foolish to spend money on things he could not use.

To some, the young Nomura's Western affectations bordered on eccentricity. Dressed in shorts in summer and trousers in winter, he pedalled around Osaka's backstreets each day on his Cleveland two-wheeler, daily stock comment in hand, knocking on people's doors and asking if they would be interested in buying stocks. Hardly anyone except hobbyists rode a bicycle around the city in 1898, a practice that did not catch on until an Osaka bicycle boom in 1901. Gradually people started listening to Shinnosuke and he opened an account with Eguchi Securities, a firm that years later merged with two other houses to become Sanyo Securities, which maintains a close relationship with Nomura Securities to this day, through which he placed orders extracted from customers.

Shinnosuke finally overplayed his hand when one loyal customer bought ten shares in a company. Shinnosuke continued to badger him until he eventually purchased more of the stock as it fell in price. The stock continued to fall. The client panicked. Shinnosuke had persuaded him to buy a total of 500 shares and before the selling melee was over, his customer had lost 1500 yen.

Although legally Shinnosuke had purchased the shares on behalf of his client in his capacity as an agent, the concept of implied accountability at the time meant that he felt he had a moral obligation to repay the money lost by his customer. Shinnosuke handled the situation in what had become his trademark style for those early years: he ran away from the problem, expecting his father to bankroll him. Once again his father did so and paid back the 1500 yen – but not before Shinnosuke had left home in despair, claiming in a note that he needed to go away to ponder his terrible misfortune. What his father had not bargained for was that his profligate son would take money from the family safe to finance this self-examination and would return to Osaka only after he had sampled the sights of Mount Fuji, the waterfalls of Nikko to the north and the excitement of the nation's new capital, Tokyo. True to form, Shinnosuke returned penniless.

4
The First Fortune

When Shinnosuke and his brother Jitsusaburo were called to join the army in December 1899, their mother was overjoyed. 'My mother thought it befitting to our samurai tradition that we serve our country,' Tokushichi later wrote in his memoirs. Their father was less concerned about the family's patriotic duty than he was about the loss of manpower in his small shop, but under the mandatory conscription laws passed during the Meiji restoration two decades earlier, he had no choice but to see his sons off. To most Osaka men, the army was Tokyo's means of extending its control over the region. They viewed the government as a *kanemushi*, a 'money-eating bug' – a term still in use to describe a spendthrift girl borrowing money from her parents to fritter away on clothes.

For Nomura the army served as a catalyst, releasing him from his anaemic adolescence and instilling in him an assertive self-confidence which bordered on impudence. He joined the second company of the Fushimi Engineering Corps near Kyoto, spending much of his time working outdoors. The long hours spent toiling under the sun, shovelling dirt and hoisting rocks, transformed him from a sickly youth into a well-built man. As his body developed, so did his outlook. Previously, physical weakness had gone hand in hand with weakness of character. For a boy of his limitations it had been easier to get things done by stealth. But now the weasel had turned hound.

The disdain felt by most Osaka men for the army was legendary: its soldiers were undisciplined and unruly, with little desire for combat. Numerous accounts of Osaka regiments chronicle their fleeing from the enemy in battle when they calculated the chances of success to be in the enemy's favour. Nomura's sergeant held Osaka men in contempt, but Nomura's brash streak seemed refreshing – even if his behaviour often overstepped the bounds of proper military codes of conduct.

On weekend leave Nomura explored the licentious underbelly of Kyoto. The binges of sake and sex sometimes extended to four or five days, ending only when scouting parties sent out by his sergeant arrived to haul him back to base. Some nights were spent intimately in the arms of a geisha, others roaming the streets with friends, brawling with rival regiments or, on one occasion, beating up a police officer who had suggested that Nomura's band of merry men retire for the evening.

In 1902, after his three obligatory years in uniform, Nomura found himself back at his father's moneychanging shop as general manager. The next three years were spent building up the family business, studying the stockmarket and persuading clients to buy and sell shares. This was his real love. He had no interest in buying and selling copper, silver and gold, a task he left to his brother Jitsusaburo. In Nomura's eyes, moneychanging had a limited role for the future. Banks were beginning to handle most money transactions and, with the introduction of the yen, Japan now had a proper currency. The future of money-making lay in the stockmarket.

Japan declared war on Russia in February 1904, following the continuing dispute over spheres of influence in Korea and Manchuria. Tokushichi decided it was the perfect time to expand Nomura Shoten from a middle-sized moneychanging house that only dabbled in stocks to a fully fledged stockbroking firm. He had seen the stockmarket gallop ahead during the Sino-Japanese War eight years earlier. At that time he had been too young to take advantage of the bull market, but now he was determined to become rich. He understood that modern war fuelled industrial expansion. There was one obstacle – his father. Although Nomura was general manager of Nomura Shoten, and his father, often drunk, was seldom in the shop, he had to uphold the tradition of filial piety and somehow persuade his father to accept the new direction for the family business. Nomura pleaded with him to see the wisdom of committing capital to the stockmarket at such a time.

His father, however, stubbornly refused Nomura access to the family funds, partly because stock dealers were detested in Osaka and partly because his son had been so unsuccessful in his previous market forays. It tortured the younger Tokushichi to think of the money he could be making in the market if only his father would allow it. He became obsessed with the thought of the money sitting idly in the company safe. Not until June 1904, when his mother died, was Nomura able to wear down his father's resistance.

'How much do you need to start a stock business?' asked his father. 'Half the family fortune,' Nomura replied. *Twenty thousand yen*, more money than the average Osaka man made in his entire working life. Tokushichi was stunned by the amount of money his son wanted as capital – speculative capital – but he suddenly relented: he intended anyway to retire one day and turn everything over to his eldest son.

Nomura quickly changed the name of Nomura Shoten to Nomura Tokushichi Shoten and later that year he married Kikuko Yamada, the daughter of a well-to-do merchant, a match arranged by his father. For Nomura it was a timely marriage, since Kiku's job was to wash, cook and care for the house, chores that had been neglected since his mother's death in the summer. Her presence was fortuitous in helping to soften his father's outrage when he suddenly hired thirteen employees in anticipation of a stockmarket boom. Later Kiku produced two sons, Yoshitaro and Tokio.

Nomura's intuition proved correct. Japanese business prospered and in 1905 Japan dealt Russia crushing defeats at Tsushima and Port Arthur, marking the nation's graduation into the world of military and industrial might. The Tokyo and Osaka stockmarkets rallied sharply.

In 1905 Nomura made his first major stockmarket investment. Fukushima Boseki was a textile company rumoured to be headed for bankruptcy. But Nomura knew otherwise. Unlike most other stock traders of the early twentieth century, he took the trouble to visit the management of companies whose shares were quoted on the stock exchange. The spinning company had been set up by his brother-in-law, Yutaro Yasuhiro, to whom he had been apprenticed. The company was located just up the street from his own shop. Nomura would occasionally stop by for tea and to discuss business with Yasuhiro. To him it was clear that the rumours were being generated by stock traders who had taken short positions, selling shares in the company they did not have, and were trying to stir up a selling panic so that they could buy shares to cover their positions.

One day, after a particularly sharp sell-off in Fukushima Boseki shares, Nomura pestered the management into showing him their order-books. What he found was that instead of being on the verge of collapse, the firm was thriving as a result of wartime demand for uniforms, socks and tents. The order-books were bulging, the spinning looms were running at full capacity and profits had never been better.

The next day, when Nomura returned to the floor of the Osaka Stock Exchange, he started quietly buying up Fukushima shares. Other traders noticed his buying and questioned him, but he casually told them he had earlier sold short, and was now buying back to cover his short positions. He began buying shares at twenty yen and within days the price hit twenty-five. He kept on buying until the price reached thirty. Nervously, some of the traders who had sold shares they did not own began to panic and scrambled to buy them back. To their alarm they found Nomura had bought up most of the available shares and they were unable to buy back their stock without forcing the price still higher. Quick-witted dealers turned the short sellers' predicament into a 'short squeeze', a buying panic that fed on itself.

Nomura sat back as the price rose each day, hitting thirty-five, then forty, forty-five, fifty. By the end of 1905 the price of Fukushima Boseki had rocketed fourfold to 100 yen and

Nomura had earned on paper the 20,000 yen he had borrowed from his father earlier. He sold a few shares in the market on the way up, but was so thrilled with his first stockmarket killing that he kept most of his shares as a long-term investment. He refused to part with his holding even later when he became rich and famous. Nomura group companies have adhered to the wish of their founding father, so that in the 1990s, over eight decades after Tokushichi Nomura II purchased his first investment, they retain a 15 per cent stake in that same textile company, now known as Shikibo. And, as if to symbolize the Nomura group's bond with Shikibo, a distant relative of Tokushichi Nomura II reigns as president.

Nomura was crudely acting out intuitive market precepts which soon amassed him a considerable fortune. He played the crowds, mastering their psychology and getting the better of them. When emotion overtook reason in the stockmarket, he was there to buy from the distressed and sell to the eager, exploiting the mass mentality that led people to make impulsive and often irrational decisions.

Nomura decided that the best way to invest and beat the crowd was to hire someone to poke around individual companies, talk to management, check order-books and, if possible, calculate stock-price movements related to cycles in the Japanese and world economies. He hired an investigative journalist named Kisaku Hashimoto to run Nomura Tokushichi Shoten's newly formed research department. Hashimoto was a star reporter for the *Osaka-Mainichi Shimbun* who had many contacts who could pass him inside information on corporate Japan. He was the ideal man to be the nation's first research analyst. Moreover, he was a college graduate and at the time no college graduate would normally have considered joining a stock-dealing firm. In hiring Hashimoto, Nomura also improved the reputation of Nomura Shoten, differentiating the firm from the crude dealers on the floor of the Osaka Stock Exchange.

Tokushichi was harsh in his criticism of his own profession: 'The biggest obstacle to our success is low-life personalities in the stock business.' Bringing Hashimoto on board in 1907 began two precedents that set the company apart from other Japanese firms. First, Nomura was subsequently able to persuade even the smartest college graduates to join stockbroking; and second, to entice these graduates and to encourage them to stay, Nomura paid his employees salaries far in excess of those paid in any other securities firm. Tokushichi compellingly relates in his autobiography how his 'blood boiled' at Japan's characterization of stock dealers as virtual outcasts. But it was not until 1987 that the status of stockbrokers – and of Nomura Securities in particular – came anywhere near that of bankers.

Hashimoto spent a lot of time visiting companies, following up rumours, formulating new ideas and writing the Nomura weekly stock comment. If one or two Kitahama dealers bought a certain spinning-company share in a conspiratorial manner because of an enormous purported contract with the government, Hashimoto would pry his way into the company and extract the truth. Some of his most valuable moles were in the nation's largest trading company, Mitsui Bussan, and by discerning which companies made the most frequent use of Mitsui as their agent to sell their manufactured products, he was able to keep track of order flows. Trading companies were – and still are – firms that acted as intermediaries in matching buyers and sellers of every imaginable product. Friends in Nippon Yusen, the large shipping company, informed Hashimoto which firms were chartering the most space in its fleet, giving Nomura Shoten a rough picture of who was exporting overseas. Tokushichi Nomura in turn used this information to buy and sell stock on the Osaka stockmarket.

In 1906 the Osaka stockmarket was in the midst of an unprecedented boom. Nomura had optimistically added ten telephones to his three existing lines, employing a woman with a seductive manner to operate the switchboard and receive customers, thinking she would encourage his male clients to place orders. Tokushichi's small sales force went knocking from door to door (as it still does), pressing clients and potential customers to buy stock in the market.

Nomura himself handled the riskier work of buying and selling stock and stock futures for the house account. For every stock he bought – and physically appropriated to stash away in his company safe as a longer-term investment – he also bought the stock's considerably more speculative futures contract. He bought shipping stocks in firms such as Japan Postal Service Shipping, the government freight operator, which in 1906 leapt from eighty to 190. At the same time, his investment in Fukushima Boseki, which had already earned him his initial start-up capital of 20,000 yen, kept hitting new highs. Fukushima Boseki reached 150 in May, inched up to 160 by June and to 175 by July. Then it really began to roar: 222 in August, 324 in October and 421 by the end of 1906.

The great 1906 bull market – one of the greatest in the history of Japan – spread like wildfire. Stocks would suddenly burst into life, setting new highs and doubling or tripling in a matter of weeks. A buying panic would ensue on the Osaka Stock Exchange floor, as dealers pushed and shoved one another to buy the latest fast-moving stock, only to find that interest had subsided, having leapt to yet another stock.

Nomura had been buying stock since 1905 and was sitting on vast profits in both his long-term portfolio and his stock-futures portfolio. To be rich in Japan in the early twentieth century meant having a net worth of at least 100,000 yen (about $50,000 then, $1.5 million in current real terms) and Tokushichi Nomura was worth ten times that amount. In December 1906 his brother Jitsusaburo, always inclined to caution, advised Nomura to sell his shares. After all, why allow excessive greed to risk the million yen he had made? Nomura saw the wisdom of his brother's advice, but his thirst for market excitement, his *need* always to be at risk in the stockmarket, exerted a stronger pull. Not content with banking his profits, he calculated he would make twice as much by betting the market would fall.

Nomura had no doubt that the 1906 bubble would

burst. He and Hashimoto did some research and found close similarities with the conditions before the stockmarket plunge following the Sino-Japanese War. They began to examine the daily data on the market closely as Nomura's scouts tracked the selling and buying patterns of major Osaka dealers. Then, on 10 December, they detected a subtle change, noting that a few big dealers had begun selling. That day Nomura took action and began selling out his long-term portfolio, eliminating one third of his holdings by the end of the week. At the same time, he started selling share futures short, betting that the market would fall and he would be able to buy back at a cheaper price. Prices continued to rise, however, as the big Tokyo dealers unexpectedly began buying Osaka shares. Jitsusaburo urged him not to take additional risks by selling short. 'Only sell your long-term holdings,' he told Nomura, but his elder brother was unmoved. His mind was set – he wanted to add another bag of gold to the swelling family coffers.

Nomura's selling had little impact on the market. Prices rose daily and Jitsusaburo pleaded desperately with Tokushichi to cover his short positions. Then, on 26 December, five medium-sized stock dealers paid a visit to Nomura's offices to ask him to persuade his childhood friend Einosuke Iwamoto, now one of Kitahama's most successful stock dealers, to start selling in the hope of triggering a big sell-off. They needed help, but Nomura refused his fellow dealers on the grounds that he would be taking advantage of his special relationship with his friend. The dealers left Nomura and decided to solicit Iwamoto's support themselves. Surprisingly, he agreed to help them and the next day led the selling charge on the floor of the Osaka Stock Exchange. But their efforts were useless. The buying spree continued.

Each day Tokushichi, who had sold out his entire long-term holdings to finance his futures positions, waited for the market to show signs of weakness and each day the market moved against him. He was now losing considerable sums of money. The bull market of 1906 carried on into 1907.

Tokushichi, distressed with the abnormal rise of the market, went so far as to place a large advertisement in a local Osaka newspaper warning investors of danger ahead.

Although the market was still moving against him, Nomura stepped up the pace of his short selling. Inevitably, margin calls from the market traders who dealt for him began to arrive. Japanese investors at that time needed little cash to make vast speculations on the market. If they made money, everything was fine and the profits were added to their trading accounts. But if the market did not go their way, they needed to remit funds on a daily basis.

The money Nomura had placed on consignment was rapidly being whittled down, so that by early January the fretful brokers began to press him even more brusquely. Years later, Nomura recounted how he had hidden under his desk to avoid creditors. He eventually resorted to hiring a rickshaw for the day and furtively wheeling around the streets of Osaka – in the middle of winter – stopping in obscure back-street cafes where he was sure not to run into irate creditors or fair-weather friends from Kitahama. Tension mounted at Nomura Shoten as salesmen, clerks and secretaries realized their jobs were in danger unless the market began falling soon. But day after day it continued to rise.

By late January 1907 Tokushichi was desperate. He decided to seek the aid of a banker named Washio Shibayama who was manager of the Konoike Bank, one of the three leading banks in Osaka at that time. Shibayama faced a delicate situation. A Nomura Shoten bankruptcy could take down the bank, but Nomura Shoten was one of his most important customers. Like his counterparts at other banks, Shibayama had virtually unlimited powers of discretion when lending to customers, playing a supportive role in nurturing Japan's early industrialization. Little documentation was needed to lend money. Instead, bankers relied on friendship, instinct and judgement – often in that order.

Nomura played with Shibayama's emotions in his bid to ensure Nomura Shoten's survival.

'How much do you need?' Shibayama asked.

'One million yen,' came the reply.

Shibayama stuttered, 'That is one third of our bank's entire paid-up capital and I am only the manager of a single branch.'

For the next hour, Tokushichi pressed his case, gradually overcoming Shibayama's doubts.

Shibayama listened carefully as Tokushichi explained in detail why he believed the stockmarket would collapse. In a crowning flourish he handed Shibayama a list of all his personal assets and pledged them to the bank. 'I am betting my life that I am correct,' said Nomura, in the ultimate Japanese pledge of honour. 'If someone considers a matter thoroughly and does nothing, the outcome is the same as if he had considered nothing at all. I have never been wrong.'

Then, in a final act of bravado, Nomura secretly offered Shibayama a high-ranking job with Nomura Shoten – conditional, of course, upon the loan. In case he should be fired by Konoike's president, Shibayama thought it prudent to accept the offer, and advanced Nomura the money.

Tokushichi now had a reprieve and could meet his consignment payments. But the next two days proved nerve-racking. The market surged still higher on a renewed wave of buying. In Osaka the index was up fifty-eight points, or nearly 8 per cent, on 16 January and jumped another fifty-one points the following day. Another peak, 774 on the index, was scaled two days later. Somehow Tokushichi and the other dealers, including Iwamoto, kept their nerve. This could not go on for ever.

Then, on a snowy 19 January, it happened: the market began to crack. Jitsusaburo was first with the news. He ran in the snow from the stock exchange to Nomura's office, only to find Tokushichi, on the brink of a vast fortune, dozing.

'Wake up!' he shouted. 'The selling has begun.'

Nomura groaned and rolled over to go back to sleep.

'Wake up!' his brother shouted again. 'Prices are falling.' This time Tokushichi heard his brother. He jumped off his futon and began hugging Jitsusaburo. 'I knew it. I saw it would happen. We are saved.'

* * * * *

Within days, the great bull market of 1906 became the great bear market of 1907, one of the most dramatic declines in the history of the Japanese stockmarket, comparable to the collapse of the St Petersburg exchange in 1917 and of the Shanghai stockmarket in 1949. In the twelve days from the peak of 19 January 1907 to the end of the month, the market shed one third of its value. By the end of 1907 the selling bloodbath had reduced the market's value by 88 per cent. The final reading on the index at the end of the year was a mere ninety-two, down from 774.

Nomura made three million yen – the equivalent of $60 million in current real terms. He became a legend. Traders, fond of labels, nicknamed him 'the great general of the stockmarket'. Aged twenty-eight, he was worth over five million yen, including the million he had made in the bull market and another million he had made speculating in property.

That same year, on the other side of the world, a twenty-two-year-old semi-pro baseball player named Charles Merrill accidentally bumped into a soda-fountain-equipment salesman named Edmund Lynch. Eight years later they set up a brokerage firm they proudly called Merrill, Lynch Co., a firm that, for thirty years after World War II, held the record as the world's largest brokerage house.

5
Gulliver's Travels

Stockmarkets all around the world plunged during 1907. In America it was called the rich man's panic, set off by the closure of the Knickerbocker Trust Company. London, New York and even Bombay share prices nosedived – a coincidence that Tokushichi noted straight away. Eighty years later, in the great crashes of 1987 and 1989, shorter, more frenetic, less traumatic, but much more chronicled declines occurred on world bourses. Ironically, it was the house that Nomura built from the first crash that saved the markets.

The fame and reputation of Tokushichi Nomura spread to surrounding cities. Stories about his money-making skills were embellished on the way, helping Nomura Shoten to build up its customer base. Nomura himself became something of a curiosity. One day Isuke Matsui, a renowned investor in his own right, appeared on Nomura's doorstep seeking the man he had heard was 'a god who can tell the market's future'. Expecting a shrine, he was surprised and somewhat embarrassed to find the celebrated stockbroker's little shop. Other merchants who called on Tokushichi to congratulate him on his success made a mental note of good-luck charms inside the shop that they might imitate, in particular Nomura's two-foot ceramic cat, which stood on its hind legs, waving one front paw and holding a fake gold coin in the other. Ceramic cats in various shapes and sizes commonly adorned Japanese merchant shops – as they do today – as a sign of welcome to customers, but after the market collapse of 1907, a number of cats remarkably similar in appearance to the one gracing the entrance to Nomura Shoten suddenly appeared in Osaka.

By the autumn of 1907, Nomura felt ready to make his entrance into respectable Japanese society. A social naif, he

50

was determined to boost the image of his company with flair. As his tight-fisted father looked on in disgust, Tokushichi spent over 2,000 yen – more than double the salary of a government minister at the time – on a grand party in a leading Osaka hotel.

The party marked the occasion of Emperor Meiji's birthday. Nomura had over 400 invitations sent out to financiers, dignitaries, politicians and high-profile businessmen. More than half of them attended. But for Tokushichi Nomura I, the strain of resentment ran too deep. He refused to attend the party. Nor, indeed, did he ever set foot in the lavish new home Nomura had built with his recent winnings. It was the beginning of a new world for Tokushichi Nomura II, a world that many Meiji men like his father found totally alien. Throughout his life Tokushichi I remained a conservative moneychanger cast in the mould of a bygone era. He found he could not adapt to twentieth-century Japan; his world had disappeared. In 1908, at the age of fifty-eight, Tokushichi Nomura I died.

His son had long yearned to visit the Western countries that had been such an influence on Japan since the Meiji restoration. He had, after all, studied in a school modelled on Western institutions, trained in a Prussian-style army, worn English clothes, ridden trams and even eaten Western food. So, in 1908, he left for a five-month tour of America and Europe, a tour sponsored by the *Asahi* newspaper, the forerunner of today's liberal *Asahi Shimbun*, Japan's third largest daily newspaper. He left his registered seal, necessary for all banking transactions, in the hands of Jitsusaburo. It was an explicit gesture of trust, since the seal was – as it remains today – one of the most closely guarded items in any businessman's possession.

Sixty, seventy and eighty years later, Westerners would point to Japan's economic and industrial might in automobiles, computers, electronics and steel, citing Japan's ability to imitate Western technology. But even in 1908 Tokushichi was borrowing American and European financial ideas. He took mental notes on everything: how the Americans and Europeans traded, recorded their bargains, settled their deals – even how they talked on the telephone.

On Wall Street and in the City of London he found models from which he could forge his own financial tiller to steer himself through Japan's business community. He was there to do what Japanese industrialists were also doing and have continued to do to this day – to improve upon the best that the West had to offer.

What Tokushichi took back from Wall Street and the City of London was no less important than the spoils of industrial pirating of Western manufacturing techniques. To be sure, financial expertise was more nebulous and its contribution to society harder to grasp. But Tokushichi understood that it was the railways, ships and factories that stocks and bonds could build that made securities houses so important.

Of Nomura's visit to New York, his biographer would later write: 'The towering skyscrapers of that city struck him as a veritable wonderland and he felt like a financial Gulliver encountering a strange incredible world.' In Japan, a land threatened by earthquakes, few structures were built more than two floors high. New York boasted offices ten, twenty, even thirty floors high. There were so many skyscrapers that the sun was barely able to filter through to the street, adding an eerie grandeur to Wall Street as Nomura made his way from Trinity Church to the New York Stock Exchange. Once there, he headed for the most famous address in finance, 23 Wall Street, the grand offices of the legendary J.P. Morgan, a man whom he had waited years to meet. But to Morgan, Tokushichi Nomura was a nobody, a Japanese in a world dominated by Americans and British. What possible advantage could Morgan derive from meeting a Japanese businessman turned tourist? Nomura was turned away at the door.

Tokushichi was depressed. He went back to look at the exchange's colonnaded facade. It left him with a feeling of envy and inferiority as he thought of his own world of fleeting financial bucketshops. Wall Street appeared not simply as a stately financial avenue, but as the financial powerhouse on which America had been built: brokers, insurance companies and banks – all were embraced by its influence.

As he relates in his autobiography, comparisons with his homeland left the impressionable young man dejected. One could hardly say Wall Street in the same breath as Kitahama or Kabutocho, the districts around the stock exchanges of Osaka and Tokyo. All they meant were a handful of grain merchants and stock dealers; they were nothing but routine addresses in two sprawling Japanese cities. Nomura later wrote of Wall Street: 'All the wealth of the world gathers here and is distributed outwards.' Not much gathered in Japan's financial districts except erstwhile rice traders ready for a day's speculation.

Nomura visited the research and trading department of Post and Flagg, a New York Stock Exchange member firm. Such was the accuracy of Post and Flagg research that the US Treasury relied on their statistics. What particularly intrigued Nomura was the way traders telephoned London every ten minutes for stockmarket updates. Suddenly he realized how easily the markets of the world could be linked. Although he had already proved he was something of a stockmarket genius, his ideas of how world markets and economies interacted were ill-formed and incomplete.

Nomura also made another important discovery. New York banks willingly funded brokers instead of viewing them as financial lepers. Behind their backs at home Nomura and his employees were called *sobashi*, a derogatory expression still in use today, literally meaning 'men who watch the rise and fall of stock prices', but connoting negative images. Few banks, except the smaller ones, were willing to lend to the Japanese stock traders. It always angered Nomura when he overheard someone using the term *sobashi*. But he knew his business had more than its fair share of shady characters. 'I suppose,' he wrote afterwards, 'we must first improve the quality of Japanese brokers before the banks will accept us. All Japanese brokers care about is speculation.'

Nomura's tour of Europe was supposed to be for sightseeing, but the culture and fine-art museums bored him. He was impatient to be back in Osaka putting into practice the lessons he had absorbed. A brand-new British car, bought by his brother Jitsusaburo, was waiting for him in front of the Osaka railway station when he returned home in 1908. 'It was one of the first cars ever imported into Japan,' he later recalled. The gift delighted him and triggered an addiction to flashy racing cars which never left him.

His first move on his return was to restructure his own research department along Post and Flagg lines, giving it four separate divisions: research, statistics, editing and translation. Translation of Japanese documents into English was necessary to enable Nomura to deal in foreign-currency bonds issued by the Japanese government to overseas countries such as England and America, whose investors had financed Japan's war against Russia. He then stepped up public-relations efforts and began spending what seemed at the time to be an exorbitant sum – 10,000 yen a month – placing stockmarket comments in local newspapers. The local business community thought Nomura crazy to spend so much on advertisements. He paid no attention. He wanted the public to buy stocks, and as always he wanted to enhance his chosen profession.

By 1909, six of the thirty workers on the Nomura Shoten payroll were men with college degrees. Training was strict and attendance at Sunday evening study meetings compulsory. Nomura was attempting to build his business as he would a family: employees learned about accounting from guest speakers, while wives and children were invited to attend other, more general lectures. He ruled over his staff with a paternal demeanour, imposing a strict code of social behaviour. Junior employees were not allowed to go out drinking at night and were required to come into work by eight each morning – often after staying in the shop until ten the previous evening.

He paid his staff more than any other financial firm of

the day, but instituted rigid internal rules to discourage his salesmen and clerks from playing the market. Naturally these rules did not apply to Tokushichi, the greatest market operator Japan had ever seen, nor to his brother Jitsusaburo or the rest of the top executives. They continued to use the market as a gaming table for the accumulation of personal riches. This double standard – an open secret – would be passed down in the firm through the years, reaching its peak in the 1960s when Nomura Securities was under the stewardship of Minoru Segawa.

6
Spoils of War

Most Japanese businessmen were not greatly affected by the outbreak of World War I; they considered it a European war which would have little effect on the Japanese economy. Though stock dealers had fervently bought shares during Japan's own wars with Russia and China, Japanese traders saw no reason to suppose that the war would affect the daily lives of Tokyo and Osaka merchants.

Nomura knew better. He was one of the few Japanese businessmen who had been to Europe and seen how the stock and bond markets of the world were linked through trade flows and improved communications. The war, he felt, was sure to have drastic implications for stockmarkets, including Japan's. What those implications would be, he was, as yet, unsure.

The answer came rapidly. Within two days of the outbreak of war, and entirely without warning, the Bank of England raised the base rate it applied to the major commercial banks from 3 to 10 per cent. Such an increase was designed to stem a run on sterling, but in fact precipitated a spectacular collapse of Western financial markets, which dwarfed even the fall of world stockmarkets in 1929 and 1987. The New York Stock Exchange closed the day after war broke out, and stayed closed for nine months.

Japanese stock traders panicked and sent their own stockmarket reeling. Depositors, demanding their money, formed a long line outside the Kitahama Bank, the main source of funds for Osaka speculators and investors. The bank quickly cut all credit to brokerage houses and called in the loans it had made to stock speculators. A selling blizzard ensued as traders were forced to sell stock to repay the bank. But most dealers were unable to repay their loans.

Every 100 yen they had borrowed was now worth only eighty yen and, worse, most traders had borrowed more than they could afford to repay. Many less reputable dealers, heavily in debt, simply left town. In August 1914 the Kitahama Bank collapsed.

Tokushichi's boyhood friend Einosuke Iwamoto, now one of Osaka's most upright citizens, suffered heavy losses. Unlike Nomura Shoten, Iwamoto's stock-dealing business had no supplementary income. Nomura bought and sold stocks and bonds for investors and received commission income whether markets were rising or falling. Iwamoto made money by intuitively guessing which way the market was headed, betting his own substantial fortune.

Normally when Iwamoto bought stock and the market fell, he just went to the Kitahama Bank to borrow more money. This time, with his credit lines cut, he had a difficult time even paying his workers, and conditions were so bad that he could not sell his stock. Nomura came to the rescue, buying up Iwamoto's entire stock portfolio to save him from bankruptcy.

Nomura was certain of one thing: the Japanese stockmarket would not keep on falling. But most market dealers were not so sure. Their judgement was guided by a string of bad omens: the volcano on Mount Sakurajima in southern Japan had erupted earlier that year; the Emperor's mother had just died; Japan was experiencing a poor rice harvest; and a government bribery scandal had been uncovered. Then came war. To Osaka's superstitious trading community, it followed that a market fall must be imminent.

Nomura, in contrast, was the only Japanese stockbroker to have sources in Europe to feed him with up-to-date information on the progress of the war. His youngest brother, Motogoro, was in England studying finance and banking at Birmingham University. After the outbreak of war, Motogoro telegraphed his brother with daily reports on events in Europe. Rival brokers had to wait for news of the war to filter through to the local Osaka newspapers, by which time it was weeks old. Nomura's second source was Mitsui Bussan, the great trading company that supplied Europeans with war material. Japan had entered the war on the side of the Allies in August 1914, and Nomura learned from Mitsui executives that the Allies were frantically purchasing supplies of shoes, combat gear, boats and ammunition. According to one executive whom Nomura plied for information, Mitsui was straining its lines of credit at every bank to purchase 'absolutely anything' it could resell to Europe.

This was the basis for Nomura's second fortune. In fact, Mitsui's overseas posts later became famous for supplying the Japanese government, during both world wars, with valuable information. But it was Tokushichi Nomura who first used their trading network to advantage. Great fortunes have been made during times of great catastrophe, adversity or strife, as Tokushichi realized. His next fortune would be a matter of timing, and so he began shoring up his own espionage ring in Japan.

Textile companies such as Fukushima Boseki, of which Nomura was both a major shareholder and a director, were selling more fabric to Europe than ever before and, despite running at full capacity, were unable to service those European orders. Nomura noted, too, that Kawasaki Steel was also busy cranking out steel and ships for export to the war zone. It soon became clear to Nomura that shortages of commodities and manufactured goods were occurring all over the world, as neither American nor European factories could deliver enough for the war effort, even while running double or triple shifts. He concluded that if the war went on sufficiently long, then increased demand for Japanese goods would send the profits of Japanese companies soaring – and the stockmarket along with them.

Late in 1914 Nomura began buying heavily. But, as in the great plunge of 1907, he had moved too soon. The Japanese market continued to fall and a rash of bankruptcies followed. Ten brokers in Kitahama closed their doors, and Nomura Shoten, full of stock bought from Iwamoto in addition to its own recent purchases, was running at a loss. Five employees were sacked – the only Japanese staff in the firm's history to date forced to leave because of poor market conditions.

Things continued to look grim for Nomura into the following year. Then came the news he had been waiting for: Japan's exports had begun rising faster than her imports. Nomura immediately increased his buying in textiles, shipping and steel stocks, both in the spot and futures markets. The local media were claiming that the war would end later that year and trade would soon be back to normal. That was not the message Nomura was getting from his brother Motogoro, who, back in Britain's industrial heartland, said the war was sure to last longer; fighting on the continent had become a bloody stalemate. World tonnage was in short supply, since there were not enough ships to transport troops and goods for either wartime or civilian use. Japan soon found itself shipping freight at three times the pre-war level, and, since most of the fighting was in Europe, Japan's merchant fleet was unharmed. Nomura bought shares in the Osaka Steamship Company, a Sumitomo family concern, and in Nippon Yusen, the Iwasaki family freight company. Traditionally most Japanese stockmarket participants cleared their trading positions in late March (as they still do today) to prepare for year-end accounts, but Nomura took advantage of the market lull and kept on buying.

As Japan prospered from the war, money became plentiful. That summer Iwamoto, solvent again, jumped into the market alongside Nomura as the market boomed. By November 1915, Japan's trade surplus had increased yet again, and, in the stockmarket, bulls became so rampant that dealing had to be suspended for three days as firms tried to absorb the backlog of buying orders. Nomura doubled his money in Osaka Steamship within the first six months of the year as the share index continued its daily climb. Then, from sixty-six in July 1915 it rose to 111 in November, and by the end of that month stood at 229. Few realized that the buying had hardly begun.

The biggest winners of that 1915 stockmarket rally were

the *zaibatsu* men, whose fortunes were usually credited to trading, banking and manufacturing rather than to the stockmarket. Their market winnings were simply staggering. Eiichi Shibusawa, the founder of the Tokyo Stock Exchange and, as we have seen, the father of Japanese industry and finance, personally amassed forty million yen in profit, the 1915 equivalent of $20 million; more than $300 million in current terms. Hachiroemon Mitsui, one of the eleven patriarchs of the great trading and banking empire, made three times Shibusawa's fortune, while Iwasaki of the Mitsubishi group brought off an even bigger coup, worth an estimated 150 million yen. A merchant called Shobo Hayashi topped them all. His winnings, at over 100 million yen – worth $3 billion at today's values – represent the single largest personal gain ever recorded on any stockmarket.

Strange as it may seem, nobody knows what became of Hayashi and his billions, but the star of a lesser-known man and his firm was rising. Tokushichi Nomura made over 700,000 yen in the rally of 1915 – modest by comparison with the *zaibatsu* titans, but enough to make him one of the country's wealthiest men. As other dealers started to realize their profits in late 1915, Nomura held on. A year later, in the winter of 1916, German victories sent the Japanese market into a nosedive. The ever-cautious Jitsusaburo advised his elder brother to sell. 'If a peace treaty is concluded, then the market will crumble,' he warned. Iwamoto, who had made almost as much as Nomura in the rally, began to sell. While clearing out his stock and futures portfolios, he began to sell short on a massive scale. Nomura relied instead on the messages from Motogoro, in Britain, who told him the war was far from over. Tokushichi held on.

The decline in the market was short-lived. As news of a Japanese trade surplus – exceeding 200 million yen – was released, the market rallied, and it remained buoyant throughout 1917. The unbending Iwamoto kept selling. Nomura, hearing that his friend's company was losing large amounts of money, became worried. Iwamoto's general manager pleaded with Nomura to intervene and persuade Iwamoto to stop selling futures. Nomura refused. 'Markets are fickle,' he told Iwamoto's manager, 'and the belief of any one man at any one time might be correct for only an instant.' He reassured the manager, telling him that Iwamoto had just donated one million yen to the building of a new public hall in Osaka. Things could not be that bad, Tokushichi argued.

The market was unheeding, and Iwamoto's creditors began to close in. Relations between Nomura Shoten and Iwamoto Shoten were especially strained, since Nomura Shoten was the biggest buyer of stock on the floor of the exchange, with Iwamoto the biggest seller. Just as Tokushichi had in 1907, Iwamoto declined social invitations and refused to be seen in public. He even gave up his directorship of the Osaka Securities Exchange. Iwamoto, once lively and outgoing, became introverted and melancholy. It was particularly painful for Nomura to witness the self-destructive anguish of his childhood friend. But Tokushichi could not reach out. Iwamoto was a man gone too far.

In the autumn of 1917, Iwamoto gave his workers a day off to pick mushrooms near Kyoto. He wrote a farewell poem, got himself a haircut, had a photograph taken outside the Mitsukoshi department store and then visited his relatives. Shortly after dinner he went up to his tea room, unwrapped a pistol wrapped in silk and shot himself through the head. He lay in a coma in hospital for five days before dying. Tokushichi lost his only true friend, a man he considered a gentleman in a den of thieves, a 'stork among hens' as he was later fond of saying. He knew that the only difference between them was that the outcome of Nomura's moment of resolve had been fortunate: both were men of unbending resolve in a business that demanded flexibility. Had the market collapsed in 1917, he, not Iwamoto, would have been wiped out.

Over 1,500 people attended Iwamoto's funeral. He left behind a wife and a three-year-old daughter. After seven

61

days of mourning, Nomura paid his respects to Iwamoto's widow. She showed him the poem her husband had written on the morning of his death: 'The red maple leaf falls without waiting for the autumn.' Iwamoto did not live to see the completion – in November 1917 – of the Osaka public hall, where today a statue stands to his memory. All the money that remained of his once huge estate was distributed to creditors by his general manager. Iwamoto's wife was left destitute, and creditors made it impossible for her to receive gifts unnoticed.

Nomura handed her 5,000 yen, enough to support her for many years, telling her he had borrowed it from Iwamoto many years before. She refused the gift, but he insisted she accept it to keep her daughter alive. Shortly afterwards the grieving Nomura, having made his second large stockmarket fortune, publicly denounced speculation. The following year another tragedy took place. His brother Jitsusaburo, who for so long had been his confidant and reliable deputy, died of pneumonia.

7
Kings and Jokers

One of the most popular pastimes of Tokushichi's era was a Meiji card-game known as *Daihimin*. It was a simple game, often played in Osaka tea-houses, but it had an interesting twist: the winner of the first hand would receive the three best cards from the loser's next hand, a rule that virtually assured the continued dominance of the winner into the next round. Everyone else fought for second, third and fourth place. Only a revolution, in this case the holding of two jokers, could change the natural order of things. Only winners could be considered winners. Those who commanded power should retain power.

Success in the highly charged business community of Osaka meant not only creating capital, but being viewed as a winner. In this context, Tokushichi Nomura faced an image problem. The real powerbrokers of the era, into whose company Nomura sought to enter, were the great *zaibatsu* houses, and he was not deemed a *zaibatsu* chieftain.

Zaibatsu, meaning financial clique or 'estate wealth', is a modest phrase for family-run industrial empires, which rose to prominence during the Taisho (1912-25) and Showa (1926-88) eras, corresponding to the respective reigns of the Taisho emperor and the Showa emperor (more commonly known as Hirohito). They were to Japan what moguls such as John D. Rockefeller, Commodore Vanderbilt, Andrew Carnegie and J. Pierpont Morgan were to America. The difference between the American titans and the Japanese *zaibatsu* was one of concentration. The *zaibatsu* concerned themselves not with control of one industry, like Rockefeller in oil or Carnegie in steel, but with a wide spectrum of enterprises.

Every *zaibatsu* house was dominated by a family patriarch, usually a man of samurai descent. (It was the samurai who, at the beginning of the Meiji period in 1868, had used their government contacts to win concessions and licences.) At the core of each *zaibatsu* lay the family bank, which funded the dozens of other family endeavours. Central to each house was also the family trading firm, with outposts worldwide, used not only to buy and sell goods, but also, as in the case of Mitsui Bussan, as key listening posts. Funded by the bank, raw materials were bought by the trading company and merchandise produced by the manufacturing arm and sold back out through the trading company. They were everywhere: from steel to railways, textiles to chemicals, banking to mining, shipbuilding to trading. Instead of one or two firms presiding over a particular segment of business, as in America, four or five *zaibatsu* towered over the entire Japanese economy.

Five *zaibatsu* ruled Japanese business at the start of World War II: Mitsui, Mitsubishi, Sumitomo, Yasuda and Suzuki. The first four remain to this day powerhouses of Japanese industry, while the fifth faded into relative obscurity, a victim of the complex financial repercussions of post-World War I deflation and the 1923 earthquake.

The house of Mitsui was the largest *zaibatsu* of them all, with origins dating back as far as 1683 when it functioned as a quasi-central bank known as the Exchange House of Mitsui. Descended from a long line of samurai, Hachiroemon Mitsui bought silk mills from the government in the late nineteenth century and turned the exchange house into a bank. By the beginning of World War II the Mitsui family was presiding over the largest company in the world: a sprawling bank, a trading company, a department store and mining and manufacturing interests, with over three million workers.

Another samurai, Yataro Iwasaki, founded the great Mitsubishi empire in the late nineteenth century and amassed a fortune by acquiring the Nagasaki shipyard from the government. Iwasaki's firm became known as Nippon Yusen Kaisha, or NYK Line, the world's largest shipping company. Mitsubishi went on to become the second largest in the world prior to World War II.

The Sumitomo family was the only major *zaibatsu* with origins near Nomura's, in western Japan. Sumitomo rose to prominence controlling the copper mines of Kyoto and through them managed the nation's coinage during the Edo period. Certain advantages naturally flowed from having a hand in the government's till. By the early twentieth century it had become the third largest concern in Japan.

Zenjiro Yasuda was the latecomer in the *zaibatsu* phenomenon. A wholesaler of dried tuna and a moneychanger, he built his business up to create the basis for the foundation, in 1880, of the Third National Bank, which he subsequently renamed after himself. (After World War II it was renamed the Fuji Bank, later becoming the fourth largest bank in the world.)

The 'big four', as the leading *zaibatsu* were known, controlled almost every sector of the economy from 1920 until the end of World War II, representing one of the greatest concentrations of wealth in the history of mankind. (The only present-day comparison, and this in one sector alone, is the stranglehold that Japan's brokerage houses wield over the stock and bond markets. Also known as the 'big four', Nomura, Daiwa, Nikko and Yamaichi account for almost half of all stock and bond transactions in Japan.)

It was this select group of *zaibatsu* that Tokushichi Nomura sought to penetrate. All his adult life he had struggled to gain the social and commercial recognition he felt he deserved. Although uneducated, he was a rich and highly successful tycoon. However, what mattered in Japan was not how much wealth a man had accumulated, but the *manner* in which he had made his fortune. Tokushichi was branded an *arriviste* by the *zaibatsu* clans, a man who had climbed to wealth during World War I with blood money made through the stockmarket.

Nomura was determined to leap over the abyss that separated the grand from the not-so-grand, the court from the courtiers, the super-wealthy from the merely wealthy. He set about making his mark on Japanese *zaibatsu* history by methodically plotting a course of action. He was, after all, descended from samurai through both his mother and his father. What he needed to do now was to start a bank and a trading company that might one day compete with the big four. Luckily, the Sumitomo family were the only major *zaibatsu* to control business in the Osaka area.

The seed of Nomura's own *zaibatsu* began gestating somewhere in the green wilderness of equatorial Asia. In 1916 Tokushichi travelled to the Dutch East Indies to discover what raw material the region had to offer. The large *zaibatsu* houses channelled their huge stockmarket and wartime trading gains into manufacturing and banking. Nomura had no footing in either. While the *zaibatsu* were interested in building a presence in Japanese-occupied Korea, Manchuria and Formosa, Nomura thought better prospects lay in the tropics, where rubber, palm oil, coffee, fruit and timber were plentiful. Perhaps he could also supply iron, petroleum, zinc, copper and sugar to Japan. Early the following year he purchased a rubber plantation in Borneo, thereby establishing the supply side of his trading firm's equation. Within years he was able to expand his offices throughout South-East Asia – from Surabaya to Singapore, from Hanoi to Bangkok.

Next came the bank. In 1918, with the help of Jinnosuke Inouye, the head of the Bank of Japan, Nomura opened the doors of the Osaka-Nomura Bank (the forerunner of the present-day Daiwa Bank, Japan's ninth largest commercial bank – not to be confused with Daiwa Securities, which is Japan's second largest stockbroking firm and Nomura's competitor). Nomura hoped the establishment of his bank – which soon had branches throughout western Japan – would give him commercial respectability, but the merchants of Osaka still considered his business largely speculative and beneath them. Instead of distancing Nomura from the passionate rice and stock traders of Osaka, the bank facilitated Nomura's own stockmarket ventures by providing him with easy access to loans. Every time the Japanese stockmarket went down (as it did frequently in the early 1920s), savers rushed to withdraw their money from the Osaka-Nomura Bank before it could be siphoned off into the stockmarket. In his drive for respectability, Tokushichi removed his name from Nomura Shoten, and in 1923 it reverted to its original name of Osakaya Shoten. Nomura had turned his back on stockbroking.

In his quest for acceptance by the landed class, Nomura made great changes in his personal life. He took up genteel pursuits such as the tea ceremony, Noh drama, horse-riding and ceramic pottery. He began building homes that would become monuments to the family's newly founded Nomura dynasty. His new house in Kobe was an overt bid for social acceptance. Situated high up on a hill overlooking the Osaka and Kobe ports, it was an ideal venue for parties, and Nomura wasted no time in using it to entertain Japan's financial elite. It was a Western-style three-storey building, with a tower in the west wing, which was occupied by his wife, younger son, nephews and nieces. Nomura himself and his elder son, Yoshitaro, lived in the east wing.

Tokushichi was very relaxed around the house; although he wore a suit and tie to work in Osaka, at home he dressed in a loose-fitting kimono. He loved to spend the afternoon in his sunroom, sitting at his writing table or in a wicker chair, reading. He warmed to the children, drawing them pictures and telling them stories – when he had the time. But they saw little of him. 'We were raised by a group of thirty servants of every type, maids, butlers, gardeners, tutors, nannies and chauffeurs,' remembers Fumihide, Nomura's eldest grandson.

Nomura's second home, his Kyoto villa (now held in trust by the Daiwa Bank and still used by Nomura group executives), was built around a pond fed by cool waters running off Lake Biwa, Japan's largest lake. The pond was filled with rare orange-and-white carp, a species treasured by the

Japanese for their longevity. (Carp can live for 200 years, and Tokushichi's carp still swim in the pond to this day.) The house remains largely unchanged since Tokushichi's time. The villa is hidden from the street by pine trees and a carefully constructed pale wooden fence and inside the grounds only the splashing of the brook and the chirping of birds can be heard. Set in the beautifully manicured gardens and lawns are one- and two-storey wooden villas – guest-houses and tea-houses.

Tokushichi took up the tea ceremony after World War I to teach himself patience and self-control as well as to improve his social standing. The tea ceremony, called *chanoyu* by the Japanese, was in many ways a negation of Tokishichi's harried and opportunistic past. It was a zen ceremony of aesthetic ritual where greatness was to be found in imperfection. Tea, served with rustic utensils, was meant to highlight the beauty of simplicity, the tranquillity of solitude and, as the utensils wore down over the years, the naturalness of decay. The ceremony put Tokushichi on a higher plane, yet he still used it as a means of promoting his business ties. He invited many influential businessmen, including various members of the Mitsui family, to elaborate tea rituals, which usually took more than four hours to perform. It was through the tea ceremony, as well as through a shared interest in road racing, that Takakimi Mitsui became a close friend. Nomura had arrived.

Now that Nomura was a man of stature within Japanese society, he and his wife, Kiku, began to lead separate lives. Family members tend to be tight-lipped about the marriage, but some recall the couple constantly bickering until Tokushichi simply decided to remove himself to the east wing of the house in Kobe and live apart from his wife (a common enough arrangement in such households in pre-war Japan). Kiku treated the Kobe manor-house as a castle and expected the servants permanently to stand guard at their posts, in constant readiness for what one member of the family called 'the return of the king'. It was as if she was frightened that her entire life was a dream and that one morning she would wake up and find herself abandoned and homeless. Like most Japanese women, she had few friends, the traditional female role being to tend the hearth. But Kiku's plight was particularly pitiful since there was no hearth to tend. She was surrounded by hired staff, whom she treated as 'common labourers' and who responded to her commands mechanically and impersonally.

When her younger son Tokio died in an automobile accident in 1928, she was left with only one child of her own, Yoshitaro, whose life was wholly directed by Tokushichi.

Much of Tokushichi's time was spent in the Kyoto retreat, thirty miles away. There he passed many months of his later years in the arms of Hiroko, his geisha. Hiroko's presence was no secret. It was entirely within the social conventions of the time to keep a mistress to act as hostess, chatting to male guests and organizing younger girls to entertain the men and ensure that the food and drink were properly served. As a secret bond between himself and Hiroko, and in accordance with custom, Tokushichi signified his loyalty by tying a small piece of her kimono below his knee. Geishas were highly trained courtesans and demanded care and respect; only after earnest courtship would a geisha subordinate herself to being the mistress of a wealthy benefactor. Hiroko bore Nomura a son, whom they named Seizo Mizuguchi. Secretly Nomura doted on him and earmarked him for a place in the family business, but the war changed all that. Mizuguchi became branch manager of the Bank of Tokyo's Kuala Lumpur office.

Kiku knew about her husband's illegitimate son and surprisingly accepted him without malice. When Seizo Mizuguchi wanted to marry at the end of World War II, he asked Tokushichi's nephew, Kozo Nomura, to act in a parental role at the marriage ceremony. Kozo asked Kiku's permission. Her response was, 'You must do this for him.'

* * * * *

Control of their far-flung fortunes was an important key to the success of the *zaibatsu* big four, and was achieved through careful placement of family members in subsidiaries throughout their realms. Tokushichi set about emulating this strategy and the perpetuation of the Nomura *zaibatsu* was a constant worry to him. Kozo Nomura remembers him grooming his family from an early age. 'The sons, brothers and nephews of Tokushichi were precious to him,' he recalled, 'but there was no doubt that he was the king and we were his princes.' Other relatives describe Tokushichi as having been a 'benevolent monarch'. His word was law in the household, where he surrounded himself with numerous members of his family. They were his future, each with his destined place in the *zaibatsu* hierarchy. When his son and nephews were older, he constantly pestered them to have more children.

Tokushichi's goal was to see his heirs accepted as members of the ruling business elite of Japan. He founded the exclusive Konan school in Kobe, where his sons, nephews and grandsons could begin from an early age to make friends with the rich. Unlike him, they would start life on the inside.

To consolidate his newly acquired wealth and to ensure that his dynasty remained in secure hands, in 1922 Tokushichi created the Nomura Partnership. Known in Japanese as Nomura Gomei, the partnership controlled most of the family subsidiaries, such as the bank and trading company (which he named Nomura East Indies). Nomura himself owned nearly 60 per cent of the partnership, while he gave his dead brother's sons 30 per cent and his youngest brother, Motogoro, 10 per cent. Upon his death, the balance of power represented by his own stake would be inherited by his elder son, Yoshitaro. The Nomura Partnership was the most tightly held *zaibatsu* of all. Other families, such as the Mitsui and the Mitsubishi, commanded their associated companies through partly owned subsidiaries. Nomura was taking no such chances.

Ironically, Nomura was helped in tightening his grip on Osaka finance by the huge and tragic Kanto earthquake of 1923, which killed over 100,000 people in the area around

Tokyo and Yokohama and left millions homeless. Nomura Securities began business early in 1926, and much of its growth was through its dealing in bonds issued to finance the reconstruction of Japan. Later, the Nomura *zaibatsu* purchased life insurance firms crippled by pay-outs to victims of the quake.

Japanese insurance policies did not cover fire losses due to earthquakes, but the government forced insurance companies to pay out 10 per cent of all existing policies; the insurance companies spent the next twenty years paying off debts, and were crippled as a result. The economy had already been in a battered state of post-war deflation, with demand for manufacturing and commodities in a slump. Now it was in a complete shambles. The fires that spread through Tokyo and Yokohama financial districts destroyed or badly damaged 121 of the 138 banking headquarters; physical securities such as banknotes and collateral simply vanished. The government tried to salvage the situation by declaring a temporary moratorium on debt repayments, and put pressure on the banks to lend more and more money to already ailing manufacturers. The demand for capital was so strong after 1923 that Japanese companies began looking abroad for funds. It was at this time that foreign capital – most of it American – began pouring into Japan. Some 80 per cent of all foreign investment in Japan before World War II came from America, an ironic fact in the light of subsequent events.

Tokushichi's business interests were, however, largely unaffected by the disaster. He had previously owned no insurance companies and had stayed clear of the manufacturing industry. As the owner of an Osaka-based bank, he made loans chiefly to businesses and individuals in western Japan, where few companies had been affected by the earthquake. He did, however, cut back the capital of his stock-trading firm, Osakaya, and appointed Kisaku Hashimoto, the investigative journalist who ran Nomura's research department, its first president. (Tokushichi sold the firm off to Hashimoto and his staff in 1929. The surviving firm, now called Cosmo

71

Securities, went on to become one of Japan's most successful stockbroking firms.) Stockmarket activity had already been very sluggish after the end of World War I and, once the earthquake hit, activity came to a standstill. Investors turned instead to government reconstruction bonds, and it was to these and to the growing corporate Japanese bond market that Nomura also turned.

Not many people knew about bonds when Nomura appointed a closet Bible-thumper named Otogo Kataoka head of the Osaka-Nomura Bank in 1918. A banker born and bred, Kataoka had been in charge of corporate lending at the Industrial Bank of Japan for twelve years. He was a quiet man and a devout Christian in a land where most people were Shinto and Buddhist. He had nothing but contempt for stock salesmen, whom he considered a decidedly lower form of life. His brief was simply to transform the Osaka-Nomura Bank from a low-grade stock-trading outfit into a first-rate banking institution.

Prodded by Nomura, Kataoka became a pioneer, for no other Osaka bank underwrote government and corporate debentures. Corporate bonds had been listed on the securities exchanges since 1912 but had rarely traded. In 1920 the government eased the regulations controlling bond dealing to encourage investment in corporate bonds, and, following the issue of reconstruction bonds after the 1923 earthquake, the bond market took off. By this time the Osaka-Nomura Bank already had a securities division to deal specifically with bond issues, and Kataoka had travelled to New York to visit the National City Company, a bond-trading house recently divested from the National City Bank. From them he learned how best to turn the bond operations of the Osaka-Nomura Bank into a separate company.

In a perverse expression of Kataoka's Christianity and a distinctly Japanese interpretation of the birth of Christ, the Nomura Securities Company Ltd was born on Christmas Day 1925. Tokushichi took 98,000 of the 100,000 issued shares for himself as the 'representative employee' of the Nomura

Partnership and another 800 shares in his role as auditor of the new company. He gave Kataoka, as president, a trifling 200 shares and a further 200 each to five other directors, including his brother Motogoro. (By 1987, when Nomura Securities' share price reached 5990 yen, those trifling 200-share stakes had multiplied in value to over $100 million each.)

On 4 January 1926 Nomura Securities opened its doors for business in Osaka, with branches in Tokyo, Nagoya, Kobe and Kyoto, and with a total of eighty-four employees.

8
Panic

In 1927 disaster struck Japan once again. Two years before the collapse of Wall Street and the folding of America's banks, Japan's own banks started going under. The roots of the 1927 Japanese banking panic lay with another upstart from western Japan, a fifth *zaibatsu* which had prospered during wartime. The Suzuki conglomerate was an empire firmly in the grip of its matriarch, Yone Suzuki – the widow of its founder – who was described by the *New York Times* in 1922 as wealthiest woman in the world. From her base in Kobe she ruled, spider-like, over 25,000 workers and a web of sixty-five companies. As a trading company hers had already overtaken Mitsui as the largest in Japan, while her manufacturing interests in steel and textiles were now threatening the supremacy of the other *zaibatsu*.

But in 1927 Yone Suzuki's empire imploded. Her dependence on the Bank of Taiwan and the Bank of Kobe brought about her downfall. Unwilling to bring in outside shareholders to finance the company's expansion, Yone Suzuki had piled up debt upon debt with these two banks. She even controlled the Bank of Kobe to ensure easy access to loans. But the unhealthy pyramid of borrowings began to totter. By 1927 Yone Suzuki had outstanding loans from the Bank of Taiwan alone totalling 350 million yen, some 100 million of them in the government-sponsored earthquake loans. If she were to default on such a debt, the bank would go under.

By the spring of that year the general public was clamouring for the government to be repaid its earthquake loans. People demanded to know why taxpayers should finance unstable companies that had obtained these loans through incestuous relations with bankers. The Japanese parliament eventually succumbed to public pressure and called for early liquidation of these debts, and promised an investigation of the Bank of Taiwan.

One by one the dominoes began to fall. The Bank of Taiwan was forced to suspend credit to the Suzuki *zaibatsu*. The Bank of Kobe, a Suzuki satellite and therefore dependent indirectly on cash flowing from the Bank of Taiwan, immediately collapsed. Suzuki itself might have survived had not the Mitsui and Mitsubishi banks been secretly supporting the Bank of Taiwan. For years they had been indirectly financing the Suzuki empire through short-term loans to the Bank of Taiwan. They now called them in with no advance warning. The Bank of Taiwan suspended business and the panic began. Suzuki businesses collapsed one after another as Mitsui and Mitsubishi rivals began feasting on the corporate remains.

Tokushichi Nomura's own bank came within weeks of crumbling during the panic that spring. One day Tokushichi noticed hordes of depositors lined up outside his Osaka-Nomura Bank headquarters. The winds of gossip had begun to sweep through Osaka. Tokushichi had actually been in no financial trouble until the rumours hit him. As local merchants angrily began to demand all their money on deposit, he realized his cash resources could not last long. His bank, with its network of fifteen branches, had an estimated 90 million yen in its vaults; between one and two million yen were being withdrawn every day by jittery savers.

According to Tokushichi's nephew Kozo Nomura, the first thing Tokushichi told bank employees was that if the bank were unable to meet its depositors' withdrawal demands, he would hand over all his personal wealth to them. The bank's tellers dutifully spread the word, but fighting panic with rhetoric was like trying to fight a house fire with a cup of water. The withdrawals continued.

Desperate to save his empire, Nomura resorted to subterfuge. He told his assistants to fill a car with all his privately owned stock and bond certificates taken from the bank's vault. They drove the short distance up the street to the Bank of Japan, exchanged the securities for cash and returned to the main branch of Nomura's bank loaded with yen notes. The sight of so much cash, readily being paid to depositors, reassured the anxious customers. A few of them left the line, then a few more. Years later it was claimed that Nomura had actually paid some of his men to stand in line with cash, posing as depositors, making those queueing up to withdraw their money feel sheepish. The withdrawals abated, the torrent became a trickle. The ruse had worked.

Even Japan's new Emperor, Hirohito, who had ascended the throne a year earlier, in 1926, did not escape the effect of the banking crisis. The Emperor's personal wealth, stored in the family's household bank, the Fifteenth Bank, was in danger of disappearing. Better known as the Peers Bank because of its noble clientele, the Peers Bank had been founded in the 1870s on the bonds issued to dispossessed nobles and samurai in the wake of the Meiji reforms. By the turn of the century it had become one of the largest banks in Japan. Its ruling cabinet was appointed by the Emperor himself.

When the Peers Bank faltered in 1927, the government and the bank cabinet decided it would not do to have their divine Emperor impoverished. His appointees acted with reverential haste in speeding legislation through parliament to shore up the foundering banking system, and billions of yen were extended to selected Japanese banks to provide indirect support for the Emperor's deposits.

By the time the banking crisis had passed, the major *zaibatsu* reigned supreme over the Japanese banking system. The big five were now four, and they had doubled their deposit base and controlled one third of all Japanese banking deposits. Meanwhile, Nomura's ability to survive the crisis had made the Nomura-Osaka Bank a major player in the nation's financial arena. Nomura began to see himself more and more as the surviving samurai of Osaka. The banking panic did nothing to discourage him from pursuing his plans to expand his financial empire. In the late spring of 1927, a month after the panic had subsided, Tokushichi opened a small Nomura Securities office on Broadway in New York. The milestone passed almost unnoticed, although his was the first Japanese securities firm to set up shop overseas. Later that year Tokushichi shortened the bank's name to Nomura Bank and began planning a larger headquarters for his burgeoning financial kingdom.

Tokushichi was now ready for the big leagues. He adopted a strategy used by the big four *zaibatsu*, and in the short span of two years, between 1928 and 1930, the Nomura Partnership increased its borrowings from 8.7 to 19.5 million yen. Most of the loans came from the Nomura Bank, giving the Nomura Partnership ultimate control over the group through its allocation of the funds. In addition, the Nomura Partnership (in fact still anything but a partnership since it was controlled almost entirely by Tokushichi himself) was the beneficial owner of the Nomura family stock portfolio. This was still worth 18 million yen, although Tokushichi himself claimed to have severed his stockbroking links in 1922.

The Japanese *zaibatsu* families were masters of the leverage game and Nomura had perfected their holding-company strategy: he borrowed money deposited by ordinary Osaka merchants in his bank, used the money to buy shares on margin, used those shares as collateral to borrow more money and in the end owned a share portfolio of the same value as his bank's net worth (18 million yen) while also owning the bank itself.

In the aftermath of the banking crisis Nomura began purchasing companies hit by the financial upheaval. The general economic depression continued until 1933 and it was then – when things looked gloomiest – that Tokushichi made his move. One of his more important purchases in the long term was a small, troubled trust company bought from the plagued Fujita *zaibatsu*, which had once ruled over a large mining, railway, banking and forestry empire. Rocked by the banking panic of 1927, their financial holdings began to disintegrate and in 1933 Nomura bought their troubled Taisho Trust at a fire-sale price, renamed it Osaka Trust and made Otogo

Kataoka president. This gave Nomura Securities – of which Kataoka was also president – yet another source of funding for its bond-underwriting ventures. The firm continued buying up small trust companies until by 1939 Nomura controlled one of the largest trust companies in Japan, which he renamed Nomura Trust and Banking.

Tokushichi's financial empire continued to grow. In 1933 he bought a second ailing Fujita firm, the Kyoho Life Insurance Company. He decided that the best way to increase life insurance policy sales was to give managers and salesmen a percentage of the annual sales figure. In a rare incentive scheme, he allowed staff to own shares in the new Nomura Life Insurance Company.

There were no financial policemen in Japan before World War II. Most life insurance companies were owned by the *zaibatsu* families, who had total discretion over the pool of funds they collected from policyholders. It was another low-cost source of money to be invested at the whim of each company owner, with little thought given to the safeguarding of assets. Internal policing was also left up to individual company owners. By the mid-twenties, the Nomura Partnership had its own auditing department to keep an eye on the finances of the growing number of companies within the empire. Locating and preventing fraud – in particular, the inflation of company earnings to increase dividends – became all the more important now that Nomura Life was allowing share ownership and sales bonuses among his own employees.

One of the first auditors Tokushichi hired was Narajiro Kamata, a short, feisty graduate of Keio University. He was given a starting salary of seventy yen a month, a princely sum for a green college student. Most managers of the bank branches of the big *zaibatsu*, men with ten years' experience, were earning 100 yen a month. Kamata's first job was to assess the performance of the Choya Shirt and Standard Shoe companies, two firms bought by Nomura during the twenties.

Kamata loved the sense of power his work gave him,

walking into the elegant chambers occupied by directors of Nomura subsidiaries and ordering senior management to hand over their papers. Kamata later claimed his department had been one of the most important in the Nomura Partnership because of the amount of money he had saved the firm by disclosing waste and in some cases fraud. Its importance could be gauged by the amount of money the general manager of the auditing division earned. 'The division was run by Mr Hamano,' Kamata recalled. 'He made 500 yen a month – more than most other *zaibatsu* executives made in half a year. You cannot have a fox in the chicken-coop.' Tokushichi had worked out that there was no way to guard the guards themselves. So he paid his auditors enough to keep them from the temptations of fraud.

After digging around in the shirt and shoe company books, Kamata was promoted to audit the Nomura Life Insurance Company. Here he found scandalous practices reminiscent of those at the old rice exchanges of the late nineteenth century, insurance salesmen being even less scrupulous than the stock traders. Kamata quickly noticed that the number of policyholders rose sharply around the end of each fiscal year and then suddenly, and seemingly without reason, dropped away at the beginning of the new fiscal year. Nomura Partnership executives had always been aware of this, but had assumed it simply reflected the fickle nature of Japanese households and, though puzzled, had never pursued the matter. Insurance was all new to them. Mr Matsuda, the company's president, enticed away from Sumitomo Life Insurance, had impressed Nomura board members with the rapid increase in the number of policyholders. They had seen no reason to question his success. Tokushichi was a bit more wary. He had sensed it was time to call in Kamata.

Kamata shared his employer's suspicion that the increase was a bit *too* spectacular and discovered that all the salesmen had been opening false accounts towards the end of the fiscal year in order to boost their bonuses. They had paid the insurance premiums themselves for the ghost policyholders and then stopped payment once their bonuses had been received. Matsuda was sacked, the scandal was hushed up and Kamata became general secretary of the Nomura Partnership.

Kamata now had access to main board meetings, where he transcribed notes on the discussion of strategy. He remembered Tokushichi studying very hard for these meetings and coming better prepared than the presidents of the subsidiaries. As the board members gave their speeches, however, Nomura would look on seriously and scribble in his notebook. Kamata sat next to him and one day, leaning over to take a peek at what Tokushichi was writing down, he found his boss was sketching comical caricatures of the assembled board members.

In 1928, when Tokushichi had reached the age of fifty, he was awarded the highest personal accolade of his life. Emperor Hirohito elevated him to the House of Peers, the noble legislative arm of the imperial family, whose members were selected by Japan's conservative aristocracy or appointed by the Emperor. Membership in the House of Peers, like most things in Japan, could be bought, and some sceptics asserted that Tokushichi's membership was acquired in just this way. But family records and family members indicate that he was appointed because he paid such high taxes to the government. In an ingenious scheme to encourage Japan's wealthy to remit their tax assessments, the highest taxpayers in each region were honoured with selection to the House of Peers.

Slightly uncomfortable, Tokushichi mingled with the titled gentry of the House. At first the highbrow members sneered at the son of an Osaka moneychanger, but eventually the quality of the speeches Tokushichi gave on financial matters won him favour. One of the men who listened intently to Nomura's speeches was Prince Konoe Fumimaro. Although nineteen years younger than Tokushichi and distinctly more refined, Prince Konoe realized that Nomura was something of a genius. He put aside the prejudices of his own background in his determination to learn from this uncouth master of the financial arts. Their relationship eventually brought Nomura close to the seat of power: the Prince became prime minister three times during the 1930s and 1940s. Prince Konoe was also to be a frequent visitor to the Nomura home in Kyoto, where he took part in the tea ceremony. As prime minister, Konoe sought to appoint Tokushichi to his cabinet as finance minister. Each time the Prince urged him to accept, Tokushichi politely refused, partly because his good friend Kaya Okinori already occupied the post and partly because it was a foolhardy position.

Political murder had become rife in Japan. Three prime ministers and a dozen cabinet ministers were assassinated between 1926 and 1945. Nomura was a patriot, but could see no reason to adopt strident views when war was imminent. Nomura family members insist that, although he served in the House of Peers during Japan's aggression in the Sino-Japanese War of 1937 and the war of the Pacific in 1941, Tokushichi opposed the fanatic militarists, but, privately and pragmatically, kept a low profile. His nephew Kozo Nomura asserts, 'Tokushichi hated militarists and that is one reason we did not have a manufacturing base in Manchuria where everyone else was expanding.' The gentler days of army life Tokushichi had enjoyed in 1899 had gone. Fanatics ruled the army now. Tokushichi could not speak out against the military aggression; there were too many right-wing secret-society zealots more than willing to kill unsympathetic members of parliament – and the threat of assassination would have been that much greater had he been a cabinet minister. He preferred to play the part of an Osaka merchant with a neutral political stance.

In the same year that Tokushichi was appointed to the House of Peers, he began to build offices in Tokyo. They were completed in 1930. The address was a prestigious one: Number One Nihonbashi – a site worthy of a financial monarch since it was the point from which all distances in Japan were traditionally measured. Nihonbashi, or Japan Bridge, was the starting point of the famous Tokaido, the principal highway of medieval Japan. Nomura had come a long way. By 1930 he had established himself in Tokyo as well as in Osaka. Through the House of Peers he had achieved the highest social standing to which he could aspire, and he held in his hands the reins of a full-fledged *zaibatsu*. At its head was the Nomura Partnership, described by Kozo Nomura as the apex of a tripod – with the Nomura Bank, Nomura Securities and Nomura East Indies the three supporting legs of the family enterprise.

9
Nomura's Men

There is a saying among Chinese families that it is better to turn the male heir of a third-generation family firm into an opium addict – and get him out of harm's way – than have him risk the family fortune through dissolute spending on women, gambling and ruinous business ventures. Universally, surviving the third generation has always been a problem for families of enormous wealth and power. The Nomura family was no exception. What undermined the perpetuation of the Nomura dynasty, however, was not so much sloth or ennui as personal tragedy.

First, in 1919, Tokushichi's younger brother Jitsusaburo, had died of pneumonia. Then, in spring 1928, tragedy had struck again when Tokio Nomura, Tokushichi's younger son, only seventeen years old, had been killed in an automobile accident. In those days driving was still regarded as something of a hobby, needing no driver's licence, and Tokio had only recently learned how to drive his father's Austin Seven. The accident happened after a party at the exclusive Konan High School, when Tokio had been driving across a railway track. With him was his friend Daisuke Kuhara, son of a *nouveau riche* family which had made a fortune in copper mining during World War I and later went on to build the Nissan *zaibatsu* of automobile fame. The Austin Seven stalled and was hit by an oncoming Hankyu Electric Railway train. Tokio died instantly and Kuhara, bleeding badly, died on the way to hospital. The two young men, whose destiny had been to rule the two fastest-growing empires in Japan, had had their lives cruelly cut short in a tragedy that ironically epitomized Japan's modernization.

After Tokio's death, family members say, Tokushichi fell apart for the first time since his brother had died. 'He wept for days,' recalls Tokio's cousin, Kozo Nomura. Only two years later there was a further disaster when Minoru Nomura, the eldest son of Tokushichi's brother Jitsusaburo, was killed by an avalanche while skiing in the Japanese Alps. These untimely deaths were more than just family tragedies: they crippled Tokushichi's plan to expand the Nomura Partnership at high speed.

Nomura's next generation of leaders was now in jeopardy, for the mantle of power would pass exclusively to Yoshitaro Nomura, Tokushichi's elder son, without a host of family supporters. At the time of Tokio's death in 1928, Yoshitaro was studying for a degree in economics at Kyoto Imperial University, the nation's second most highly regarded college after Tokyo Imperial University. With his academic turn of mind and love of the humanities, he was not the most promising heir to the Nomura empire. Meanwhile, however, Tokushichi forcefully conscripted every remaining Nomura male into the family firm.

Management of the principal subsidiary, the Nomura Bank, had already been resolved. Motogoro Nomura, Tokushichi's English-educated younger brother, had been at the bank's helm since 1925, when he had taken over from the strait-laced Otogo Kataoka, who had been pushed into the presidency of Nomura Securities. That left Keiji and Kozo Nomura, the two surviving sons of Tokushichi's dead brother Jitsusaburo. By 1930, both had entered their freshman year at Kyoto Imperial University. 'I wanted to study English,' says Kozo Nomura, 'but after Minoru died, the last thing we needed was another academic.' In the eyes of Tokushichi, Keiji and Kozo were now valuable commodities and both were ordered to learn economics.

While Keiji and Kozo were busy studying in 1930, Yoshitaro Nomura returned to the Kobe mansion from a year abroad in England enamoured with everything British, like many Japanese in the first four decades of the century. The bond between Japanese and British culture had been cemented after the signing of the Anglo-Japanese treaty in 1902, which was soon followed by an import boom into Japan. Anything British – automobiles, clothes, manufacturing technology and literature – was seen as a quality product and eagerly bought up by wealthy families anxious to demonstrate their *savoir vivre*. Rich *zaibatsu* families such as the Mitsui, Iwasaki and Sumitomo bought the most fashionable British cars. Tokushichi bought a British Daimler and an Armstrong Siddeley Special. Yoshitaro excitedly purchased an Invicta and joined a racing club. Donning hat and goggles, he would race along Kobe's tortuous, pitted roadways.

To the Japanese this was the era when Britain ruled the world. Although American investment in Japan was substantial, the British pound held sway over the world currency markets while British rail and ships dominated world transport. But while other *zaibatsu* families laid claim to being internationalist, their understanding tended to be superficial. Yoshitaro, however, was a true advocate of British literature, democracy and economic liberalism. One practice he brought back to Japan was the British club, which was a big hit in Osaka. Liking the way the mere presence of a businessman at a British club seemed to ensure his plans financial support, Yoshitaro, while training as his father's understudy in the Nomura Partnership, began the Nomura Club, to which he also attached a putting green, to satisfy the new Japanese fervour for playing golf. Amidst the chummy confines of the Nomura Club, family members and Nomura *zaibatsu* executives could relax with clients, mimicking the British by intertwining their private lives with those of business associates for the prospect of a deal.

Kiku, Tokushichi's wife and the family's thorny matriarch, meanwhile impressed upon Yoshitaro the importance of marrying a suitable wife and producing a male heir to carry on the Nomura name. Not only was he being groomed for the top slot at the Nomura Partnership, but, more important, he was the last direct blood link of the Nomura family. After an exhaustive investigation of her background Yoshitaro settled on a lovely twenty-one-year-old girl named Sae, the daughter of a well-to-do textile merchant. Sae was introduced to Yoshitaro at a tea ceremony and, although she liked him, was hesitant about taking on the large Kobe house and organizing the household maids, gardeners, chauffeur and cooks. But Yoshitaro was not only handsome and rich, he was persuasive as well and in 1933 they were married.

A year later Sae bore the family its next Nomura heir, a boy called Fumihide. From the moment of his birth, he became 'Kiku's treasure', as Sae later recalled, and grew up to be the ideal successor to the Nomura legacy – tall and powerful, with the noble bearing of his secret samurai heritage.

Tokushichi knew only too well that his own son did not have the driving personality or physical stamina needed to run the family business, and he accepted him for what he was: the family thinker. A new form of control would have to be created. As the Nomura kingdom moved ahead in the 1930s, he devised a power structure that balanced insider and outsider, family and non-family members. Rule over the holding company, the Nomura Partnership, would be delegated temporarily to an outsider, the firm's general manager, until 1938, when Yoshitaro would reach the age of thirty-two. That left the now-gentrified Tokushichi with more time to pursue esoteric hobbies – time he spent in Kyoto riding his white stallions, performing Noh drama, drinking tea in formal ceremonies and making ceramic pottery.

As Tokushichi mellowed, he preferred the sedate business of banking to the harried world of broking. This was exemplified by his appointment in 1925 of the outsider, Otogo Kataoka, to run the stockbroking business of Nomura Securities, while Motogoro Nomura ran the bank. Stockbroking in the interwar years was not only unimportant, it was still a dirty business. 'My uncle thought stockbroking was too risky for family members other that himself. Besides it was not very glamorous,' said Kozo Nomura. Nomura Securities thus became the only major branch of the group that would never be run by a family member. Outsiders were thereby enabled, during the years from 1925 until World War II, to run Nomura Securities.

Without direct family supervision and unshackled by the constraints of the who-do-you-know banking world, the firm's salesmen were able to rise by doing exactly what Nomura Securities president Kataoka personally found so contemptible – churning speculative accounts.

Out of pre-war Nomura Securities sprang two of Japan's most powerful post-war financiers, Tsunao Okumura and Minoru Segawa, one a spoiled playboy who barely made it through college, the other an impoverished, hard-working peasant who graduated at the top of his college class. Okumura became the firm's first post-war president and Segawa the second. Okumura was good-natured and care-free, and loved by most, while Segawa was cold and stoic, and feared by all.

10
The Playboy and the Hustler

Tsunao Okumura, who was to be king of Japanese stock-broking in the 1950s (and friend of every post-war prime minister until his death in 1972), was born in 1903, the only child of a wealthy confectioner. He spent a pleasant childhood in Shiga prefecture just east of Kyoto near Lake Biwa. 'Since I was an only child, my father raised me in quite a lavish style,' Okumura later mused.

At nineteen he entered Kyoto University where he learned about the softer pleasures that life offered a well-to-do college man. 'My father gave me 100 yen a month spending money in the days when twenty yen was enough to support a fancy life style,' he reminisced years later, after he had retired as president of Nomura Securities. The 100 yen he received in play money equalled the starting salaries in the best banks. He cavorted around the dance halls of Kyoto with other rich young men, taking life, and classes, lightly.

Okumura's free-wheeling habits were reflected in his grades and consequently he was rejected by the Mitsubishi, Mitsui and Yamaguchi Banks. However, through a personal introduction he entered Nomura's research department in an undemanding job perfectly suited to his temperament. Immediately after graduation in 1926, only a year after Nomura Securities' foundation, Okumura became a Nomura man.

Of those joining Nomura at this time Okumura was the least likely to take command of Nomura Securities twenty-two years later. With only a handful of exceptions, every Nomura director who rose to power after the war rose through the sales side. 'While the other men were fighting their way through the trenches, Okumura was prancing around on a white steed,' recalled one colleague. He was pleasant and self-assured, but he lacked the hunger that would later become the hallmark of Nomura Securities men.

Okumura's professional enthusiasm was further diluted by his marriage into real wealth. Shortly after joining Nomura Securities, his parents arranged for him to marry the eldest daughter of a prominent Osaka landowner. His own father had been well off but the family of his new bride, Masiko, was extremely rich and in 1926, the first year of the reign of the new Emperor, Hirohito, Okumura and his young bride of eighteen moved into a splendid new house with tennis courts, built by Masiko's parents next to their own home.

Despite his affluence, Okumura was miserable during the mid-1930s. His seven-year-old daughter died, leaving him and his wife heart-broken, and shortly afterwards he lost his entire fortune in the stockmarket crash. His wife recalled, 'I had to go to my parents' home with my daughter's bones and somehow, at the same time, ask my father for money.' Masiko's father gave them over 10,000 yen in stocks – a fortune – but her parents secretly pressed Masiko to leave her husband, which she refused to do. In his later years, Okumura claimed he was so moved by his wife's act of loyalty that each night, out of respect, he honoured a traditional Japanese custom by never placing his feet in her direction when he slept. This added a slight inconvenience to his nocturnal infidelities. Okumura, a playboy from college in 1922 to his death fifty years later, was frequently in the arms of some dancing girl or geisha.

Meanwhile, fellow workers at Nomura, superstitious when it came to tragedy, blamed Okumura's bad luck on his lazy character. He came to work late, was despondent and left early. The stressful business of securities figured low on his list of priorities. Colleagues were constantly criticizing him. After he became president he recalled (with ironic pleasure) in his autobiography, 'Ten years after joining, my friends were all branch managers while I had fallen behind three years and was only a deputy manager. I didn't care, though.'

Then in 1935, Okumura made an error which nearly cost him his career. In his capacity as a research analyst-cum-marketing man, Okumura published a secret booklet for investors, explaining the merits of purchasing overseas bonds. It was an egregious mistake, for the Bank of Japan explicitly prohibited Japanese purchase of foreign bonds – it had needed all the money it could get to expand the Japanese war machine and did not want money to be siphoned overseas. Somehow the brochure found its way into the hands of Bank of Japan officials, who reprimanded the president of Nomura Securities, Otoga Kataoka. Okumura's booklet was not only unpopular within Nomura but also seen as threatening, since Japan was awash with patriotic fervour. Life was clear-cut: things Japanese were good and things foreign were bad. Furious, Kataoka ordered Okumura's resignation, but was eventually persuaded by other senior Nomura men simply to demote him. Okumura was transferred in disgrace to the registration section, where only women worked; his primary task was numbering by hand each security as it was bought and sold. 'A prison' he later called it, but there was the compensation that the women spoiled him shamelessly.

* * * * *

Meanwhile, Minoru Segawa was developing a notoriety quite different from that of Okumura. He had entered Nomura Securities in 1929 as a common, overweight, hard-drinking, loud-mouthed salesman and twenty-eight years later, to no one's surprise, became its president and one of the most influential men in Japan. He was an outsider whose ascent mirrored the rise to respectability of Japanese stockbroking.

Born in 1906 in the small town of Oofuka, not far from Osaka, he had known from a young age that he would have to bully his way through Japanese society. Segawa's father had been a respected local school teacher, but poor eyesight had forced him to leave the job and haul firewood to eke out an existence. Watching his father pull his cart of wood around the town was a painful memory that haunted Segawa for the rest of his life. Nonetheless, his youth was relatively carefree; he spent much of his time sumo wrestling and resented the time he had to spend in the classroom. Osaka men seldom studied beyond secondary school, but when they did it was to pursue business and trade at a commercial college, not to flirt with art and literature at one of the Imperial universities. Segawa was very much in the Osaka merchant mould and hated school, but when his father's fuel business briefly picked up, bringing in a little extra money, he was prodded into continuing his secondary education. Segawa did everything he could to fail the entrance examinations before telling his father he wanted to find a job. They compromised: Segawa worked as an errand boy at the Bank of Taiwan while attending classes in the evening. He handed his paycheck over to his family. When the family business improved, Segawa quit his job to attend the Seiki Commercial School full-time.

Then disaster struck. His father and his brother died within a few months of each other, leaving him, as the eldest male in the family, to run the fuel business. Segawa's dilemma over school and work was a familiar one to Osaka teachers and one of them told Segawa that he was bright enough to take examinations without attending every class. In later years Segawa recalled those high school days as the toughest of his life. Each morning he rose at five, showed up briefly for school, went to work and then studied into the night. He kept up this routine for months until he could hire a boy to haul firewood.

Segawa performed so well in his examinations that a teacher alleged that he had cheated, a charge that he vehemently denied. Those close to Segawa remember him telling the story years later – 'I passed my exams with honours, which shows I didn't cheat' – as if he still needed to prove his innocence. Graduating from high school at the age of twenty, he refused, against his relatives' wishes, to enter the family business. With his father dead, he felt no obligation to carry on what he considered a menial existence lugging wood from house to house. He was restless and worked for a few months at the Kajima Bank before deciding to devote himself to a college degree at the Osaka University of Commerce. There Segawa knew he could distinguish himself and climb out of the miserable lower class into which he had been born.

There he was also conscious of his inferior status. The other young men in college were there because they had money, while Segawa was there because he had none. But his humiliation drove him harder than anyone else and by his own admission he turned himself into an uncouth, unromantic studying machine. He rejected the slightest frivolity. Every sport or hobby he took up in later life was for business purposes only, killing any joy he might have derived from them. The opportunistic Segawa had one extracurricular activity in college: selling used textbooks to fellow students at a generous mark-up.

Hard-headed and calculating by the age of twenty-three, Segawa graduated at the top of his class and his finance professor suggested that he join Nomura Securities. Segawa, however, wanted to work for the prestigious Sumitomo Bank, the core company of the Sumitomo *zaibatsu* and Osaka's largest company, staffed by sons of the best families of Osaka. Segawa hated the thought of competing in the domain of the wealthy but was attracted by the high pay of Sumitomo – a handsome seventy yen a month, a king's ransom for the poor Segawa. Then he looked at Nomura Securities and found that they were paying a monthly wage of 110 yen per month. His choice was clear.

The young Segawa borrowed an ill-fitting suit to take the Nomura entrance examinations and became the first student in his college's history to pass the Nomura test. He joined Nomura in 1929 with the other green recruits, this time buying his own suit for the occasion. Nomura Securities was the only brokerage house to have a formal training programme and Segawa was anxious to push his way through such effeminate tasks as letter writing (which reminded him of learning calligraphy in primary school), telephoning and accounting – clerks could do that. An aggressive, hands-on man, Segawa felt he was meant to be a salesman, not an errand boy.

A few months after joining, he got a chance to prove himself when he was transferred to the Hiroshima branch of Nomura Securities, a four-hour train ride west of Osaka. This was his first time away from his family and the farthest he had ever travelled from Osaka. Hiroshima was to become what he later described as his second home, for it was here that he learned to drink, smoke and play mah-jong. Playing mah-jong with friends and listening to the clickety-clack of the tiles while he drank gave him a feeling of security. He no longer felt like a refugee. Mah-jong became his favourite hobby and he played to win: members of the Nomura family recall playing with him in the 1960s and being surprised at his business-like approach to the game and strict adherence to the rules, especially when they were in his favour. Segawa hated to lose.

Business was slow in the stockmarket of the early 1930s owing to the world depression and Japan's slow recovery from the banking panic of 1927. Persistently Segawa went around Hiroshima on foot every day to drum up orders. Stockbrokers hardly used telephones in pre-war Japan; business was conducted in person and the salesman later delivered the stock in return for payment, an approach still in use today.

One day Segawa called on a powerful, local businessman named Tanaka with a fierce reputation for 'eating up salesman and spitting them out', as Segawa recalled later in his autobiography. Everyone in the office had given up on the tight-fisted Tanaka except Segawa, who visited him day after day to explain why he should buy foreign bonds, an opportunity few were familiar with. (It was one thing to publish public reports on foreign bonds; it was quite another to make money for the firm by quietly selling them.) Tanaka held back but at the end of the second week he bought $10,000 worth of foreign bonds, one of the largest orders ever received by any branch salesman. Instantly Segawa was the hero of the Hiroshima office.

Secure in his job at Nomura, Segawa set about finding a wife. His newly found friendship with Tanaka bore fruit when the powerbroker suggested he could arrange a marriage with a friend's daughter. The marriage took place in the autumn on 1932.

As Segawa entered his fourth year of service at Nomura he was suddenly ordered to Moji, a busy port on the northern tip of Japan's southern island, Kyushu, to be second in command of a new branch office. The distance caused Segawa to relocate without his wife, a practice called *tanshin funin*, which still operates in the Japan of the 1990s. The rationale is that children cannot afford to lose out on the competitive schooling needed to pass the examinations that determine one's place in Japanese society. The arrangement was not disagreeable to Segawa, whose wife was pregnant and could remain at home near her parents; besides, he could concentrate full-time on his work.

He was now enjoying a prosperity he had never known before. Nomura Securities even put him up in a Western-style hotel in Moji, the first he had ever slept in and which he found confusing. He had never slept with a bed raised off the floor, but always on roll-out futons. A bed that was a permanent fixture seemed to him a waste of space, as if sleeping were a full-time occupation. The bathroom was also strange and, not understanding how to use the bath, he stood outside it with the taps running and washed himself; similarly the toilet came as a complete surprise to a man used to squatting down over a hole in the ground.

The Moji branch was opened with three dozen workers. Segawa's job was to set up the office and buy equipment and phones, and then to rally the young salesmen to find customers. First he boosted the morale of the workers by forming a baseball team to play at weekends and by buying tables and tiles for mah-jong after work. He then set about generating business, and in one year found enough active and highly speculative dealing accounts to make Moji the second most profitable office after Tokyo. Segawa was not the branch manager of Moji, but he brought in most of the business and everyone thought of it as his office.

Unfortunately, Nomura Securities' chief, Otogo Kataoka, and the other executives called Moji a gambling den and gave no praise to Segawa and his achievements. Kataoka preferred bonds and considered Segawa an inveterate gambler – the type of man Kataoka was hired to polish. Segawa thought of bonds as cash and cash needed to be invested. His natural instincts turned him away from the slow, plodding business of bond sales. He wanted to make real money for Nomura, himself and his clients by buying as much stock as he could. He built up a network of friends who knew when a stock was about to shoot up and soon, with a client base, his prophecies became self-fulfilling. He discovered he could move a stock on his own, by first buying for his clients and then spreading a rumour into the market so that other speculators came piling into the stock. It gave him a delicious feeling of power over the upper class that had once despised him. Thirty years later, through his ability to manipulate Japanese society, he would become one of that society's most powerful members.

11
Winds of War

The real power in Japan in the 1930s lay with bankers. The stockmarket was a game for small-timers. It would not be until after the war that men of action like Segawa, men without social connections but men of ability, could rise in stockbroking. Meanwhile the upper classes of Japan were pursuing a policy of international economic and military expansion, consolidating their power. The purchase of fancy European goods was not enough – the *zaibatsu* families wanted to produce their own goods and increase their market share, and formed a colony to this end in Manchuria, now the northernmost part of China directly across the Sea of Japan. Manchuria had what Japan lacked: wide-open spaces on which to build factories and lay track; natural mineral resources and a proximity to China. Japan's imperialists hoped it would one day become a colony. From 1931 until the onset of the Sino-Japanese War in 1937, Japan increased its hold over Manchuria, while Tokushichi was continuing to build the Dutch East Indies empire he had begun in 1917.

In 1934, Japan installed China's deposed Emperor Pu Yi as puppet emperor and chief executive of Manchukuo, as the Japanese called it, and a year later ambitiously announced that it would settle five million Japanese there over the next twenty years. Immediately the government sent hundreds of thousands of farmers and factory workers from Japan to Manchukuo to work in state- and *zaibatsu*-run facilities. Paradoxically, it was Japan's international plans for expansion that would bring about the downfall of the major *zaibatsu* families.

Tokushichi took a pragmatic approach to Japan's imperialism. He knew that all business ventures abroad had to be cleared through the Yokohama Specie Bank, a quasi-governmental bank; known today as the Bank of Tokyo, it was, as it still is, the nation's primary foreign exchange bank. Many of its workers spoke English – and the company still demands that all employees have a command of written English. By placing his nephew Kozo Nomura in the bank in 1934, Tokushichi aimed to gain access to the secret workings of Japanese international finance. Finance was the mechanism to Japan's growth. Moreover, the bank resembled a social register of the sons of Japan's ruling politicians, bureaucrats and businessmen. The Yokohama Specie Bank was filled with young clerks with surnames like Mitsui, Yasuda and Uchida (the son of a former foreign minister). Tokushichi had always been considered a *parvenu*, but members of the next Nomura generation such as Kozo were educated and monied and now part of Japan's aristocracy. Kozo became close friends with noblemen such as Matsudaira, the elder brother of Prince Setsuko Chichibu. Kozo's closest friend in the bank was Kenji Hirota, whose father was foreign minister in 1934 and later prime minister in 1936.

Kozo Nomura spent five lazy years in the Yokohama Specie Bank in Tokyo, seldom taking the train back home to Kobe. His carefree days were occupied as a clerk, while his nights were spent rollicking in the dance halls of Ginza, the first urban area where the Japanese could spend their leisure hours, strolling the streets, sitting in French cafes (Tokyo still has hundreds of French restaurants) and window-shopping. Here, Kozo, a self-admitted playboy, spent many late evenings with Reniichi Takenaka, who later became head of Japan's largest privately owned construction firm.

Meanwhile, Minoru Segawa was doing well. In 1936, at a time when Nomura Securities was still known as a regional bond house, his big chance finally came. Since Segawa hated the boredom of selling bonds he had concentrated on making a name for himself by racking up stock commissions in the Moji branch and he was now allowed to set up his own branch in Shizuoka, a middle-sized coastal city between

Tokyo and Osaka. Slowly he was edging closer to the centre of Japan's new financial power base in Tokyo.

If he could make it in Shizuoka, Segawa reasoned, he could make it anywhere. Selling stock had by now become a well-tried formula for him: the first thing he did was buy baseball and mah-jong equipment for his salesmen. Within two years, with morale high and profits higher, Segawa was beginning to stand out. The bond market was in a slump in 1936 and 1937, as were the firm's profits: Nomura Securities earned only 228,000 yen in the second half of 1937, a quarter of its earnings from a year earlier. The cautious President Kataoka was beginning to reconsider his stance on stock dealings when he visited the Shizuoka branch in 1937. Duly impressed with the earnings of Segawa's branch, he discovered that most of the profits came from Segawa's stock dealing at a time when Segawa was supposed to be selling bonds. Instead of rebuking him, he issued a conciliatory statement. 'I am not saying that entering the stock business is a bad thing, and perhaps one day we can focus on the stockmarket.' The eager Segawa read into those words a mandate to plough all branch efforts into stock sales and trading. In 1937 the Shizuoka branch was the only Nomura office to post a profit.

A year later Nomura Securities upgraded its stock section within Nomura Securities to division status, which meant stock sales were now an accepted part of the firm, technically ranking *pari passu* with bond sales. It was to this division that Segawa was assigned. He reported to a man in Tokyo he described as 'an incompetent boss' and spent a year quarrelling with him. All his superiors were knowledgeable about bonds but slow to take up the finer points of stock trading. They felt threatened by Segawa's bull-like attitude: he was just not Japanese. Momentum had built to have him transferred to the Tokyo office. Then suddenly Segawa's wife died, leaving him with a six-year-old son. Distressed and charged with misplaced anger, he began fighting with everyone in the office until at length the firm told him they wanted to send him to Manchuria. It would, he was told, take five years to turn the Nomura Manchuria office into the black. The big accounts were in Tokyo where the money was. The outraged Segawa became obstinate and, calming down, politely but firmly refused to move.

While Manchuria was unattractive to Segawa, it proved to be Okumura's big step. As quickly as Okumura's career had nosedived, it took off again. Disgraced by his internationalist stance in 1935, he now, with those same outspoken views on overseas investment, attracted the attention of Tokushichi Nomura. In 1937, two years after being demoted, Okumura was asked to look into expanding Nomura's business in Manchukuo. Thereafter he became infamous throughout Nomura Securities as the man who spoke his mind, regardless of consequence – one of those rare people whose candour was at times naive but evoked trust. Tokushichi sent him along on a study group with other businessmen visiting Manchukuo at the request of the government, and here he met Pu Yi, Manchukuo's Emperor. 'I trembled at the thought,' he recalled many years later. Okumura was so ashamed at going to China in the presence of so many senior businessmen that he secretly printed up name cards with a fictitious title, 'director of planning'.

While Okumura was beginning his rise to the top, Yoshitaro Nomura received the crown of the Nomura Partnership, passed on by his father in 1938. That year Tokushichi reached his sixtieth birthday and completed his magnificent new villa at Atami, on the coast south of Tokyo, a tribute to himself, a great merchant prince of western Japan. No expense had been spared in building this monument to wealth: heavy blocks of granite sloped upward to vertical whitewashed walls, while a turret with large glass windows ran up one side of the house; one of the villa's tea rooms had been modelled on the famous Katsuura Imperial Villa in Kyoto, with wood panelling brought up from the old Imperial capital.

But the villa was less for Tokushichi's use than for Yoshitaro's. Only thirty-two, the Nomura heir was physically frail and it was thought that sea air would benefit his failing health. From 1938 till his death seven years later Yoshitaro spent most of his time at the villa.

Living in Atami, Yoshitaro was not the power broker his father once was. The Partnership was still an Osaka concern and was now fully run by Mitsugu Yamanouchi, the general manager (a position comparable to that of a present-day chief executive). Although some operations had moved to Tokyo, only Nomura Life Insurance Company kept its main office in Tokyo. Even forty years after Yoshitaro took over Nomura, many descendants of the Nomura *zaibatsu* – Daiwa Bank, Cosmo Securities, Osaka Gas, Nomura Construction and Shikobo – retained their headquarters in Osaka in western Japan. The Nomura Group in the late thirties was still a provincial firm in Japanese eyes. Even Nomura Securities, with ten offices across the country, was considered parochial and had not even become a member of the Tokyo Stock Exchange. It had of course a licence to trade on the Osaka Securities Exchange, but when it came to deal in Tokyo stocks the firm had to go through another broker, who charged Nomura a fee.

Shortly before Yoshitaro's appointment in 1938, Japan had declared war on China.

PART II
WAR AND REBUILDING

12
Paradise Lost

The war changed everybody's life. The Nomura family was divided in its feelings over Japanese imperialism. Tokushichi took war as a matter of course and worked with the establishment. Yoshitaro deplored Japan's burgeoning nationalism and found the Japanese military unbearably arrogant. He told the family he would rather be under occupation by the British Army or Navy than by his own countrymen. 'The Japanese army is barbaric,' he told his cousin Kozo, 'but the English act like gentlemen even in time of war.'

In 1938, Kozo was the first Nomura to be dragged into the Sino-Japanese conflict. After five unexacting years at the Yokohama Specie Bank, he suddenly found himself called up by an Osaka infantry unit. He felt sure he would be commissioned as an officer, having gone through military training at Kyoto University, but the army refused to give him a commission, telling him he was short of the required 100 training hours. At the end of the training course Kozo had tried to win over his commanding officer with supplies of sweetcakes, but the ploy did not work. For that reason he survived the war. 'All the other officers died in combat,' he recalled later. 'But as a common foot soldier stationed in southern China I saw no action.'

He was sent off to Canton after the main theatre of war had moved north, a humbling experience for a member of a *zaibatsu* family. 'The meals were awful and we slept like sardines,' he later complained. Feeling he deserved better, Kozo arranged for the underpaid captain of a naval ship to have his staff prepare meals for him during the week. At weekends, he dropped into the Canton branch of the Yokohama Specie Bank where the resident servant would prepare toast and coffee for him while he read one of the scarce English

103

newspapers. Later in the day he would shower — a luxury unavailable to enlisted men. There were few distractions at night, so Kozo and his friends spent a year getting drunk and paying for the services of Chinese women. He was then shipped off to Nannei, the border between China and French Indochina, to spend another year before returning home. Back in Japan in 1941 Kozo found many of his Ginza watering-holes in Tokyo shut down. Foreign goods were scarce and the Parisian cafes that lined the willowed streets had been boarded up.

Japan attacked the United States shortly after Kozo returned, but the war did not prevent Nomura Securities from flourishing. In fact, with twelve branch offices throughout Japan, Nomura generated hefty commission income as the Japanese government issued more bonds to raise money for armaments. Nomura's share of the Japanese bond market rose to 19 per cent by 1942 – almost the same share as it was to be forty-eight years later.

Encouraged by the war ministry, Nomura launched a new investment vehicle for its clients, one that would unwittingly propel it to greatness four decades later. This was the investment trust, an idea pirated from Britain but destined to become one of the most important products in Japan's rise as a financial power. The trusts – pools of money collected from individual clients – were put in the stockmarket. After World War II had ended, this thriving investment trust business enabled Nomura to wrest control of the stockmarket from Yamaichi Securities.

However, Otogo Kataoka, the head of Nomura Securities, was outraged at an idea which had been put forward by his second in command, Seizo Iida, namely that Nomura guarantee investors compensation for 20 per cent of any losses they might suffer. Kataoka thought the idea dangerous, but was overruled by Tokushichi Nomura himself. Believing it would strengthen the stockmarket and raise new capital for manufacturers, the Japanese military sought and won Tokushichi's support to ensure that Nomura would give its backing. As he travelled from Kyoto to Osaka for the crucial board meeting, Tokushichi declared: 'If the country singles us out to take the lead in establishing investment trusts, I believe we should go ahead and do it right.'

Humiliated, Kataoka resigned as Nomura Securities' chief and was replaced by the victorious Seizo Iida. Behind Iida, however, stood Minoru Segawa. Segawa was the man who pushed the new fund hardest when it was launched in November 1941. The Nomura Investment Trust was fabulously successful. More than 7,000 Nomura clients bought into the fund and with this precedent Nomura went on to capture almost half of all the investment trust business generated during the war.

A month after the launch of the fund the Japanese bombed Pearl Harbor. British colonies in South-East Asia were invaded simultaneously and by Christmas Day 1941 Singapore fell. Kozo Nomura read about the Singapore victory over the British and remembered thinking what a great triumph it was for Japan 'but for Britain a small fire in a small barn on a large estate'. It was, however, an ignominious loss and an ominous sign for the future.

The Pacific War was at its height as Kozo Nomura set out for an eight-month tour of the Nomura interests in South-East Asia in 1943. Although Kozo was not the head of his branch of the Nomura household – he was younger than his brother Keiji by ten months — he was chosen by Tokushichi to run Nomura East Indies where much of the family fortune was staked. But Tokushichi's good relations with the Japanese military did little to prevent their intrusion into Nomura family affairs. The Nomura properties were run for the sole benefit of the army and the Japanese subjugation of South-East Asia included requisitioning of Nomura rubber, oil plantations and refineries. Although the government lent the Nomura Partnership money via the Yokohama Specie Bank, Tokushichi was alarmed. Nomura East Indies was the Nomura crown jewel purchased with heavy borrowings from the Nomura Bank. The family gem was now a non-performing asset on loan to the military. It was Kozo's job to see that these enterprises were not run into the ground.

At the same time, the Nomura Securities research team quietly predicted Japan's defeat. It was a view discreetly passed among the senior Nomura men to protect their assets, but never spoken of in public. Even as early as the Battle of Midway in 1942, the turning point in the Pacific War, the Nomura family began to sell off most of their stockmarket assets. Nomura Securities also sold stock for its 'house' account, with Segawa taking his usual bold stance and shorting the market. Nomura Securities would later ride out the tough post-war years with these funds stashed away.

* * * * *

Meanwhile, the Nomura family was agonizing over its South-East Asian assets. The Japanese military had expropriated the Nomura land and refineries in the Dutch East Indies but allowed the family to run Nomura East Indies for the benefit of the war, buying all Nomura refined rubber and palm oil at cost. It was important to Tokushichi that Kozo keep tight controls on the facilities, not letting them run down, in anticipation that demand would revert back to market forces after the war. The military agreed and allowed Kozo a military exemption for the rest of the war.

A large portion of the Nomura family wealth had been invested in Nomura East Indies, and the firm was the largest client of the family bank. The Nomura Partnership had borrowed heavily from the Nomura Bank to finance this expansion into South-East Asia, and a huge flow of cash had been channelled from Japan to Nomura East Indies. In the hands of the Japanese government it was now a non-performing asset. When Kozo flew to Borneo in a Dutch Fokker plane in 1943, his task was to protect the family's crown jewels. His problem was that the jewels were now on loan to the Japanese military, and he was unsure that he would ever get them back.

Most of Nomura's valuable property was in Borneo and Sumatra, and although there were Nomura offices strewn across the archipelago from Surabaya to Singapore, Jakarta to Hanoi and Bangkok to Balibiya, these were mainly trading outposts that sold Nomura's rubber and palm oil. The hardy Japanese managers of the Nomura plantations oversaw 2,000 local workers and spoke the native dialect. After examining the plantations, Kozo visited the Nomura Trading and Yokohama Specie Bank offices in Surabaya, Jakarta and Singapore, before returning home.

Throughout the rest of the war, Segawa tightened his grip on Nomura Securities. In time-honoured Japanese fashion he cleverly extended favours to influential men whose obligations he could call in later. By 1939 he had become director of Nomura's Tokyo branch, a position that gave him full discretion in placing Tokyo orders. Some even suggested Segawa lined his own pockets by granting business favours to Tokyo's stockbrokers, who were hungry for Nomura's order flow. One man he had befriended was Yozaburo Tsuchiya, whose family were powerful stockbrokers. This friendship blossomed and years later Nomura Securities took a minority shareholding in Tsuchiya's family firm. Although Yozaburo Tsuchiya was rich, Segawa made him even wealthier. In the autumn of 1939 Segawa had begun funnelling much of Nomura's Tokyo business through the Tsuchiya Shoten. Tsuchiya received a fee for each deal and exchanged tips with Segawa. Other than their mutual interest in making money, there could hardly have been a more unlikely duo. Yozaburo Tsuchiya had been born to wealth and into a family of Japan's intellectual elite. A graduate of Hitotsubashi, Tokyo's business school, he had hoped to go into the China trade, but in 1937 his mother had died and his heart-broken father had handed the family business over to Yozaburo. In 1943 Yozaburo Tsuchiya, as the eldest son of the house, tried to find his unmarried sister a spouse. Segawa, in what became typical of his way of operating in later years, promptly set up a marriage with Masao Ono of Nomura Life Insurance.

* * * * *

The two years up until the end of the war were as tumultuous a time for Japanese stockbroking as for the rest of society. The government was assuming greater and greater control over all aspects of Japanese business, in an all-out effort to win the war. In a bid to control stockbroking activities, it wiped out the smaller houses and consolidated the rest into larger groupings. The only major Japanese securities firm to come out of the 1943-44 purge intact was Nomura Securities. Tokushichi violently opposed any consolidation for Nomura Securities and other group companies. In the chaos, his empire emerged unscathed, with the younger men in the Ministry of Finance unwilling to challenge the nation's now retired financial kingpin, the man who had once been asked to rule the very ministry in which they worked.

Under wartime government directives the foundations of modern Nomura's three fierce competitors were laid. Before the war, however, Nomura had not been Japan's largest stockbroker. The Tokyo-based Yamaichi Securities had been the biggest. In 1943 it was merged with Koike Securities but retained the Yamaichi name. Nomura's main rival in Osaka had always been Fujimoto Securities, part of the Sumitomo *zaibatsu* which merged with Nippon Trust Bank to form Daiwa Securities in 1943. Twenty years later Daiwa emerged as Japan's second most powerful brokerage house – slightly ahead of Nikko Securities, an affiliate of the Mitsubishi *zaibatsu* which merged in 1944 with Kawashimaya. Smaller brokers disappeared, although Yozaburo Tsuchiya's firm managed to survive with the help of an injection of funds from Nomura, which took a 2.5 per cent stake in the renamed Nitto Securities.

Tokushichi had fought successfully to keep the Nomura empire together during 1943-44 but Japan's defeat in the war spelt the doom of the House of Nomura – and of the seemingly unassailable power that the ten wealthiest families in Japan exercised over their country and the world. Until defeat in 1945 these ten families lorded it over three-quarters of all industry, finance and commerce in Japan. Success had bred arrogance and arrogance a sense of infallibility.

The resilient Nomura family had prepared itself better than most for what the victors would inevitably deliver. For years the Nomura Research Department had predicted defeat at the end of the war, a view never made public for fear of military reprisals. According to Narajiro Kamata, Nomura's short, sprightly auditor, the family holding company began dispersing staff to subsidiaries while the main board directors went into hiding. 'By 1945, I was one of the only senior men left around the firm.' His job was to alter, destroy and hide any company documents the authorities could use to trace the Nomura riches. But before Kamata could finish that task, Tokushichi Nomura died.

It was not a bomb that finally killed him, as everyone thought it would be, for he stubbornly refused to take shelter from air-raids in the hole that had been dug outside the Kobe home, but rather the toll that the war took on him. In 1944, a Japanese cargo ship carrying Nomura employees was sunk on its way to the East Indian plantations and on hearing the news, Tokushichi broke down. Distraught, he began suffering chest pains, which became more insistent over the year as news came of the Americans fighting their way up from the Philippines. Tokushichi knew the downfall of Japan was near. In January 1945 American forces retook Leyte, an island in the northern Philippines, where they could establish a base from which to bomb ships bound from the East Indies to Japan. This would sever Japan's lifeline for vital shipments of oil, copper, nickel, palm oil and rubber. With that Tokushichi realized that the Nomura Group's plantations in the southern hemisphere would be lost for ever.

By early January 1945, the Japanese setbacks were too much for Tokushichi and after several small heart attacks, he slipped into unconsciousness. Doctors and nurses watched over him while the children were ordered to keep silent. 'The war is over,' his grandchildren heard him stammer in his sleep, 'Japan is finished.' On 13 January he suffered

109

a final massive heart attack. At the age of sixty-seven, one of Japan's greatest stockmarket speculators had died. Tokushichi's death was a fortunate release since he escaped the grief of the dissolution of the Nomura *zaibatsu*. Nine months afterwards the Nomura group was torn apart. 'He was lucky to die with Nomura in one piece,' his grandson Tomohide said later.

Within six months of his father's death, Yoshitaro suffered his first heart attack. The stress of the war he had never supported proved too much for him. A little over a month later, on 6 August, the Americans bombed Hiroshima and the following day Yoshitaro received a call at his Atami retreat that the Nomura mansion in Kobe had been bombed. Nobody had been harmed, but the war that had once been so far away was closing in. Yoshitaro went into shock. On 9 August, Nagasaki was destroyed and on the following day Yoshitaro, still in Atami, sat in formal dress as he listened to the Emperor address the nation over the radio. It was the first time the Japanese people had heard Hirohito's high-pitched, crane-like voice. Yoshitaro's contacts in the military had already informed him of what the Emperor would say. It was one of the most moving moments in Japanese history, as much for Yoshitaro as for any of his countrymen. His wife, Sae, listened to the broadcast from the Nomura villa in Kyoto. 'I was relieved,' Sae sighed. 'I was really afraid we were going to have to fight with bamboo spears.'

Two weeks later General Douglas MacArthur landed in Japan. It was 24 August and it was on that memorable day that Yoshitaro Nomura died as the world he had known began to fall apart. Sae received a frantic phone call from one of the maids in Atami, telling her of Yoshitaro's death. Japan had come to a standstill, as the country prepared to be raped by America. Everyone remained at home, partly out of uncertainty, partly because all forms of transport were disrupted. But Sae, out of devotion to her husband and to tradition, had herself and a tutor driven from Kyoto to Atami

110

in a charcoal-powered car, a twenty-four hour journey. The roads were pitted from the debris of war and three times during the journey the tires were punctured by rocks and had to be repaired. 'If he had died four weeks later we would have had a problem,' said Sae. 'It was then that the armed bandits and looters started coming out.'

Yoshitaro was cremated in Atami and his ashes brought back to the Nomura Kyoto villa where a ceremony was held a few days later – on a dark day, heavy with rain – which seemed to epitomize the misery of a nation in defeat. Those family friends still alive or not in hiding were packed together, sodden, in the special funeral room that remains untouched to this day, where Yoshitaro's spirit was allowed by Japanese custom to wander in comfort and freedom.

Thus it was that ten days after the end of World War II, twelve-year-old Fumihide Nomura, the eldest son of Yoshitaro Nomura and grandson of the founder of the Nomura *zaibatsu*, became the titular head of the entire family. But the glory of Fumihide was but a passing moment. The boy reigned only in name over a wealth held only on paper. Four months later the Allied powers stripped him of his assets. Fumihide Nomura later joked, 'I was a multimillionaire for four months.' A shooting star, the Nomura *zaibatsu* had burned brightly for twenty years. Now it was expiring. But although Fumihide was the biggest loser of the purge in material terms, the young heir suffered little psychological damage from the experience. The older Nomura generation, Kozo, Keiji and Motogoro, were ruined and broken men. The power of the once great Nomura group seemed lost for ever, its subsidiary companies no more than debris that later came to settle around two firms: Nomura Securities and Daiwa Bank.

Although 1945 had been a cruel year for the Nomura children – with the loss of their grandfather and father – the war's end was such a tumultuous time that they were quickly taken up in its excitement. It held no political or social significance for Sae's three sons, Fumihide, Tomohide, and Harukate, only twelve, eleven and nine, and her daughter, just six years old, Kazuko. Many years later, the thrill of wartime 1945 still lingered in their memories as they recalled being moved with the entire primary school from Kobe to the safety of the Kyoto hills. Separated from their parents, they were left in the charge of teachers and little time was spent on school work as the children explored Kyoto's forests, rivers and temples. Sae lived nearby in the Nomura villa with Kiku.

As MacArthur's forces began taking over the country in the autumn of 1945, it gradually became clear that the Japanese had little to fear. The Americans took over the large European houses in Kyoto, finding the diminutive wooden Japanese houses unfit for habitation, with their matchstick furniture and rush matting. Just to be safe, Sae rented part of the villa to the Japanese Ministry of Foreign Affairs, and that autumn, she decided to uproot the children and move to Tokyo. Widowed and alone in the chaos of 1945 Japan, she thought it best to make a new start in life where she would teach her children how to be strong, independent, and how to survive. They would live like everyone else. They would use public transport and eat as normal Japanese ate. She knew the great *zaibatsu* days were gone and her children could not survive if they tried to live in the past — a past where Japanese people were either rich or poor. The Americans made it clear that the new Japan would be free and democratic, freed from the rule of the few. A middle class would emerge. Sae realized that everything would be different.

So, late in 1945, Sae, accompanied by only two maids, moved with the children to a small Japanese home in the suburbs of Tokyo. Feeding the children was her principal concern, a difficult task since rice, fish and vegetables were strictly rationed. Now Sae was simply a widow fending for herself, able to call on favours from Nomura Securities executives only sparingly since they too were faced with trying to feed their families. As food became more scarce, it became dangerous for Sae to go out of the house. Scavengers barely clothed in rags roamed the streets. Those Japanese too proud to beg died of starvation – a little discussed but very real horror of the immediate post-war period – and starvation drove those less proud to armed robbery. Day or night the streets were best left untrodden. Resentment against *zaibatsu* families ran high and it was dangerous to be associated with wealth. Masumi Nomura, the wife of Kozo, recalled wearing her beautiful silk kimono in public, only to have one woman try to rip it off her and another throw ink over her.

While Sae Nomura was fighting to keep her children alive, others were fighting to keep the Nomura *zaibatsu* assets hidden from the Americans. The largest companies in Japan were viewed by the Americans as forces of evil – malignant instruments of the Japanese military. This was not entirely the case but it was nonetheless clear to all the top brass of Nomura that they would be counted in with the other *zaibatsu* when recriminations came due.

By the war's end, the Nomura *zaibatsu* was a tightly knit financial conglomerate, with the Nomura Bank at its centre. The Nomura Bank had become the eighth largest bank in the nation, while Nomura Securities had gained the number one market share in investment trusts sales. Nomura Life Insurance was the fifth largest in its field, Nomura Trust and Banking sixth. The family business had not been immune from military pressure, however. Near the end of the war it had been forced to start up a steel factory as well as a mercury mine in Hokkaido to provide base paint for warships. When the war ended, the Nomura group were the largest shareholders in Osaka Gas, one of the nation's largest utility companies, and held the controlling interest in Fukushima Boseki, the textile firm on which Tokushichi had made a fortune in the first decade of the century.

* * * * *

Under pressure from American public opinion, with its demands for imprisonment and in some cases death for the Japanese imperialists, the US government decided to act. In the autumn of 1945 the powerful Japanese conglomerates would be dismantled as part of a larger plan to do away with world trade cartels. General MacArthur himself, Supreme Commander of the Allied powers, felt that the *zaibatsu* had in any case directly financed the Japanese war machine.

Others, like Eleanor Hadley, the Princeton scholar of Japanese anti-trust, did not agree with the blanket stigma that had been placed on Japan's noble banking and trading houses. 'Obviously neither the *zaibatsu* families nor their hand-picked officers were a bunch of criminals ...' What both General MacArthur and Eleanor Hadley did agree on was that the economy had been ruled by a few for the benefit of a few and in the process the average Japanese, working for slave wages, had no money to buy consumer goods. The House of Mitsui alone, which began as a small moneychanging firm 350 years before World War II, employed over three million workers by 1945 – probably more employees than any firm in the history of mankind. Such power had to be destroyed, reasoned the Americans. The subjugation of many for the benefit of a few was hardly the American way. It was economic totalitarianism.

On the last day of October 1945, the assets of the great houses of Japan were frozen by order of General MacArthur. Fourteen *zaibatsu* were targeted for destruction. Mitsui, Mitsubishi, Sumitomo, Yasuda, Asano, Furukawa, Fuyo, Kawasaki, Nisso, Nichitsu, Nomura, Okura, Riken and Shibusawa. (Only ten of the fourteen were actually dissolved.) American examiners were startled to find the four biggest *zaibatsu* controlled a quarter of the paid-up capital of the nation's enterprise. Half of the financial sector and a third of heavy industry were under their sway. By liquidating the holding companies of these industrial giants, MacArthur hoped to sell off the subsidiaries to the general public through the stockmarket and pave the way for what Japanese society lacked: a middle class.

The Nomura men in the meantime, like all other *zaibatsu* leaders, had the stock of their companies frozen and were forbidden to take more than 500 yen a month from their bank accounts, a pitiful allowance. A final directors' meeting of the Nomura Partnership was held on 15 October to formally abolish the holding company and its subsidiaries. Then came the purge of all family members from the Nomura boards. Their salaries were suspended and properties confiscated. The Allies recorded the Nomura family household items and Kozo even recalled them counting the shoes in his closet. Finally they were even banned from setting foot in any of the Nomura offices, a ban Kozo defied, as he came into the Osaka office each day to read his English language newspapers. Although the deaths of the two Nomura patriarchs earlier that year presaged the break-up of the family fortune, the American directive stripping Motogoro, Keiji and Kozo of their titles hastened its demise.

In the autumn of 1945, before the Americans realized the intricacies of the Japanese *zaibatsu*, General MacArthur proposed that the *zaibatsu* themselves determine how best to unravel their extensive cross-holdings. The *zaibatsu* chieftains could barely believe this extraordinary piece of good fortune. They had spent their lives concocting schemes and now they were told, by someone who did not understand the Japanese language or Japanese business methods, to form a plan to break themselves up. An innocuous dissolution was duly formulated and delivered with barely contained enthusiasm. When wiser, more experienced Americans with some knowledge of Japanese ways arrived in Tokyo, they gave the plan short shrift. Finally in the winter of 1948 they completed the process of wading through piles of convoluted and altered company holdings and came up with the names of 325 firms (many subsidiaries of the large *zaibatsu*) with a large market share, workforce or asset value to be broken up. Only eighteen were, however, ever actually broken up.

MacArthur placed ultimate responsibility for the break-up of these gargantuan corporate structures with the Ministry of Finance and its blue-blooded leader, Keizo Shibusawa.

115

MacArthur was beginning to understand the not-so-subtle loyalties in Japan that tied together the interests of ministers, politicians and businessmen, and was afraid a bureaucrat would undermine what he was trying to achieve. So he specifically forbade Shibusawa from selecting an overseer from within the Japanese bureaucracy. Instead he told him to use his high-level contacts to seek out an impartial Japanese businessman to dissolve the *zaibatsu*, someone who understood the complex web of cross-holdings, family ties and friendships.

MacArthur could not have relied on a better connected man as finance minister. Shibusawa was the grandson of the Meiji industrialist Eiichi Shibusawa. Keizo Shibusawa was now supposed to rip industrial Japan apart. He ruled his grandfather's banking *zaibatsu*, an inheritance that posed a conflict of interest since his own mandate was to hire a man to liquidate the top fourteen *zaibatsu*, including his own. (He was later to convince the Americans to leave his family firm untouched, modestly claiming it to be too small to be worth bothering with.) The search for the right businessman for the demolition job was not easy. Most of those who understood the workings of the *zaibatsu* had been or were about to be purged by MacArthur. Shibusawa's first point of contact was with Mr Nakane, the head of the Sanwa Bank, who was not merely a banker but a respected humanist who wrote poetry in his spare time. He seemed the right person to carry out the task in an honourable way, but shortly after Shibusawa had chosen him, Nakane was blacklisted by the Americans, who purged him of all positions of responsibility for a poem he had written. Only much later did the Americans realize that the offending poem had been mistakenly translated, with the word 'Roosevelt' given for Nakane's word 'loose belt'!

Shibusawa finally chose a banker called Tadao Sasayama to become the chairman of the Holding Company Liquidation Commission. Sasayama had come from the Bank of Japan and had not been purged, since bankers had been regarded as pacifists during the war. However, he spoke no English and had little understanding of Western ways of thinking, which would make his value limited.

While scouting Sasayama, Shibusawa had come across Iwajiro Noda, an eloquent Mitsui man conversant in English who had sat out the war in a prison camp in America. Noda, born in Kyushu, was a product of Japan's best schooling as a graduate of Hitotsubashi University in Tokyo. He was a Meiji man, westernized and bright, landing a job at the pre-war choice of every aristocrat's son: the giant trading firm of Mitsui and Company. Luckily for Noda, Mitsui had shipped him off to New York and, when the war broke out, he was quickly interned.

Returning to Japan in the winter of 1946, Noda was approached by Shibusawa with the offer of overseeing the dismantling of the Japanese *zaibatsu*. At first Noda, appalled by the sheer scale of the task and the weight of the responsibilities, was not interested. Shibusawa, though a gentle man, could be persistent and persuasive. He pointed out to Noda that in the course of history there had never been such a defeat as that of Japan. Shibusawa put the job in context: never before had there existed such power as the *zaibatsu* wielded and never had the victors in war allowed the vanquished so much mercy. With no precedent for this job, Shibusawa told Noda, there would be no shame in any mistakes he might make for posterity.

The problem remained over who would be the chairman, but Noda solved the dilemma by nobly suggesting Sasayama for the initial three-year term, knowing his own term would last more than five years. With his fluency in English Iwajiro Noda managed to dismantle the *zaibatsu* while at the same time preserving a modicum of wealth for the *zaibatsu* families. Noda was later to claim 'I was the only competent person left after the war who was not dead or purged. Very few people have ever been told the story of how Japan was systematically picked apart only to be put back together again once the Americans had left.'

In the years after the war and the dismantling, Noda would

go on to become the head of the prestigious Okura Hotel group. It was an important role since hotels, and the Okura in particular, had become a post-war meeting place for Japanese high society. Here Noda later carried on his unofficial diplomatic role and befriended most heads of state, including Reagan and Thatcher. Whenever anyone of senior diplomatic or professional note visited Japan, they almost inevitably paid a courtesy call on Noda.

Noda dismembered corporate Japan with a staff of five hundred, most of them the finest university graduates the country could offer. Jobs were scarce elsewhere and most jumped at the chance of employment. The first three years entailed endless negotiations with the Americans and through it all Sasayama sat smiling, unable to understand English and missing much of the translation. When finally Noda succeeded Sasayama, he had a very clear idea of what he wanted to do. At root, he had every sympathy with the fallen *zaibatsu* families. Noda was a personal friend of Hachiroemon Mitsui himself, the head of the largest *zaibatsu* and arguably the richest family on earth before the war. Mitsui now lived on 500 yen a month and Noda was privately disgusted with such treatment of Japan's aristocracy. He was deeply upset when such men had to borrow from him. In later years he defended the *zaibatsu*: 'The *zaibatsu* had no part in the war. It was the military who were to blame, not the families.'

Noda's refined manner made him a natural go-between for the Americans and the Japanese. It was a tricky balancing act for the Chairman of the Liquidating Committee. He made many friends but even more enemies. His job, as the Americans saw it, was to bring ruin upon the wealthy Japanese families. On the other hand, most Americans assumed that because he was Japanese, he would inevitably become the lapdog of the *zaibatsu* families. In fact, he was at first loathed by the *zaibatsu* families, who saw him as bent on making them destitute. In time, however, Noda won everyone's respect, especially the esteem of the once-wealthy. In his heart he wanted to hide as much wealth as possible for

118

his fellow countrymen so they might claim it back once the occupying forces had left Japan. This he was able to achieve only to a very limited degree.

The *zaibatsu* families, including Nomura, lost all the money they had hidden away in Japanese bank accounts and any funds not confiscated were wiped out in the post-war inflation. Noda's dissolution committee ended the industrial autocratic reign of family patriarchs like Tokushichi Nomura, Hachiroemon Mitsui and Kichizaemon Sumitomo, and ownership passed from the wealthy few to much larger numbers of individual Japanese investors. In 1946 one in every four stocks held was in the hands of the *zaibatsu* and other corporations. By 1950 only one in twenty stocks was held by them. Eventually the ownership of stock passed into the hands of the major financial institutions and individual investors.

In the end, the only assets Noda was able to protect for the families were large tracts of seemingly worthless landholdings. What was the use of land, thought the Americans, since most of the nation had been razed? Later, one of the wealthiest men in Japan, and indeed in the world, was Kichizaemon Sumitomo, who retained huge tracts of forests after the war.

Noda spent the first period of his tenure tearing apart the big four *zaibatsu* and the final two years dismantling the six medium-sized *zaibatsu*, including Nomura. Working closely with Narajiro Kamata, the auditor of the Nomura Holding Company, and the only director left from the original team, Noda began systematically liquidating the remains of Tokushichi's empire. Theoretically nothing should have survived the dissolution since all Nomura shareholdings and money were to be confiscated along with property and other belongings. Collusion between Kamata and Noda ensured that that was not the case.

Kamata had been hiding and altering Nomura family documents since the early part of 1945. When in the autumn the Americans, through Noda, demanded the family papers,

119

Kamata feigned innocence and told the authorities he had no idea where they might be. The Americans got tough with the Nomura family and threatened Kamata with court-martial if he did not hand over all the documents by the end of the year. The threat was enough: Kamata magically appeared with Nomura's figures. But that scarcely made the liquidators' task any easier. Even with access to the company records 'they were soon hopelessly tangled in a web of contracts, loans and accounts, joint and nominee shareholdings, common directorships, family ties and *oyabun-kobun* patterns which held the business world together; as fast as they severed connections, the strands rejoined silently behind them'.

After the Americans had finished dissecting Nomura, they gave the house a nominal value of 165 million yen, a figure Kamata purposely understated to soften the authorities' stance towards the firm. He hoped for leniency when it came to redistributing the family fortune. The 165 million yen was the paid-up capital of the empire, the amount of money originally put up to finance the business. It bore no relation to the earning power, market value or influence the House of Nomura had within the Japanese financial community. To put the value of the Nomura family holdings into present-day terms, Nomura Securities was worth $70 billion in the spring of 1987, Daiwa Bank (renamed from Nomura Bank) was worth over $20 billion and Osaka Gas more than $15 billion. Retaining a mere 5 per cent of these firms would have placed the Nomura family among the wealthiest in the world.

Even the optimistic Kamata realized in 1945 that the Nomura family and the Nomura companies would never regroup. He was resolved, however, to salvage as much of their wealth as possible while trying to ensure that the firms within the group did not drift apart. In the summer of 1948, those shares of Nomura's subsidiaries that had been frozen by the Americans in 1945 were confiscated. The intent was all too clear: Nomura shares were to be auctioned off to the public. A frantic Kamata went to Noda to plead with him to stop the public tender. 'You will destroy one of the nation's proudest firms,' he said.

The plea fell on sympathetic ears and together the two men worked out an ingenious plan to give employees the first option of purchasing shares in Nomura subsidiaries. It was a plan the Americans could hardly refuse. Their objective was to promote widespread ownership of corporate Japan. There was little danger of hard-pressed Nomura employees themselves taking the whole share distribution. Unknown to the American authorities, however, each Nomura firm, at the instigation of Kamata, had lent money to trusted workers to buy shares. These workers agreed to sell the shares back to the firm at a later date, ensuring that control of the Nomura group did not fall into unfriendly hands. In effect what transpired was a shift of ownership from the Nomura family to institutional cross-holdings in related firms. When it was over, Nomura Securities owned shares in the Nomura Bank and Nomura Bank held shares in Nomura Securities. Nomura was forever indebted to Noda. Even after his death Nomura Securities paid its respects to Iwajiro Noda for helping the firm through the post-war years by renting out the Okura Hotel for most of its company parties.

Although Nomura group firms took shareholdings in one another, other Japanese companies used this same strategy for more pressing reasons. Hostile takeover attempts after the war posed a threat to many companies and triggered the structure of Japanese cross-holdings which remains in place to this day. Iwajiro Noda liked telling the story of the Mitsubishi break-up at a time when he was forced by the Americans to split Mitsubishi into more than 120 different entities. All of the Mitsubishi land near Tokyo Station in what is now central Tokyo was to be sold off and Noda, sympathetic towards Mitsubishi, thought that giving it away to an unrelated company would be a pity. Instead he approached a sister firm in the Mitsubishi group called Yowa Real Estate and, at negligible cost, put the *zaibatsu* land into Yowa. Everything was fine until 1949. That year the Tokyo Stock Exchange reopened and Yowa's shares were listed on the exchange. Immediately Yowa's share price raced ahead as Kuniro Fujizuna, a wealthy black-market operator, bought up 35 per cent of Yowa shares. This turned out to be Japan's first post-war case of greenmail and Fujizuna was bought out at a hefty profit. This scare sent listed firms flying into the protective arms of friendly companies and by 1953, after the Americans left, the Japanese rewrote the nation's anti-trust rules to allow companies to hold cross-holdings in each other.

Kamata's task of protecting the Nomura assets proved more difficult. Towards the end of the war Kamata had helped set up a firm called Nomura Construction (which survives to this day as the repository of the Nomura family wealth) and at its head had placed one of Japan's leading architects, Kaishi Yasui, since Kamata anticipated the need for reconstruction after the war. Kamata began secretly transferring remnants of Nomura *zaibatsu* land into the construction company, including three prime sites in Osaka and further sites in Tokyo. As soon as property values began to recover after the war, the Nomura family achieved a modicum of wealth and Kamata himself became known as the 'father and protector' of the Nomura children. Noda turned a blind eye to Kamata's wheeling and dealing. Later the land held by Nomura Construction was valued at more than $40 million. The Nomura Construction company managed secretly to retain a 1.5 million shareholding in Nomura Securities whose value on the Tokyo Stock Market in 1987 was as high as $50 billion.

The Americans did, however, achieve much of what they had aimed for when Noda was hired. The Nomura family portfolio was shattered into irrecoverable fragments. Today, instead of total ownership, the family holds one tenth of one per cent of Nomura Securities. Similarly, the family was stripped of its holdings in what is now Japan's ninth largest bank, the once pivotal money centre of the Nomura group. The renamed Daiwa Bank was sold off to sister firms, listed on the stock exchange and placed under the control of a vehemently anti-*zaibatsu* leader, Takeo Terao, a once lowly bank clerk. This fiercely independent man broke the Nomura group into two camps: those under the influence of Nomura Securities and those under the Daiwa Bank's sway.

Osaka Gas, which Tokushichi had saved from hostile hands in the twenties, also had its shares listed and sold off to the public. Nomura Life Insurance, which had been Japan's sixth largest life company, also fell from the family's grasp. The post-war financial reforms changed life insurance companies from *de facto* vaults, with cash on call waiting for accidents to happen, into mutual companies which, under MacArthur's new democracy, were theoretically owned by the life insurance policyholders. Nomura Life was renamed Tokyo Mutual Life Insurance Company and later became Japan's sixteenth largest life insurance company. Other companies which had helped the war effort, such as Nomura Steel and Nitto Aviation, never reopened. Nomura East Indies was lost without compensation to the Dutch East Indies. Fukushima Boseki changed its name to Shikibo and remains one of Osaka's leading textile firms, still in part owned by the Nomura group.

13
The Prison and the Picture Palace

Life in Tokyo was bleak after the war. 'Japan of the late 1940s was like Africa during the 1980s, with little food and little hope until slowly, very slowly, aid arrived in the form of bags of wheat and rice,' recalled Tadashi Ishida, Nomura Securities recruit from the class of 1946. Though welcome, American aid was never enough. Families sent their oldest boys into the countryside by train in hope that they would return with a few vegetables or a handful of rice. The trains bound for the country were so crammed that station attendants were unable to close train doors, and Ishida remembers the poignant scene of hundreds of starving people left on the platform, with the more agile boys able to climb and squeeze their way through a window to be assured passage.

As food prices soared, Japanese families withdrew their savings just to purchase meagre amounts of rice, fish and vegetables. Inflation fed on itself as banks turned to the nation's central bank to borrow money to replenish their vaults.

Prompted by the occupying American forces, the government took the only action it could. It froze all bank deposits and issued a new currency in a bid to prevent a further run on the banks. Tough new rules were imposed, allowing households to withdraw only 100 yen a month from their accounts – a sum barely adequate to feed a family of four. Old bank deposits could be converted to the new currency at the painfully slow rate of 100 yen at a time. Old yen could be used to pay taxes, but for the man in the street the overriding fear was that his trifling savings were about to become worthless.

In bitter irony, catastrophe for Japan meant prosperity for Nomura, for a loophole was uncovered in these draconian banking controls. No law prevented the transfer of blocked savings to the brokerage houses. Banks began transferring money to brokers, who in turn bought stock for their clients. Although the Tokyo Stock Exchange was officially closed, a huge underground stockmarket had emerged. Individual investors immediately sold the stock and collected new yen.

Minoru Segawa, the most adroit of Japan's black-market operators, was the head of the Tokyo branch office of Nomura Securities in the spring of 1946 when he boldly confronted Nomura's president, Seizo Iida. Segawa showed Iida how Nomura could profit by buying stock illegally with old yen, selling the stock and then converting it into new yen. Ethically upright, Iida was in principle opposed to the idea but allowed his concern for Nomura's staff and their families to override his scruples. 'I give you,' he told Segawa, 'authority to make money any way you can to ensure that our people are fed.'

Segawa acted quickly. Within five months he had made Nomura Securities a sizeable fortune operating the currency black market. Then on 10 August 1946, just one day before Nomura Securities was due to become an independent company, free from *zaibatsu* constraints, the Ministry of Finance declared that frozen bank deposits were illegal for use in any stockmarket transactions. But it took more than utterances from the Ministry to stop Segawa. Defiantly, he continued trading in the black market. Every yen he had earned in the first six months of 1946 was the result of converting old yen into new by laundering the money through the stockmarket.

Unknown to him, however, the public prosecutor's office was quietly undertaking its own investigation of Nomura, Yamaichi and Yamazaki Securities in search of precisely such violations of the law. On 9 September, the Tokyo police burst into Nomura's Nihonbashi offices, demanding to see the president. Segawa calmly explained that Nomura Securities was an Osaka-based company with none of its executive officers located in Tokyo. 'I am the one in charge,' he blustered. That was good enough for the police, who hauled him off to prison and threw him into a cell.

Years later in his autobiography, Segawa recounted being grilled by detectives in a room stacked high with sequestered Nomura documents. He realized that the interrogators were clueless about financial markets and simply expected Segawa to confess. Aware of the weakness of the authorities' case against him, even if they could understand the Nomura records, Segawa refused to talk, an insolence that landed him a two-week jail term. Japanese authorities were permitted, as they still are, to incarcerate suspects without evidence of wrongdoing and they hoped, by leaving Segawa to sweat it out in a detention cell, that he would break down. Segawa, however, had no such intention. He was not exactly a small man and instead of wasting away inside prison, he actually put on weight. 'My friends from Nomura brought me food every day and after two weeks I had grown fat.'

The heat was unbearable, however, and one of his favourite stories later was of the time he went to wash up under the courtyard faucet. He sauntered up to the well like a rhinoceros to a watering hole, removed all his clothes, put his head under the faucet and started splashing cold water all over his body. The guard yelled over to him, 'Get your clothes on now.' 'What's the problem?' asked Segawa. 'Just put your uniform back on, now!' the guard snapped. Later Segawa discovered that the female prison cells faced the courtyard and he was thrilled at the thought that 'the women might have seen my private parts'.

Segawa broke his silence sufficiently to mislead the police investigators into believing that Nomura Securities had broken no rules. He explained about stock transactions, steering them away from the trail of his firm's illegal activities. Although their Tokyo chief was still in jail, Nomura continued to earn substantial sums by buying stock with blocked deposits, just as Segawa had done.

New yen notes were essential for other thriving businesses during those lean years – in particular covert but extremely active black market dealing. Segawa thrived on confusion and anarchy, buying and selling anything that was profitable for Nomura. On his release from jail, near the end of September 1946, he ordered Nomura employees to sell lottery tickets issued by the Kango Bank from a wooden stall in Ginza, the main shopping area of Japan. For only one yen, people bought a chance to dream and win a million yen. On another occasion Segawa was caught smuggling vegetable oil through a military checkpoint. Some Nomura salesmen even peddled kitchenware, made by Nippon Light Metal, door-to-door in the hope of bringing in commission revenue.

Post-war Japan was made for men like Segawa: everyone was on equal terms, with no hierarchy and no rules. Survival was all. Gambling, legal and illegal, swept the country as pachinko parlours operated by underworld syndicates became the rage. For one sen, a hundredth of a yen, compulsive gamblers loaded up vertical pinball machines with silver metal balls in hopes of winning yet more balls, exchanging their winnings for cash or returning home broke. Mahjong parlours sprang up and soon the back streets of Tokyo were filled with the clickety-clack of the tiles until late into the night.

But it was not blackmarketeering that made Segawa such a hero to upper management. The reality was that there was a power vacuum in the firm and Nomura needed leadership. Most of the able-bodied men in Nomura Securities had been killed or wounded in the war. So, after his release from jail, Segawa was promoted to director, then rising to become managing director by April 1948, the month Tsunao Okumura became president.

* * * * *

By the time the war ended, Okumura the playboy had had enough of the chaos of Osaka. Everything was destroyed. He wanted to begin a new, more peaceful life with his wife and requested a transfer to nearby Kyoto which Allied planes had left untouched and where he had spent his happy college days. Nomura president Seizo Iida agreed to his appointment as head of the Kyoto branch and the choice unwittingly made him a rich and powerful man.

Amid the tranquil beauty of Kyoto, while the rest of Japan starved, Okumura became a millionaire – though not primarily through stockbroking. Instead, Okumura converted a munitions warehouse into a cinema and the masses, unable to afford any other form of leisure, flocked there day and night. Families used their food money to see movies and keep warm in the cinema, losing themselves for three hours in another world, far from the hardships that awaited them outside. The cinema was always filled to capacity. Audiences overflowed into the aisles to get a chance to see their favourite Hollywood stars: Maurice Chevalier, Greta Garbo, Ingrid Bergman and most popular of all, Clark Gable. *Gone With the Wind* was the biggest hit. Crowds who had never seen a colour movie before were enthralled, coming back night after night to see the bright orange flames of Atlanta burning. According to Tokushichi Nomura's grandson Tomohide, Atlanta and the Civil War reminded the Japanese of their own bombing, fire and destruction, and finally the hope of resurrection.

By charging an exorbitant forty new yen to get into his picture palace, Okumura quickly became one of Kyoto's more prosperous citizens. He funnelled his rising pile of new yen into a dummy company and used it to finance the lavish entertainment of his stockbroking clients. It was a brilliant move that helped Nomura's rise to power after the war. Tomohide Nomura, who also spent the immediate post-war years in Kyoto, recalled how Okumura loved having a good time. 'Clients were Nomura's future. Okumura knew the poverty would not last for ever. Some day there would be business again.'

To win over clients, Okumura had to find a source of food. No matter how much cash a man had, it was still difficult to gather clients at a local restaurant and provide them with enough food. Food had to be supplied by the customer since, to prevent an active blackmarket in food, restaurants were prohibited from serving their own food after the war. More fortunate patrons such as Okumura brought their own food with them to be cooked by the chefs and eaten in a convivial atmosphere. One client recalled Okumura buying a fish and inviting a group of hungry businessmen over to a restaurant. Then to everyone's surprise, he opened a bottle of scotch. Food was rare but scotch was unheard of. Okumura had found himself an American soldier who sold him food and drink at a huge mark-up. Scotch was nectar to the deprived men, who were able to get drunk only on poorly fermented potato wine, distilled from rotten potatoes. 'We never forgot him for that, and when business picked up in the 1950s, Nomura Securities got all our trades,' the client remembered.

The food shortages became so acute that in Tokyo policemen went to extraordinary lengths to ensure that restaurants prepared food only brought by customers. If they caught a restaurant-owner serving food on one of the restaurant's own plates he was likely to be arrested. 'We got round that by bringing our own aluminium lunch-box plates which any policeman recognized had been brought from home,' Tadashi Ishida recalled. 'The restaurant-owner then secretly portioned out a helping of rice and vegetables from a bin hidden in the back room.'

Okumura's parties soon became legendary. He struck up a friendship with one of the bosses of the Gion, the famous high-class geisha area in Kyoto, where exquisitely trained geisha sang, danced and played the three-stringed shamisen. There his clients drank and ate into the night. The customers loved this treatment and Okumura quickly became friends with the leading businessmen and politicians of Japan. Any dignitary knew that he could rely on Okumura to arrange a night on the town whenever he passed through Kyoto. Okumura even hired the women of Gion to join him at the Nomura family villa in Kyoto, where he entertained Prime Minister Shigeru Yoshida and later made friends with Finance Minister Hayato Ikeda.

Although Okumura's ability to throw a good party was the basis of his rise to power in Japan, he found himself elected president of Nomura Securities in April 1948 by a fortuitous process of elimination. When the American authorities purged Nomura Securities of its ranking executives, Okumura, only a branch manager in Kyoto, became *ipso facto* one of the firm's most senior executives. A nobody before the war, he was now thrust into the top slot at one of the country's largest brokerage houses.

Okumura's socializing concealed a shrewd business judgement, and immediately after being elected by a committee of Nomura executives as president of Nomura Securities, he forged ahead, thinking of ways to make up for the losses Nomura had incurred in wartime. In his opinion, his predecessor, Seizo Iida, had been too conservative. He promptly set about rebuilding the securities business which had lain dormant for three years. The first thing he did was expand the firm's capital base from twelve to fifty million yen. There was nowhere to go but up: over half of the fourteen Nomura branch offices had been damaged by bombs and fires, leaving only Nomura's Kyoto, Niigata and Sapporo buildings untouched. Most of the Nomura men had been killed or wounded during the war and only half of the 800 salesmen from the pre-war period returned in 1945. Nomura's overseas offices in the former colonial cities of Mudken and Dalien in Manchuria were seized by the Russians and Chinese. None of the employees in Manchuria was ever heard from again; most of them it was assumed had been left to die in Siberian labour camps.

The Nomura Hiroshima office had been vaporized in the atomic blast of 6 August 1945, and only the firm's sturdy cast-iron safes survived. When Nomura men finally located the remains of the office, they opened the safe to find a single glass of water kept to cool the thirst of some employee in the humid Hiroshima summer.

Okumura revived everyone's spirits, with a cheery bearing that put those around him at ease. But for his smile, he was an undistinguished looking man. Each morning he greased back his hair, an action which highlighted his beaming face. 'The eyes and smile were the key to Okumura. His eyes would open up and enlarge when he spoke with you, until you thought you were the only person in the world who mattered,' recalled Shuzo Nagata, a close colleague who later became president of Kokusai Europe, a Nomura affiliate.

Okumura had charmed the other Nomura executives into electing him president by playing the part of the warm-hearted bundle of humanity. One close colleague, however, compared him to a raccoon, able to cheat people without their knowing it. 'The fox and the raccoon symbolize traditional cheaters to the Japanese,' he said. 'The fox is sly while the raccoon is humorous. Alarm bells go off when you spot a fox but a raccoon plays the comic and lures you into a pleasant fit of laughter while he picks your pocket.' That was Okumura.

His smile won him a lot of support. Younger people thought of him as an avuncular 'godfather' of Nomura Securities, a man who understood their problems and was able and willing to solve them. Even shy people could talk to Okumura, while women were especially attracted to his apparent humanity. He listened and in a country where men treated women like hired help, that was an endearing quality. Playing the 'sensitive man' won him many female conquests and he steadily added women to his coterie until, at his death in 1972, he had four mistresses, and a wife.

* * * * *

The post-war securities business had been a nightmare for three years. Legalized stock trading had ceased on 25 September 1945 as the Supreme Allied Command shut down all Japanese stock exchanges. They were not reopened for three and a half years, but brokers were soon able to conduct business beyond the confines of the exchanges at informal gatherings. Since the inception of the Tokyo Stock Exchange in

1878, most Japanese stock trading had been in stock futures. Dealers did not buy shares in the normal way, taking delivery of a share certificate in exchange for a payment. Instead of a straightforward money for share swap, they bet on which way shares would move over the coming three months. Cash only ever changed hands with these bets on future trends in share prices. So by October 1945 hundreds of stockmarket operators were waiting for money they had been promised in the previous three months. The Tokyo *saitori*, the men who had worked on the floor of the exchange matching buyers and sellers, started by trying to reconcile these outstanding trades. Dealing soon began to snowball and eventually a giant unofficial market emerged, lasting up to the official reopening of the Tokyo Stock Exchange in May 1949. The occupation authorities turned a blind eye.

The war's end ushered in one of Japan's biggest stockmarket booms. Nomura Securities decided Tokyo now had to be the focal point of any development of the securities business instead of Osaka. By December 1945 trading became active as individuals sold shares to buy food and Nomura, sensing opportunity, sold private customers' stock to the cash-rich institutions. When a salesman won an order from an institution, he had one of Nomura's messengers run over to the Japan Securities Building, an old property near the Tokyo Exchange where thirty stock dealers used to congregate. 'We could not use the Tokyo Stock Exchange floor because it had been taken over by the Americans for use as a gym,' recalled Shoshi Kawashima, a Nomura salesman who later became President of Kokusai Securities.

While the Tokyo Stock Exchange was a gym, the Osaka Stock Exchange buildings in Kitahama had become an American hospital. Fujio Kodama, a salesman in 1945 who later became chairman of Osaka-based Wako Securities, a competitor of Nomura and one of Japan's top ten brokers, recalled how the back office buildings of the Osaka exchange were used as an infirmary while the main trading floor had been converted into a dance hall. 'No Japanese was allowed into the dance hall and the Americans posted a huge MP at the door of the exchange just in case anyone tried to sneak in.'

Seven Osaka traders began stock trading in the autumn of 1945 in tiny back rooms near the stock exchange. Salesmen such as Kodama had a tough time earning money for their firms. 'Eating was the big thing back then,' he remembered. 'We traded food, not shares at first.'

Although the Tokyo Stock Exchange did not officially exist, its index, called the Nikkei-Dow Jones Average, was faithfully recorded each day by the newspapers and was riding the wave of the greatest bull market since World War I. The index rose from sixty-five in the autumn of 1946 to 700 by the time the exchange reopened in May 1949. Slowly, new stock issues began to appear as the government began the process of dismantling the *zaibatsu* holding companies and their hundreds of subsidiaries. Before the war, when stock had been tightly held in the hands of the founding families, the physical trading of shares was by-passed for the more speculative trading in stock futures. Now things were going to be different as the newly spun-off corporate fragments of the *zaibatsu* were listed on the unofficial stock exchange. Japan needed money to rebuild its burned-out factories, and what better way to raise the money while freeing the firms from the oppressive ownership of the *zaibatsu* than to sell them to institutions and individuals through the stockmarket? It was not long before the first new stock issue, New Japan Chemical, arrived in April 1946, followed by two dozen more issues in the next six months. Brokers were eager for the business and allowed investors to buy these issues with their old yen bank savings.

The rise of Japan from shantytown to superpower was staggering. 'Think of post-war Tokyo as a giant slum,' said Richard Devine, a leading historian of the Japanese, 'an eyesore as far as you could see, with hovels erected everywhere from anything which would keep the rain out – metal, bits of wood, string.' Tokyo was a patchwork of tin huts except for occasional structures like those left standing in front of the Imperial Palace in Marunouchi, central Tokyo. These buildings had been spared owing to their proximity to the Emperor's residence and after the war were requisitioned by the American forces.

Finding suitable office space amidst the rubble of Tokyo was difficult. Most offices, including Nomura's, had no air-conditioning in the summer and no heat in the winter. Few offices could afford electric heaters so they used kerosene heaters. Young boys made extra money in Nomura by cleaning the wicks of heaters, a morning priority. Nobody owned electric heaters – they were too unreliable with the electricity going on and off all day long. Most nights in the Nomura offices were finished by candlelight when heavy power usage blacked out Tokyo. Amenities to which Nomura men later became accustomed did not exist: there was no telex, and cables had to be written in shorthand to save money. Most customers' orders were received and reported by hand.

One of the biggest headaches facing Tsunao Okumura when he took the reins of power in 1948 was getting enough telephone lines into the Nomura Tokyo office in Nihonbashi. Phones were the ears and mouth of daily stockbroking, but there were almost no available phone lines in Tokyo. Nomura had to sign on a two-year waiting list just to procure a single line. A black market sprang up in the sale and leasing of phone lines and Nomura cleverly assigned a man whose sole task was to procure telephone lines from Nippon Telephone and Telegraph (NTT). Then in 1948 the government decided it needed money and awarded anyone purchasing a certain amount of its bonds a telephone line. Everyone rushed to trade government bonds, including manufacturing firms totally unfamiliar with fixed income securities, who bought up bonds in exchange for a phone allocation and then immediately sold them.

Getting the telephone installed was the first problem but even then each phone call from the Nomura office had to be put through an NTT operator, who took requests each morning and put calls through some time later in the day. One only hoped to be near a phone when the call was returned. When it rained nothing worked. An extreme distrust of telephones ensued, which reinforced the inclination to do business face-to-face. To this day, stockbrokers leave their desks at the market close to have tea and chat with customers.

Yukio Aida was another Nomura salesman of this period. (Forty years later he became chairman of the powerful Nomura Investment Management Company, with over $20 billion under his wing.) Between 1947 and 1958 he worked as an institutional salesman and covered all the biggest players in the Japanese stockmarket. 'I had ten or fifteen accounts, mainly life insurance, banks and casualty insurance companies. Then, as today, Nippon Life was the largest participant in the market.'

Aida started selling stocks for Nomura from the first day he joined the firm in 1947. There was only a handful of active stocks traded and he was able to monitor them at a glance. Four decades later there would be over 2,000 different issues divided into dozens of industrial and financial sectors. In those days a Nomura salesman was a jack of all trades and very knowledgeable about the companies he discussed with clients. Many years later, Aida was surprised at how much more Nomura men had to know about the Japanese market than their counterparts at Merrill Lynch knew about the American one. 'We knew the business of the companies whose shares we were selling. We knew our client, made the sale, executed the trade and then delivered the report by hand to our client. The Merrill salesmen just pushed stocks of companies they had never visited and barely understood, with no idea how their trade was settled and paid for.'

Selling stock was a tiring business, since the Tokyo transportation system consisted of one subway, one tram, buses, taxis and the occasional privately owned car. Aida jumped on the tram every afternoon (running from Shinagawa in southern Tokyo to Ueno in the north) and got off at the Ginza stop, where he walked over to see his banking and insurance clients in Marunouchi. Charcoal-burning Renault taxis just after the war were relatively plentiful. Gasoline was impossible to procure, since only American troops and well-connected officials were allocated fuel, and the drivers removed their car trunks and put charcoal burners in the rear. Because they needed to conserve fuel, taxi drivers did not roam the streets looking for passengers but waited until a passenger arrived, when they would stoke up the burner in the rear by lighting the coals. The flames sometimes spread to other parts of the car and it was not an uncommon sight to see drivers dousing their blazing cars. Buses ran by the same method but used slow-burning chunks of wood to fuel their engines.

'We tried to live like the common people after 1945,' said Tomohide Nomura. 'Other families hired chauffeurs who were so cheap that if you could afford one, you usually had two.' Driving was not a practical means of transport. Special licences were necessary and any time a Japanese drove out alone he was usually stopped by the Japanese or American police for simply being Japanese. Everyone knew that only Americans drove cars in Japan.

14
Paradise Regained

'Buy a share for a pack of Peace,' ran the brokers' sales pitch in the late forties and early fifties. Peace – the name of a popular brand of Japanese cigarette – cost about fifty yen a pack, roughly the same as the cost of buying one share from the local stockbroker. Fifty yen was a considerable amount of money for the average Japanese, and cigarettes were a great luxury. A pack would often have to be eked out over a fortnight. Any Japanese, however, who fought off the fleeting satisfaction offered by Peace and instead put his money into a share like Toshiba or Nomura would years later have reaped a spectacular reward.

By the spring of 1949 the clandestine Japanese stockmarket was out of control. There were 360 dealers, forty floor clerks and twenty-four newspaper reporters jockeying for position in a 216-square-foot room in the Securities Association next to the Tokyo Stock Exchange. Trading volumes exceeded the million share a day mark, far above the volume in 1944 when only 68 million shares had changed hands in the entire year.

The occupation authorities had little choice but to reopen the Tokyo Stock Exchange. Trading resumed on 16 May 1949 with much drunken celebration, festive banqueting and general euphoria. The partying seemed to symbolize the emergence of the new Japan. Pre-war Japanese markets had been obsessed with bonds – but this was the new era of stocks, where individually owned companies, stripped of *zaibatsu* control, were traded on the exchange. Tokyo began with 120 stock exchange members and Osaka with eighty-three. A new company, Heiwa Real Estate, was formed to preserve the buildings and land which belonged to the pre-war shareholders (mainly stock dealers) of the Tokyo Stock Exchange. Before the war members of the Exchange both

137

owned and ran the trading floor for their own profit and the shareholders who had owned the exchange were now given Heiwa shares as compensation. Heiwa was, however, only a real-estate company leasing its assets to the Exchange and had no involvement in the running of the Exchange, which was the prerogative of a membership committee overseen by the Ministry of Finance.

The celebratory mood of Kabutocho, Japan's Wall Street, turned sour a year after the exchange opened. By 6 July 1950, just eleven days after the outbreak of the Korean War, the stockmarket had halved from its opening level, plunging from 176 to eighty-five. This was the lowest point the post-war Japanese stockmarket reached, and anyone quick enough to have bought a significant number of shares on that day, and held on, would likely have become one of the world's richest men. Whose crystal ball would have foretold that the Nikkei-Dow Jones Average, pausing for breath here and there, would motor past the 100, 1000, 5000, 20,000, and finally even the 30,000 barrier – all within the span of a generation?

Tsunao Okumura laid the groundwork for Japan's post-war bull market, the most prolonged rally in the history of mankind – a rally that began in 1945 and, except for a few blips here and there, is still going on. In doing so, as the head of Nomura Securities, he made the interests of Nomura the interests of the Japanese government. Though it was a remarkable feat, Okumura's solicitation of high-ranking government support for the stockmarket was simply the way the Japanese got things done. When he lavished entertainment on Prime Minister Shigeru Yoshida and Finance Minister Hayato Ikeda in Nomura's luxurious Kyoto villa after the war, there was a serious purpose behind his Sybaritic activity. His party-giving brought Nomura stature within Japan's financial community. Hayato Ikeda built his own power base and was responsible for moulding the Japanese industrial juggernaut. Ikeda became known as the saviour of Japan and Okumura hung firmly on to his coat-tails.

Ikeda's beneficence towards Nomura and the stockbroking community set a pattern of reciprocity between Japan's prime ministers and financiers that would continue until the late 1980s. Ikeda was born at the turn of the century, the son of an affluent Hiroshima sake brewer; at secondary school he was the classmate of Eisaku Sato, who went on to become prime minister in 1964. He went to Kyoto Imperial University, where he was one year ahead of Okumura, and then joined the government revenue office. There, as an obscure tax officer, he was spotted in 1944 by Japan's financial kingpins as an astute influence peddler, favourably settling estates for payment in kind. Ikeda's payment in kind did not take the form of under the table payments, for he was much more ambitious. He wanted real power and in 1946, as a result of his favourable tax ratings, he was named by Prime Minister Shigeru Yoshida as the nation's finance minister.

Amazingly, Japanese politics after the war were dictated not by the will of the people, nor even by the seemingly omnipotent American officials, but rather by the doyens of Japanese business, who were known as the Four Heavenly Kings: Takeshi Sakuada of Nisshinbo (a large textile company), Shigeo Nizuno of the Sankei Newspaper, Ataru Kobayashi of the Japan Development Bank and Shigeo Nagano of Fuji Iron Works. Together, these four funded the ascent of Japanese politicians. They chose Yoshida as prime minister and in turn ensured that Ikeda would be his finance minister. More importantly for Nomura Securities, these four men belonged to the powerful Kayokai or Tuesday Club, whose other key members included Okumura, Ikeda, and the governor of the Bank of Japan.

By 1950 Ikeda had consolidated his position by taking over the Ministry of International Trade and Industry in addition to his role as minister of finance. He and Okumura spent much of their time in Ogawaken, a notoriously expensive steak house in Shimbashi, where they would drink Hennessey brandy late into the night. At other times they would eat fresh raw fish just feet away from where the tuna and bream were hauled off the fishing vessels to the Tsukiji sushi shops at the Tokyo Bay docks. Afterwards they usually moved on to the bars of Ginza or Akasaka. Even after Ikeda became prime minister years later, the pair maintained their habit of taking in sushi at Tsukiji, trailed, as Okumura recalled, by an entourage of bodyguards and a Tokyo Metropolitan Police car. (In fact Okumura dined out so much that by the time he retired as president in 1958 he was as overweight as Segawa.)

The temporary downfall of Ikeda came without warning. In November 1952 he addressed the Diet about his selective lending policies to Japan's cash-starved companies. 'It makes no difference to me if five or ten small businessmen are forced to commit suicide,' he told the assembly. 'The poor can eat wheat instead of rice,' he went on. It was one of the gravest Japanese political blunders, since rice was – as it still is – the staple of the Japanese diet. Thousands of small businessmen clamoured for his head and Ikeda was forced to resign as finance minister and minister of trade.

Suddenly the great powerbroker was abandoned, jobless and forsaken by friends – except for one, Okumura. Tsunao Okumura had once wallowed in the trough of ill-fortune and he gave the sullen Ikeda free use of the Nomura family seaside villa in Atami to restore his fighting spirit. The two men went fishing together and Ikeda enjoyed the culinary delights of a full-time tempura cook provided by Okumura. At about the same time another ex-finance minister was given a hand up by Okumura. Kaya Okinori, the much-feared and all-powerful pre-war friend of Tokushichi Nomura, was released from Sugamo Prison where he had been jailed for class 'A' war crimes. Okumura immediately took him on as senior adviser to Nomura Securities.

Before Ikeda was sacked, however, he had allowed Nomura to relaunch the investment trust (what Americans called a mutual fund), the concept Nomura had created back in 1941. The occupying authorities had banned investment trust activity after the war, even though Nomura had by

1949 reimbursed all holders of the fifteen trusts in which clients had lost money. Okumura spent 1950 petitioning his friend Ikeda and John R. Allison, the occupation official in charge of the Japanese economy, for the reinstatement of investment trusts. Finally, late in the year, Allison relented: 'You win, Mr Okumura. Since I will be going home soon, I am giving you a going-away present.' The deal was that Allison would raise no objections when the Japanese government pressed the Americans for approval of investment trusts.

If one were to pinpoint one statement, one action, on which the fortunes of the post-war Japanese stockmarket hinged, and indeed the wealth of Japan was based, it was Allison's 'You win, Mr Okumura.' Okumura left Allison's office that day on the verge of tears. Instinctively he knew he had opened up a new era of dominance for Nomura. His firm had created the investment trust in Japan and his salesmen knew far better than any securities industry rival how they should market it. He quickly broke the news to Ikeda, who saw to it that by the spring of 1951 a new law was passed allowing securities firms to solicit individuals for funds to be invested on their behalf in the market. It was to be the buying power of these investment trusts, led by Nomura, which sent the index on its skyward trajectory into the 1960s and again in the 1980s.

Investment trusts became to Nomura Securities what savings deposits were to the banks: a low-cost source of funds with which Nomura could control the stockmarket. Whereas banks remained stagnant icons of bricks and mortar within every local community, waiting for customers to beat a path to their door, securities firms were mobile, aggressive solicitors of business. Banks were like gentle ruminants compared to the predatory brokers. Though only four Nomura offices were fully functional as the war ended, by 1953 Okumura had built a network of thirty-three offices scattered all over Japan. Each day Nomura salesmen combed the streets and byways of urban and rural Japan in search of solvent individuals whom they could pressure into the market.

But Okumura did not rely solely on his salesmen. Women

controlled the family budget in Japanese society, so Nomura approached large department stores like Daimaru and Matsuzakaya to set up investment consulting centres to explain about the stockmarket. This was the forerunner of the American stock retailing technique used by Sears Roebuck which, after purchasing the leading Wall Street firm, Dean Witter Reynolds, set up stock sales desks in major Sears stores. The Japanese were able to buy their stocks where they bought their socks even before the market had officially reopened in 1949. And by 1953 these Nomura consulting centres had blossomed into more than 600 customer 'service stations' across the nation, agencies which pulled more and more ordinary Japanese into the Nomura web.

Still, it was an uphill struggle for Okumura and his growing sales force. The Japanese still eyed stockbrokers with suspicion and the market itself remained volatile, rising sharply between 1950 and 1953, owing partly to the Korean War; Japanese industry boomed as it fed the West's military build-up. Then came a short-lived market shock in 1953 when Joseph Stalin died. With his death, it was reasoned, the chill between the Soviets and the West would be sure to subside and such thoughts were enough to send the Japanese stockmarket plunging 10 per cent in one day. Such events undid much of the effort Okumura had put into improving the image of stockmarkets. Clients who had been sitting on large profits and thinking how astute they had been were now blaming, and indeed hating, their stockbroker for allowing those profits to be eaten away.

Okumura found it impossible to manipulate the market's direction. Nomura was still too small to do that. But in his frustration he began building up Nomura's influence over the market, so that one day his successors could dictate its movement. Much in the manner of Tokushichi Nomura, Okumura understood the need to expand the firm in a time of crisis. As he well knew, having once lost everything he owned, crises pass and when the market rallied again some day, as it was sure to do, Nomura would be ready.

The year 1953 was bad for Yozaburo Tsuchiya, head of Nitto Securities, now known as Sanyo Securities, Japan's largest family-controlled brokerage house. The stockmarket plunge brought his firm to the brink of bankruptcy. Nitto was particularly vulnerable because it had carved itself a huge chunk of an emerging, but speculative, market known to the Japanese as 'the blue sky market'. This was an unofficial market dealing in splintered *zaibatsu* companies that were being listed on the stock exchange. Tsuchiya had formed a profitable business in buying and selling the rights to trade in these new companies before they came to the market.

The 'blue sky market' was so called because trading took place without an official roof, mostly in the corridors of the Tokyo Stock Exchange. The division of the large Japanese conglomerates into smaller companies had created hundreds of new firms. Flagrant speculation centred on the division of Mitsubishi Chemical, only one of many Mitsubishi *zaibatsu* subsidiaries, a firm divided into Asahi Glass, Shinko Rayon and Nippon Chemical. Stock vouchers were issued by these three companies which were certificates for shares to be issued in the future. Tokyo and Osaka traders, excited by something resembling the old rice future tickets, began actively buying and selling these rights. Many dealers saw it as an easy way to make a quick profit and bought rights in hopes of selling them on rapidly at a profit without having to put up any cash. This practice, known as trading on balance, was popular in the spring of 1950 and the three Mitsubishi splinter companies were bought aggressively day after day. Eventually the bubble burst and the share prices of the companies collapsed, sending many Osaka stockbrokers into bankruptcy.

The occupying forces had done their best to curtail such trading, but by 1953 stockbrokers were again vigorously buying 'blue sky' stocks. When the stockmarket fell sharply in 1953, Nitto was nearly wiped out. 'You might say my customers were at the speculative edge of the credit system,' Tsuchiya regretfully recalled. 'When Stalin died in March and the market collapsed, my clients walked away from their debts. By the following September they owed me 70 million yen.' The creditors, smelling blood, started closing in to nibble at any flesh still left on the Nitto skeleton.

On 28 September Tsuchiya called on Tsunao Okumura and, samurai-like, unfolded his story. 'I need your help,' he said bluntly. 'I will resign my post as president of Nitto if you can save my firm.'

Okumura was gracious. 'How much do you need?' Okumura enquired.

'One hundred million yen' (a fortune in those days) came the reply.

Then, with the charm that won Okumura friends throughout Tokyo's political and financial circles, the Nomura president responded: 'Nomura Securities will not lend to Nitto Securities. It will only lend to the honourable Tsuchiya, personally, if you stay on at Nitto.' Shortly thereafter Tsuchiya received 100 million yen at a low rate of interest. Nomura group companies increased their stake to 10 per cent of Nitto and, with the consent of Tsuchiya, sent in a host of managers to beef up the sales and financial controls. The Japanese began referring to Nomura as a *bakemono* – a goblin-like master company with tentacles everywhere.

Tactics such as these – gaining control over stock exchange member firms in time of crisis and creating a new sales force to market investment trusts and stocks – helped Nomura build a commanding 20 per cent share of the Japanese stockmarket by the 1990s.

Okumura figured that the only way to put his hand in the pocket of the small investor in Japan was to gain his trust. In a brilliant manoeuvre to win over the Japanese public he launched the 'Million Ryo Savings Chest' campaign in 1953. A ryo was an ancient form of Japanese currency and much as Americans would use the phrase 'I wish I had a million dollars' so would the Japanese sometimes sigh for a million ryo. To create the illusion that this dream was possible, Nomura built thousands of traditional wooden strong-boxes,

capable of holding 1,000 ten-yen coins, which salesmen peddled throughout Japan. These locked piggy banks were lent
to customers who, when the coins filled over half the box,
called their Nomura salesmen for the key. The savings were
then placed in a Nomura investment trust of equal value.

Okumura's nephew, Tetsuo, recalled how as a novice
Nomura salesman in the fifties he trundled round the streets
of Tokyo delivering the Million Ryo boxes. 'I placed them
out every day, targeting particularly the wealthy sushi shop
owners.' With intestinal fortitude, he ate his way through six
sushi shops every day and at the end of each meal asked the
owner if he would mind putting the Million Ryo box in the
sushi shop. Tetsuo Okumura guessed that he ate in about 500
sushi shops before being saved by a transfer.

If Allison's parting statement 'You win, Mr Okumura'
launched Nomura and investment trusts on the path to the
top of the world securities market, then the mechanism by
which that dominance was achieved was the Million Ryo
Savings Box. This was the key to unlocking the legendary
appetite for saving of the ordinary Japanese, the key which
little by little turned the psychology of the man in the street
back in favour of the stockmarket. By 1962 Nomura's once
tattered sales force had put Million Ryo boxes into more than
one million homes across the nation. Okumura found that
housewives – prospective customers – trusted other women
with their money, so Nomura began hiring low-paid women
– more than 2,000 of them – to explain about the stockmarket
to their friends and neighbours.

Okumura, 'the smiling raccoon', knew that trust preceded
exploitation. Nomura had in many senses become a bank
with a steady source of deposit money. There was an important difference, however. Nomura charged its clients to put
money into its investment trusts while banks foolishly had to
pay out interest. The clink of every ten-yen coin squirrelled
away in a Million Ryo Box by the housewife in Saitama,
the corner-store in Aomori or the monk in Nikko was a
victory over the sensibility of the Japanese public. At first

Nomura's competitors – banks and other securities companies – laughed at the hollow clink of single coins in Nomura's coffers. But slowly the boxes were distributed across the country and by 1962 Nomura needed over 150 women to collect boxes each day, count the coins and pour their ringing contents into the growing pot that would one day enable Nomura to dominate the stockmarket.

15
The Go-Go Years

A new political party, the Liberal Democrats, was formed in Japan in 1955, and immediately became the dominant political force in the country. This was just the opening Tsunao Okumura was looking for to lure his friend Hayato Ikeda out of his exile. Ikeda eagerly agreed to join the new party and within a year the Tuesday Club had selected him again as minister of finance. So powerful was the Tuesday Club and its affiliates that between 1946 and 1972 they controlled the office of the prime minister in eighteen of twenty-six years; in 1960 Hayato Ikeda was selected as party president and therefore prime minister. Japan was not like Western democracies where popular vote decided leadership. Control was wielded by the amount of money raised to pay off electors and not until 1972 did someone outside the Tuesday Club have deeper pockets. This was Kakuei Tanaka who made world headlines in 1976 in the Lockheed bribery affair.

In the summer of 1959 Okumura became Nomura Securities' first chairman, leaving day-to-day management of the firm to Segawa. When Ikeda ran for prime minister that year Okumura helped underwrite his campaign and Ikeda himself raised more money than any of his rivals – some 232 million yen (about $650,000 in those days) – to guarantee his victory. He is estimated to have spent in all over one billion yen (more than $2.7 million) currying favour with electors and a large chunk of that extra cash pile was raised courtesy of Okumura.

In many ways it was Okumura's kindness to Ikeda that brought Japanese stockbrokers to power. Ikeda showered the securities industry with benefits throughout the rest of his career. Any hint, for example, of a capital gains tax in

Japan during the reign of Ikeda was immediately dispelled and investment trust laws were strengthened to increase Nomura's sway over the securities markets. Capital expansion plans by means of stock issues accelerated in the late fifties as the economy made its great leap forward. Japan's economy grew by over 11 per cent in 1959, 12 per cent in 1960 and 13 per cent in 1961. These years of glorious growth became known as the Iwato boom – a name conjured from the sun goddess of Japanese mythology.

The return of sunlight to the Japanese economy after the gloom of war was Ikeda's triumph. He was dubbed by Chalmers Johnson, a political economist and author of *MITI and the Japanese Miracle* (the bible of Japan's rise to economic power), as the 'architect of the Japanese miracle'. Ikeda ruled Japan during the golden years of Japan's growth – the go-go years leading up to 1964 when Tokyo hosted the Olympic Games. They were the most exciting that modern Japan had ever seen. The entire country appeared under the spell of Prime Minister Ikeda's economic magic. It was as if the Japanese decided to put aside the warrior gear of a samurai nation and take up the robes of a merchant society. Money that once poured into national defence was funnelled into industrial production.

Life through the 1940s had been an inferno, life through the 1950s a greyish purgatory, while the 1960s gave Japan a new spirit and a new life. Nothing symbolized the acceptance of Japan into world society better than the Olympics of 1964, the year that provides a dividing line between the old and new post-war Japan. The streets were empty and flat in the late 1950s before the Olympic skyscrapers started appearing. Ever since the great Kanto earthquake of 1923, the city of Tokyo had imposed a thirteen-storey restriction on building height but now, with the advance of light, tensile-strength materials, buildings could be put up that swayed with tremors, like bamboo, instead of holding fast and cracking like oak.

Transportation also improved. Although there were numerous trains throughout Japan, there had only been one subway and one streetcar line in Tokyo until the Olympic Games, when 'like a mole let loose', subway stations started popping up all over. The pre-Olympic intercity trains still had wooden floors and each morning the smell of disinfectant in the cars, washed by hand the night before, was overpowering. Officials tried to cut down on the proliferations of bugs that burrowed into the wooden floorboards, but, according to Richard Devine, a scholar of Japanese history who moved to Tokyo in the late 1950s, the cleaners missed scrubbing behind the seat boards, the preferred breeding spot of fleas each September. 'You could always tell the people who were lucky enough to get a seat in the autumn since they were the ones who scratched all over.'

New methods of sewage, sanitation and agricultural fertilization appeared after the Olympics so that the stench of human waste (although still apparent in Japan's cities and towns owing to open drains) was cut down remarkably. Food became more plentiful as the Japanese prospered and slowly whale meat, the common man's sushi, was replaced by more exotic cuts of tuna and shellfish. As in most cycles of poverty and wealth, form followed content in everything from food to architecture, fashion to design. Japanese footwear told this tale of rags to riches. 'At first after the war,' said Devine, 'the kids were all running around barefoot, then they wore wooden shoes, or *geta*, then plastic shoes, until finally after the Olympics, leather became more fashionable.'

The new affluence was reflected in Japan's stockmarket, which tripled between 1957 and 1961. Stocks like Toshiba, then an affiliate of General Electric, surged from thirty-five to 280 yen. It was the age of the growth stock, a concept Nomura pirated from Wall Street where during those same years the chase was on in earnest for investors to 'buy Control Data' and 'load up on Burroughs' and every other maker of the latest electronic widgets of the new age of technology.

Nomura coaxed investors into unfamiliar stocks like Matsushita Electrical Industrial Company, a medium-sized

Osaka-based producer of everyday household appliances. Matsushita would become the world's largest maker of consumer electronics products by the late 1970s, but in 1961 it was just another promising dream stock. When the Iwato boom began in 1957, investors could buy a share in Matsushita for under fifty yen. By the end of the boom in 1961, the price was up to 430 yen. And so it went ... Sony had just begun producing its first radios out of a back-street garage in Nagoya and investors were so enchanted by its prospects that they bid the price up by 117 yen in two days of panic buying during June 1960.

Buying reached such frenzied levels that the stock exchange, under pressure from the Ministry of Finance, was forced to put daily limits on price increases and decreases. Investors piled into Nomura's investment trusts, now numbering over a hundred and the nation's third largest investment medium. They were golden years for Nomura Securities and the other three brokerage firms as well. Okumura tripled the network of branches to ninety-seven and the firm's net profits soared from 700 million yen ($1.9 million) in 1959 to over four billion yen (more than $11 million) by 1961.

Shuzo Nagata, a novice salesman in the go-go years, who later became president of Kokusai Europe, was typical of Nomura's expansion. He recalled those years as 'one big blur'. He had joined Nomura in the remote seaside town of Miyazaki, in the mountainous region of Kyushu, and was one of Okumura's infantry men, traipsing the countryside looking for stockmarket orders. But the distance between villages and even between houses was too far to cover on foot and to help men like Nagata, Nomura bought a fleet of the new Mitsubishi 500cc cars, Japan's answer to the Volkswagen Beetle. With its rear-mounted, two-cylinder engine it chugged its way through pitted roads and the hilly terrain, often taking five or six hours to cover twenty kilometres, and the khaki-coloured Mitsubishis, gears grinding because of the inexperience of their drivers, became a familiar feature of rural Japan in the fifties.

Nagata had the good fortune to be in the right place when many of Kyushu's landowners became rich overnight. The government was busy building hydro-electric dams in the region and landowners whose property was to be submerged received generous compensation. Many found they had money to spare even after they had bought a new home, and they had little idea how to spend it. Japan in the fifties was not yet a consumer society of dishwashers, TV sets and automobiles and the Kumamoto and Miyazaki prefectures, where Nagata plied Nomura investment trusts, were even less endowed with consumer products than the rest of Japan. Most of the locals were simple folk with simple ambitions. The contractors were the first to become wealthy once the dam construction was under way. Nomura targeted the Miyazaki office as the firm's hottest new growth area and soon Nagata's colleagues had more Mitsubishi 500s than they could use. Nagata himself kept two cars, one at the Nomura dormitory and one at the office. 'If I got drunk I got a lift home and drove straight into work the next morning.'

Back in Tokyo, companies were taking full advantage of the buying hysteria which had gripped the stockmarket. In 1961 some 293 firms arranged to have their shares listed on the exchange. Lines formed outside Nomura offices to subscribe for initial public offerings, many of which traded 30 or 40 per cent above the subscription price on their first day of dealing.

The most speculative game in town became the over-the-counter market. This was a second-class stockmarket with no real listing requirements and lax settlement procedures, which had sprouted in its own corner of the Tokyo Stock Exchange. Prices were easily manipulated on low volume so that 10, 20 and 30 per cent price movements – down as well as up – commonly occurred in a matter of days or even hours. The king of the over-the-counter market was Yamaichi Securities, a Tokyo-based stockbroker and Nomura's main rival. Yamaichi was the undisputed heavyweight of Japanese corporate underwriting and when it came to advising companies on how and when to list their shares on the Tokyo Exchange or on the over-the counter market, everyone turned to Yamaichi.

16
The Grave-robbers

The popularity of the over-the-counter market spurred Yamaichi to bring dubious companies, many no more than bucketshops, to the stockmarket, so that the hapless Japanese investor was unable to distinguish between the good, the bad and the downright ugly companies. Disclosure rules were non-existent and pricing was in an anarchic state. Investors found they could get different prices, varying as much as 5 per cent, for the same stock from different brokers, who gouged clients by selling stock on to the customer at a much higher price than they had actually paid, pocketing the balance.

Finally, in October 1961, the Ministry of Finance tried to bring some order into the chaos of over-the-counter trading by formally creating a second section to the Tokyo Stock Exchange. The aim was to upgrade this speculative market by trading in a central marketplace, thus making accurate prices available to the public, increasing marketability and improving settlement of stock. Some 385 companies entered the second section in October 1961, many of them spon-sored by Yamaichi. No one knew it, but the seeds of disaster were being sown.

Yamaichi was the acknowledged powerhouse of Japanese underwriting in the early 1960s but in achieving such a distinction it had overextended itself. It was the role of Yamaichi, as underwriter to over 40 per cent of the sec-ond section firms, to provide a liquid market in firms to which they acted as adviser and by 1965 Yamaichi was underwriter to 160 of the 462 second section firms. It lent a helping hand in illiquid stocks, much like specialists on the floor of the New York Stock Exchange, which meant that it had to provide each stock issue with marketability. 'It was our job to buy shares if there were too many sellers in the market,' said Masayoshi Katsuta, a salesman for Yamaichi in the early 1960s, who later became president of Kleinwort Benson Investment Management in Japan, 'a dangerous game in a bear market'.

In addition to the responsibility for second section firms, Yamaichi had its blue-chip clientele to advise – names like Mitsubishi Heavy Industries, Ajinomoto, Kanebo and Asahi Glass. Yamaichi, like most Japanese firms and individuals, believed the good times would keep on rolling. Unfortunately, company presidents in Japan also believed that their company was better than that of a competitor if its quoted share price was higher. There was no such thing in Japan as valuation, except by absolute price. Japanese investors dismissed the price earning ratios that American investors prattled on about: the stockmarket was the barometer of prestige in Japan – the highest share price indicated the best company. 'There was a social prestige within each industrial grouping on the stock exchange and if you could not keep up the stock price of your client, then the underwriting deals went to someone else,' explained Katsuta. Matsushita trading at 350 yen a share was markedly superior in the minds of the Japanese to Hitachi trading at 150 yen a share. To support a client's share price required buying power and only Yamaichi had that clout, the ability to command a 30, 40 or 50 per cent market share in the stocks of those firms for whom it acted as financial adviser.

When the stockmarket took a tumble, as it did more or less continuously from 1960 until 1965, Yamaichi lost a fortune. Things had been looking bleak as early as November 1963 and symbolic of the nation's concern were the constant phone calls in November 1963 from Prime Minister Hayato Ikeda, while attending the funeral ceremonies for President Kennedy, worriedly asking for stock quotations. Yamaichi was faltering. Part of the problem was that there were 1,700 stocks quoted on the Tokyo Stock Exchange by 1965, compared to 790 just four years earlier. The financing got bigger and bigger. Companies came to the market in droves and were knocking on Yamaichi's door to go public. The firm's capital base began to creak.

Silver-haired Fujio Kodama, who became the adviser and chairman of Wako Securities and who was in 1963 a senior manager at Oi Securities (a firm that went belly-up in 1965), twenty-seven years later looked back and stated unequivocally that the size of the stockmarket, as opposed to the share index, grew too fast in the late 1950s. The index fell, from 1,800 in 1960 to nearly 1,000 in 1965, as a result of the investment trusts. 'They were like a whale in a short wooden wash tub,' said Kodama. 'They ripped it apart – there was too much demand for stocks for too small a market.' His reasoning is that the 'rocks' got pushed up along with the 'diamonds' of the second section. His small firm of Oi alone hired 600 extra staff to sell stocks. But when investors realized the indiscriminate nature of their stock purchases, they sold stock off rapidly and brokerage houses found themselves with too many fixed costs. 'We had it too good for too many years,' stated Kodama.

One man foresaw the 1965 collapse of the Japanese securities industry but his warnings to the Ministry of Finance officials went unheeded. The Cassandra of stockbroking in the early 1960s was Akira Miyazawa, chief of the securities bureau at the Bank of Japan from 1963. Later, when he became chairman of Nippon Telephone and Telegraph Systems Technology, Miyazawa looked back: 'I predicted a crisis two years before it happened, but the Ministry of Finance did not listen.' Miyazawa's job as head of the Bank of Japan's four-man securities bureau was to keep the bank informed of any problems in the industry. Under the aegis of the Ministry of Finance, the main role of the Bank of Japan was to lend money to industrial and commercial firms using commercial banks as intermediaries.

Miyazawa's natural wariness of stockbrokers, a trait he learned from his father, a liberal-minded professor of law at Tokyo University, made him a good watchdog. His father had constantly stressed the importance of giving and Miyazawa remembers his lecturing that 'stockbrokers use other people's money and give nothing back to society'. Technically the Bank of Japan was forbidden to lend directly to brokers, and was supposed only to monitor their operations, but even monitoring securities firms was a problem for Miyazawa – stockbrokers were of such low status that they had never been allowed access to the Bank of Japan premises. His first task in his new job had been to walk over from his majestic offices to the nearby Nihonbashi headquarters of the big four. He had called on the senior executives at Yamaichi, Nomura, Nikko and Daiwa and informed them that they would be permitted to visit him at the Bank of Japan. He added that he would like their cooperation in the future. What he really wanted was a weekly copy of each broker's financial statement.

What Miyazawa discovered in 1963 was startling. The major Japanese brokerage firms were issuing attractive, 6 per cent bonds to individuals, then taking this money and plunging it into the stockmarket on their own account. Yamaichi was especially aggressive in using individual clients' money for purchasing stock of their favoured, publicly quoted corporate clients, to shore up their declining shares. In the years leading up to the 1965 crisis, 'Yamaichi made more money from trading on its own account than it did for customers,' remarked T.F.M. Adams, the foremost authority on financial Japan, in his notable 1972 book, *A Financial History of the New Japan*. This worried Miyazawa. The Japanese hated speculators and would have caused a run on the financial system if they had realized that their bonds could become irrecoverable.

Miyazawa knew trouble was looming and told his superiors that the bank should be prepared to lend money to help the brokers. The board of directors remained impassive, and, prohibited from lending to securities firms directly, were not keen to bend the rules. The Ministry of Finance was the only body that could authorize the bank to make payments to brokerage houses, but the Ministry of Finance had no grasp of the day-to-day activity of the stockmarket. 'They were too high level,' complained Miyazawa, who was a lone voice pleading for help. Each week, executives from the big four came by with their income and reserve statements. It was clear that all the firms except Nomura Securities were in dire need of assistance, but nobody wanted to lend to stockbrokers. Even the Industrial Bank of Japan refused to lend to brokers. 'So they came to me, as last resort,' boasted Miyazawa. 'I held the purse.' But Bank of Japan officials turned down brokers' requests for money.

Secretly, however, Miyazawa found a means to transfer loans to the big four. 'I was not a big fan of broking in general but something had to be done to save the industry.' In one of the most intrepid and yet little-known episodes in Bank of Japan history, Miyazawa authorized the Bank of Japan money market window to lend each of the big four a huge sum of money, but in order to leave no trace of the transaction, Miyazawa memorized the figures. In February 1965 he lent Nikko 13.5, Daiwa 8.6, Yamaichi 8.2 and Nomura 5.2 billion yen ($37.5, 23.8, 22.7 and 14.5 million respectively), money he never told the board of directors about. Although Nomura Securities was not under any financial duress Miyazawa felt it was only fair to provide funds at the same low rate of interest. The relative strength of Nomura was underscored by a list of valuations Miyazawa had tallied, figures he still kept in his files years later. In March 1965, as usual, Miyazawa gathered the financial statements of all the stockbrokers: Nomura had a net asset value of 17.1 billion yen, Daiwa 2.6, Nikko 9; and Yamaichi had a negative net worth of 18.2 billion yen. Two months later only Nomura Securities was left standing in the plus column.

The money was, however, of little help. A panic was coming. Yamaichi customers had been cashing in their discount bonds at a furious pace. Moreover, unknown to the general public, 'Nikko Securities was on the verge on bankruptcy,' Miyazawa stated twenty-three years after the crisis. He was convinced that the only way to solve the crisis was to take the problem to the newspapers. In that way pressure would come to bear on the Ministry of Finance to lend money to the entire securities industry. 'We decided to use Yamaichi as the scapegoat,' admitted Miyazawa. 'Nikko Securities was about to go under as well but we could not tell the public that. It would have created more of a panic.' By May 1965, the newspapers were well aware of the impending financial disaster but agreed among themselves, in what they decided was in the interest of the nation, to hold this sensational head-line story until 23 May. Some of the executives of NHK, the Japan Broadcasting Association and the nation's powerful, government-held television station, were made privy to the news but ordered to hold it back. 'If NHK releases this,' a Ministry of Finance official warned an NHK reporter, 'I will bet some people will hang themselves in front of your house.'

Meanwhile, an obscure newspaper reporter named Tsutomu Matsuo was about to blow the lid off Japan. Working for the *Nishi-Nippon Shimbun*, a medium-sized regional daily, Matsuo was a financial reporter for a second-string newspaper in the burned out, coal-mining city of Fukuoka in northern Kyushu. In the middle of May, one of his contacts in Yamaichi, Mr S., a junior manager who had kept his ears open, spilled the beans about the reorganization plan he had caught wind of. Matsuo's paper had not taken the vow of silence that Japan's seven major dailies had and his superiors were eager to investigate the matter: circulation had been faltering in recent years and a scandal would revive subscriber demand. Many years later, Matsuo admitted he was unsure about the code of ethics he might be violating but, pressed by his superiors, on 21 May 1965 Matsuo broke the sensation of the post-war financial era: the collapse of Yamaichi Securities, the nation's largest brokerage house. The headline may seem uninspiring to Western readers but to the Japanese it was one of scandalous proportion: '*Yamaichi Ready For Reconstruction*'.

Matsuo had done the unthinkable and scooped a story not due for release. Not only had it been an open secret in the financial community that Japan's brokerage industry was about to crumble, but the issue of a brokerage bail-out had not yet been fully arranged by the government and, further, the Japan Socialist Party, the government's outspoken but tiny opposition party, which had caught on to the Yamaichi disaster, had promised to keep it quiet in exchange for being allowed to break the news on the Diet floor at the appropriate time. Matsuo, by having the courage to print what other newspapers feared, had caught Japan Inc. with its pants down. The giant, collusive PR machine that brought politicians, bureaucrats, business and the media together had for once been upstaged. The public, usually so well manipulated, was now aware of an impending disaster.

At first there was a lot of blustering and many red faces and nobody was quite sure how the crisis would be resolved. One thing was certain, however: the implosion of Yamaichi Securities on that fateful day propelled Nomura Securities to the top of the Japanese stockmarket and for the next decade, Nomura men would poke the twitching corpse of Yamaichi.

Tsutomu Matsuo himself became famous overnight. Although bylines are rare in Japan, the entire press community knew it was Matsuo's story and he was besieged by requests for interviews. 'Even in retirement, twenty-three years later, I get calls about that story.' His salary more than doubled.

The paper was not available as far north as Tokyo but Miyazawa was rung up at the Bank of Japan early the same morning by his Kyushu branch. 'I was very happy,' he stated, 'I *wanted* it leaked.' Everyone had feared causing a panic by releasing the truth but Miyazawa recognized that press coverage was the only way to save the brokerage industry. Matsuo forced the hand of the government and at 11.30 am Tanaka, the minister of finance, gave a press conference to reassure individual investors. 'The Bank of Japan is prepared to lend money to Yamaichi, if necessary.' That hardly helped. To make matters worse, the head of the Bank of Japan hated Tanaka, who wanted control of the bank. To undermine the

authority of the Ministry of Finance after the press conference, the Bank of Japan issued a statement expressing the
Bank's reservations on lending to Yamaichi Securities.

By noon, pandemonium had broken out in Yamaichi's
ninety branch offices. Lines formed outside as everyone
rushed to redeem their Yamaichi bonds and pick up any
stock held in custody. By Saturday, 22 May, over 14,000
people had taken out their money. More than 10 billion
yen had been withdrawn by the following week. By July
over 35 billion – about $100 million in 1965 terms – had
left Yamaichi's coffers and over 20 per cent of the quoted
stocks that Yamaichi supported on the second section had
fallen by more than 80 per cent. As it turned out, a year
before Matsuo's revelation, the firm, according to Miyazawa,
had been fraudulently hiving off loss-making stock positions
to affiliated companies and had begun to carry two sets of
accounts: one for itself and one for Ministry of Finance officials.

'Please lend us some money. Nobody will lend us even a
million yen,' pleaded one Yamaichi man to a ministry official, who overheard weeping on the other end of the line.
Officials from the Bank of Japan, Fuji Bank, Mitsubishi Bank,
Industrial Bank of Japan and the Ministry of Finance gathered after the stockmarket close on 28 May to decide how
to stem investor panic. 'Let us be careful,' the president of
Mitsubishi Bank remarked. Tanaka, the Minister of Finance,
got angry: 'You call yourself the president of a bank?' Shortly
thereafter, at the instigation of Tanaka, all parties agreed to
tell the press that the government was prepared to lend an
unlimited amount to save Yamaichi and the Japanese securities industry. On 7 June, the Bank of Japan agreed to lend
Yamaichi 28 billion yen and Oi Securities 5.3 billion yen,
withholding from the public that they would also lend vast
sums to other impoverished stock houses.

Fujio Kodama, a director of Oi Securities at the time, later
insisted paradoxically that the industry would have collapsed
if the first firm to go under had not been a major name. 'Only

the prestige of Yamaichi forced the Bank of Japan to step in,' he explained. Moreover, Kodama said the decision by Tanaka to lend freely and willingly to brokers was not an obvious one. 'The Japanese financial world would be a lot different if Tanaka had not forced the Bank of Japan to lend money.' Everyone but Tanaka was fighting to prevent money being lent to the brokers and the taxpayers resented bailing out stockbrokers, men whom they considered financial parasites. In return for the government bail-out, there were numerous resignations in the Japanese stockbroking industry as the chairman of Yamaichi, the son of the founder, was himself forced to resign. Yamaichi's president also went and was replaced by Teru Hidaka, an ex-Industrial Bank of Japan man and president of Nissan Chemical. IBJ's speciality was turning around corporate Japan and Hidaka was one of the best.

The entire broking industry underwent chaotic change: Daiwa, Nikko and Osakaya sacked their presidents and only Nomura retained its man, Minoru Segawa, at the helm. In total, Japan's stockbroking branches were slashed from 2,424 to 2,166, and almost 20,000 workers were fired or laid off in 1964 and 1965. The phrase 'bye bye brokers, hello banks' became popular. Stock salesmen, instead of proudly displaying their company name when carrying packages down the street, 'snuck around trying to hide they were from Yamaichi,' according to Katsuta. They refused to put stickers on their cars for fear they would be abused or beaten up. Before the crisis, it was common for Tsunao Okumura and Minoru Segawa to pay courtesy calls to Yamaichi's office during the course of the year. From 1965 onward, it became customary for the Yamaichi president to call on Nomura.

17
Innocents Abroad

Shoshi Kawashima had no idea why he had been called into Segawa's office that winter day in 1953, but he assumed the worst. Segawa, the second most powerful man in Nomura Securities after President Okumura, had a reputation for blunt and abrasive criticism, an un-Japanese quality which left many of his salesmen cringing. On this occasion, though, Segawa was unusually polite and took the anxious Kawashima by surprise. Segawa was only five years his senior, having joined Nomura Securities in 1929, but he had remained in the firm throughout the war and had thus built up fifteen more years service than the man now facing him across the desk, who had joined in 1936 and then spent almost ten years in the army.

'Kawashima-chan,' Segawa began, a suffix generally used with children, and it was a sure indication that Segawa was about to ask something delicate of a junior. Segawa continued: 'I want you to become a securities immigrant. I want you to go to New York and reopen our first overseas office.'

Nomura's first overseas office in New York, opened in 1927, had been shut down in 1936 after the Japanese military had persuaded the government to ban overseas investment. Since most of Nomura's New York income had come from wealthy Japanese individuals and corporations investing in US Treasury Bonds, business had in any case ground to a halt. While Japanese banks, trading and shipping companies all had long histories abroad and their activities were spread around the globe, Nomura's New York office had been the first venture overseas by a Japanese securities house. Mitsubishi Bank, trading houses like Mitsui and Marubeni and shipping firms like Nippon Yusen Kaisha had long had a presence in New York. Families on overseas postings were considered to have semi-diplomatic status. Their employees came from the wealthiest Japanese families and spoke many languages, while their children attended American and British universities.

Now Segawa told Kawashima: 'Nomura has no such international ambassadors abroad. You will be our first overseas link. You will live your life in New York and give up all ties with Tokyo. You must learn how to survive there.' As a securities immigrant, Kawashima's first mission was to gain acceptance into the elite Japanese overseas community of established trading firms and banks – something both Segawa and Okumura desperately wanted.

Nomura's keenness to return to New York also stemmed from the growing interest among American institutions in Japanese stocks. But conducting international business was difficult for Nomura, as it was for most Japanese companies in the early fifties. Japanese who were proficient in spoken or written English were rare and procuring secretaries with ability in English was a costly business. Foreign housewives, who had to be paid more than chief executives at most Japanese firms, were the only alternative for those wanting to draft letters or interpret business meetings. Virtually the only form of international business done by the Japanese in 1952 was import and export.

The man whom Segawa had entrusted with this international mission was to prove well suited to the task, although this was by no means clear to Kawashima himself as he set off for New York with his family in 1953. Born into a prosperous merchant family in Omi, near the rising industrial city of Nagoya between Tokyo and Osaka, Kawashima had graduated from Nagoya Commercial College in 1935 and had followed his father's wish that he should go into the securities business, his father telling him, 'Believe me, one day stock traders will not be looked down on as they are today.' Kawashima got a job in Osaka with what was then informally called the Nomura Bond House and after ten months was called into the army, where he remained until

1946. 'Most of my time,' recalled Kawashima, 'was spent in China fighting the Communists but I managed not to get shot.' He then picked up his career as a stock salesman in Tokyo, this time with more success, for the American-inspired sale of tightly held, pre-war company stocks to the masses of Japan was in full swing.

Kawashima had studied English at college but during war service in China and in his stock-selling job later in Tokyo, he had forgotten most of it. When he left for New York he knew only two sentences: 'The spring has come. There is no snow upon the ground.' Fortunately many Americans had become sympathetic to the Japanese after the war, their hatred turned to pity by the total humiliation of Japan's defeat. American correspondents portrayed their hungry and homeless plight, and the American public had been moved by photographs of the Japanese people, weary and shorn of their pride.

Kawashima's task was to introduce Japanese industry to Americans in the hope that investors might be interested in buying Japanese shares, but it was more difficult than Nomura's senior executives had anticipated. The same emotions which evoked pity also prevented Americans from accepting Japanese companies as being commercially viable investments. As far as Americans were concerned the Japanese economy was still convalescing. The three years Kawashima spent in New York were tough and isolated. The Japanese community there at that time was small and it banded together for comfort – aliens in a foreign land. He did not call Tokyo once. Calls to Japan took more than ten hours to place and there was no telling at what hour they would be put through. Nor did Nomura have a telex machine in New York, although that was not a problem because Kawashima had little business to transact. Soon after he arrived, however, he had one major stroke of good fortune. He received a phone call from General Electric saying it wanted to sell its rights to new shares it had been offered in Toshiba, the electronics company in which it already owned a sizeable stake.

General Electric's ties to Japan went back to the turn of the century when it had begun offering manufacturing expertise to companies in the hope of breaking into the consumer market; at one time it had a controlling interest in a light-bulb maker named Tokyo Electric. In 1939 Toshiba had been created by a merger with Shibaura Engineering where GE retained a minority holding and after the Korean War boom Nomura advised Toshiba directors to fund expansion by the issue of new shares at a discount to its share price. Unfortunately Toshiba did not register these new shares with the Securities Exchange Commission in the US, thereby forcing GE to sell the rights to these new shares. Toshiba, anxious to see GE's influence in the company reduced, was delighted. So too was Kawashima, as Nomura arranged for the huge block of shares to be placed in friendly Japanese hands like the Mitsui Bank. For Nomura's new man in New York it was a major coup.

Kawashima's life in New York developed its own routine. Settled in their Brooklyn house, he and his wife often met other Japanese for lunch and dinner, if only to converse in their native tongue rather than in faltering English. Mrs Kawashima found a group of friends who taught her where to shop and how to get around the neighbourhood. In Japan, women seldom ventured out of the house except to buy groceries, but in America Mrs Kawashima was amazed to find other women travelling in public and even taking jobs. On weekends there were guests in the Kawashima home – simply to be Japanese and passing through the New York area meant an open invitation to call upon a fellow countryman in a strange land. No matter how remote the connection with Nomura Securities, visiting Japanese businessmen and travellers would often find themselves at dinners hosted by the sociable Kawashima family.

One frequent house guest was Keisuke Egashira, a postgraduate student at Princeton University who twenty-five years later rose to become chairman of Nomura's highly profitable European offices. Though a student, Egashira was on the Nomura payroll and had entered the firm officially in

1954, leaving for America on a scholarship to study money and banking. 'I was a poor student back then and split the gas bill to drive to New York with a friend to stay at the Kawashima house. It saved me the cost of a hotel room.'

Egashira was one of Segawa's first recruits in the Nomura international department. He did not consider himself a Nomura man while attending Princeton. 'Segawa tricked me into joining Nomura,' he later ruefully admitted. Born and raised in rural Kyushu, where he was quickly recognized as a brilliant student, he had passed the difficult entrance examinations to Tokyo's Keio university where he excelled and won a Fulbright Scholarship to study in America. Late in the winter of 1954, before graduating from Keio University, he was called in to see the university's finance director, Mr Kanzaki, the most senior man at Keio, whose connections enabled students to find jobs after graduation. He told Egashira that he had been asked by Mr Segawa of Nomura Securities if there were any students at Keio he could recommend to work in Nomura's New York office and he had put forward Egashira's name. Egashira was not looking for employment since he was off to Princeton in the autumn but, a polite and gracious young man, he did not see how to object without causing offence and decided at least to go to the meeting arranged with Segawa.

Segawa, after an exchange of generalities, congratulated Egashira on his new career. Thoroughly alarmed by Segawa's assumption that he was joining Nomura, Egashira was about to tell Segawa that he had no intention of working for him when the meeting was interrupted by the announcement that Ambassador Iguchi had arrived. Iguchi was Japan's new ambassador to the United States and a personal friend of President Okumura. Segawa introduced the ambassador to Egashira, saying, 'This is our new recruit from Nomura who will be going to the States to study at Princeton.' Iguchi invited him to visit Washington when he had a holiday, an invitation for which Egashira humbly thanked him. Within ten minutes he found that he had joined Nomura without even being asked. He tried to state his objection but Segawa was not to be put off and used the sales tactics for which he was famed. Egashira was left with no words with which to turn him down without being rude.

* * * * *

When Egashira finished his graduate studies in 1956, the Nomura international web had slowly begun to grow. That year Kawashima was brought home to be replaced by Tadashi Ishida, a man with some English ability who looked forward to his new challenge. The quality of life was still low in Japan and Ishida hoped America would offer a grand lifestyle. 'We had not even worn suits to work until 1950,' he later recalled, 'and even then they were made of brown and white canvas. I thought things might be different in America.' Ishida was to receive $650 a month, or over 230,000 yen – a huge salary by Japanese standards. When he arrived in New York he realized that college graduates there were earning $480, more than ten times the earnings of Japan's new graduates, and it rankled Ishida to hear young Americans complain about their low salaries. Thirty years later American expatriates in Tokyo would be complaining about how tough it was to get by on $600 a day.

The long flight from Tokyo to New York was an ordeal, but it had its compensations for Ishida who had, like most of the other seventy passengers, never been on an aeroplane. Sightseeing was still not permitted by the Japanese government and business visas were issued sparingly. The airline buffet included food that most Japanese had not seen in a dozen years: beef, bread, coffee with sugar and milk, bananas and watermelon. Ishida thought he was in heaven; in Japan the only people who ever got bananas were the patients in hospitals.

Ishida settled in Greenwich Village near Washington Square. He had left his wife behind for six months so that he could save some money and he soon found he could put almost half his monthly income into savings. Nomura Securities allowed Ishida only $5,000 a month for office expenses, including the rental of the Nomura office on Broadway, although, unlike Kawashima, he was allowed to call Japan once a week, a call which by then took a mere eight hours to place. There was still no telex machine.

As emissary for Nomura in New York, Ishida's task was to ensure that all Japanese visitors were properly entertained. Since Nomura was then one of a select band of just ten branch offices of Japanese corporations in the city, the stream of guests became overwhelming and Ishida would drive out to La Guardia airport five times a week in a tank-like Buick Electra, a car he had bought because it could swallow four or five suitcases. To many Japanese entering the US in the late fifties, the first memory is of the smiling face of their fellow-countryman Tadashi Ishida, meeting them at the gate. It was a reassuring presence and one which did wonders for Nomura's reputation back home. In effect Nomura New York was a travel agency and Ishida its tour guide. By the time he left New York Ishida had seen *My Fair Lady* eighty-five times, the *Sound of Music* fifty times and had been to the Barnum & Bailey Circus over thirty times.

Tsunao Okumura applied his well-tested, free-spending approach to the Nomura New York operation. Although it was still struggling to find business, Ishida was ordered to spend money in a manner befitting the most prestigious Wall Street firm. Okumura told him to make sure his staff ate in restaurants that served lunch with a napkin service and insisted they avoid the Dunkin Donuts or Chock Full O'Nuts fast food shops. Nomura's New York venture in the early years was anything but profitable, a loss-leading beachhead in American finance. Nonetheless, Okumura believed so deeply in the symbolic importance of the New York office that he paid a visit in February 1959 to mark the occasion when Nomura was allocated a derisory $100,000 in the first post-war Japanese government bond issue.

Although it was a freezing New York winter, Okumura

A group of investors in the late nineteenth century trade shares on the street in Kabutocho, Tokyo's financial district, near the Tokyo Stock Exchange. The man on the far left is selling sushi.

The start of stock trading was heralded by a man who walked around the city with wooden clappers. The sweaty traders were cooled down by attendants with huge fans.

見張　　　帳付　　　帳場係

創業当時
上場の銘柄
金禄公債
秩禄公債
第一国立銀行
東京株式
米商株

*A superintendent and a smiling clerk watch as a registrar makes stock
entries. On the left is the special slow-burning rope called the* hinawa
that was lit each morning; trading was halted when the rope burned out.

*News of stockmarket changes spread quickly via young singsong boys,
who, after peeking through the stock-exchange windows, ran through
the streets shouting and gesticulating to relay market information.*

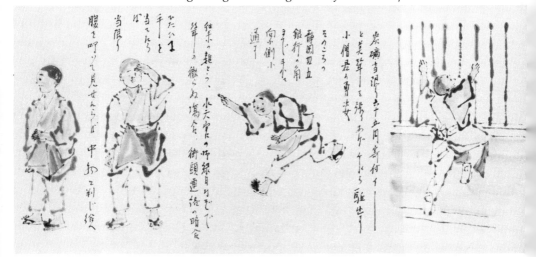

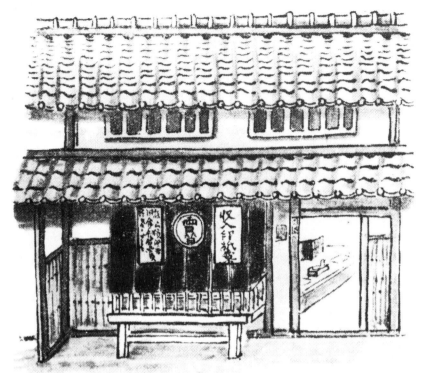

The Nomura shoten or 'shop' as sketched by Tokushichi Nomura around the turn of the century.

A photograph of the shoten at about the same time. The rickshaw standing outside would be used to carry Tokushichi around Osaka.

Tokushichi Nomura II's mother, Takiko Yamanouchi.

Tokushichi Nomura after his appointment to the House of Peers in 1928.

The founder, Tokushichi Nomura II (1878–1945) in dress kimono.

Motogoro Nomura at
Birmingham University in the
UK in 1908. He went on to run
the Nomura Bank, but was
dispossessed in 1945.

The scholarly
Yoshitaro Nomura
with his wife, Sae.
Yoshitaro loved
smoking Romeo y
Julieta cigars.

The Nomura villa in Atami, completed for Tokushichi's sixtieth birthday in 1878. The sickly Yoshitaro died here in 1945. Nomura Securities bought the villa from the family in the 1980s when upkeep had become too expensive.

The Nomura family villa in Kobe in the 1930s. The watchtower was spotted by Allied bombers in the last days of the war and the villa was bombed.

The tranquil Nomura villa in Kyoto, built by Tokushichi after he had
made his second fortune on the stockmarket rise of World War I. The
house is now home to Fumihide Nomura; it is secretly owned by Daiwa
Bank, which pays for its upkeep.

Tokushichi kept three white stallions at his Kyoto villa. He is pictured
here with his wife, Kiku (left), and son Yoshitaro (right).

Tokushichi's son Yoshitaro, the heir to the Nomura zaibatsu founded by his father. A British-car enthusiast, he is pictured here with his two sons, Fumihide (centre) and Tomohide (left).

Kozo Nomura in uniform, in preparation for the Sino-Japanese war, 1939.

American officers at the Nomura Kyoto villa during the occupation.
Tokushichi Nomura's widow, Kiku, stands second from right.

Tsunao Okumura (Nomura Securities president:1948–1959).

Minoru Segawa (Nomura Securities president 1959–1968).

Setsuya Tabuchi, president of Nomura Securities from 1978 to 1985 (left), with Ryoichi Sasakawa, one of the world's richest and most powerful men. An underworld kingpin turned philanthropist, Sasakawa loved to boast that he had given away more than twelve billion dollars.

Toshio Komoto, Japan's Economic Planning Agency chief, greets US Treasury Secretary Regan in Tokyo in March 1984. Komoto by this time had lost his bid for the prime ministership and had watched his company Sanko Steamship founder.

The Tokyo Stock Exchange.

Stock dealers clap their hands in celebration of the New Year before the first trading on the Tokyo Stock Exchange, 4 January 1989. The New Year ritual was more subdued than usual, in deference to the ailing Emperor Hirohito.

A kimono-clad worker scurries through the crowd of navy-suited stock dealers during New Year first trading at the TSE on 4 January 1989.

A 7.50 a.m. meeting at the Nomura Shinjuku branch office.

A Nomura woman works with an abacus in the Nomura vault.

A tea-training class for Nomura office ladies is held twice a week on the ninth floor.

An aerobics class for new Nomura recruits.

Morning exercises at the Nomura Shinjuku branch office, 7.40 a.m.

insisted on being taken to the top of the Empire State Building. His guide was Keisuke Egashira, who later recounted how Okumura looked silently out over the other skyscrapers, trying to find meaning in the vast cityscape. He had been moved by a written account by Ichizo Kobayashi, the founder of the Hankyu railway conglomerate, who had made the same pilgrimage to wonder at the New York skyline before the war. It had been the turning point of Kobayashi's life. From that trip and that vision he returned to Japan to build one of the country's largest entertainment empires.

Okumura, like Kobayashi, felt the sheer power of America and thought back to Japan, convinced of his own country's potential for greatness. On the drive back to the Plaza Hotel, he told Egashira: 'Americans still look down on Japan and pay no attention to our country. We must educate the Americans. We will convince Wall Street about Japan. This is now my task.' He flew back to Japan with this personal pledge and immediately began meetings with Japan's power brokers. His first port of call was his old friend, Hayato Ikeda, now prime minister, to whom he recommended a government-sponsored trip to bring prominent Wall Street financiers to Japan.

With Ikeda's blessing, a high-powered delegation of Wall Street's financiers arrived in Tokyo in autumn 1960. The trip was organized by an amiable twenty-nine-year-old Nomura man named Yoshio Terasawa, who was put in charge of organizing the trip simply because he spoke English. It turned out to be the biggest break of his life. A 1954 graduate of Waseda University, he had joined Nomura on a delayed entry basis after winning a Fulbright scholarship to study finance at the Wharton School in Philadelphia. Like his contemporary Egashira, Terasawa became a valuable commodity within Nomura because of his ability in English and Ivy League polish. To Nomura's status-conscious top executives this qualified the pair perfectly to lead the build-up of Nomura's international operations.

The snobbish element in the filling of posts in the

international operations did not, however, apply to the career structure of those who stayed at home. The international and domestic divisions of Nomura were to become like two companies. The bright young English-speaking recruits whom Nomura hired in the fifties and sixties found that as they aged into greying denizens of international finance their paths to elevated positions back home were blocked. Egashira and Terasawa, though respected, even famous, in Europe and America, were later to be discounted in the Nomura power structure in Japan. In essence the two cultures parted because it was felt a waste to send a trainee with English ability on the usual grind of door-to-door stock selling, still the vital honing process for any home-based Nomura man. In some sense the international Nomura man could never be considered a *real* 'Nomura man'. For this reason not all Nomura staff who could speak English wanted to work in the international department. Many of them felt it was like being a glorified translator and it was not uncommon for them to feign ignorance of English to avoid having to spend hours poring over texts, translating them into Japanese or English.

Yoshio Terasawa, however, was happy to be known as an English expert. Nomura executives would invite him along as interpreter when they were travelling abroad on a marketing trip and by the time the American delegation arrived in Tokyo in 1960 Terasawa had already met with many American and European institutions to discuss the merits of Japanese stocks and bonds. Over time he found that he evolved from mere translator to full-fledged adviser, an 'ideas man' whose presence when foreigners were at hand became indispensable.

Terasawa became Nomura's self-proclaimed 'Mr America' and, after his return from Philadelphia in 1958, he had developed certain Western mannerisms. He took up golf, drank the finest American whisky, drove big cars and tucked into huge steaks.

He became Nomura's golden boy, and as such it was only to be expected that Minoru Segawa, who had been appointed president of Nomura in June 1959, would have a hand in his future. Shortly after he became Nomura Securities' president, Segawa called Terasawa into his office.

'Do you know Mariko Inagaki?' he asked.

Terasawa replied that of course he knew her, for it was Segawa himself who had introduced them.

'What do you think of her?' the plain-speaking Segawa inquired.

'Well, I don't really know her, but she seems like a nice enough girl,' came the embarrassed response.

'Would you be open to the idea of an arranged marriage with her? You are under no obligation of course. Just take her out a couple of times, meet her parents and see if you get along.'

Recalling that meeting years later, Terasawa realized he had been set up by Segawa months beforehand. Both Segawa and Nomura's managing director, Fumio Yamamoto, had talked with Mariko's father, the owner of the successful Inagaki restaurant chain, about staging spontaneous meetings between the couple, bringing Terasawa frequently to their Chinese restaurant. Mariko worked there part-time and soon, everywhere Terasawa turned, he was accidentally running into Mariko. It was typical of Segawa's manipulative style, and Terasawa found himself borne along by his boss's desire to have his own way.

Yamamoto stood in for Terasawa's sick father at the first formal meeting between the couple, at Tokyo Kaikan, a famous restaurant and gathering place of wealthy Japanese. With Mariko's parents present, Terasawa asked polite questions about her hobbies. Mariko kept her sentences to a minimum and smiled sweetly. Terasawa found they did have similar interests; she was a blackbelt in karate and he a master of the samurai sport, kendo, the art of combat with a bamboo pole. He was taken in by this apparently demure and yielding flower. Ruefully he admitted years later: 'She should have been a movie actress for the part she played that day.' Mariko was anything but an obsequious woman.

Thus the courtship began, although Terasawa was too

busy to spend much time with Mariko. During the day he worked in the Nomura research department and at night translated Japanese stock recommendations into English. His boss, Shoshi Kawashima, the man who had re-opened the New York office six years earlier, had arranged with a news magazine, the *Tokyo Keizai Shimposa*, to provide Nomura with 100 Japanese company outlines, in Japanese. Terasawa hired an English teacher with no Japanese ability to write the reports in English as he slowly dictated them. They would meet at a cheap hotel popular with businessmen travelling back and forth from Osaka and there the two of them would work until ten in the evening. By October 1960 they had put together profiles of 100 of the best-known Japanese companies, names that American and European investors had then never heard: Sony, the Toyota Motor Corporation, the Nissan Motor Company, Japan Airlines, Fuji Photo Film and Matsushita Electronics. Thus Terasawa's translations of the *Tokyo Keizai Shimposa* outlines became the basis of Nomura's international research department.

The only time Terasawa – or Terry as he was to become known because of his American connections – could see his bride-to-be was after eleven in the evening, with the maid present as chaperone. They would sometimes talk until two or three in the morning, after which Terasawa would come into work exhausted. They were formally engaged on Christmas Eve 1960 at a ceremony neither participated in, as Japanese custom dictated. Performing the engagement ritual, Minoru Segawa acted as Terasawa's go-between. Dressed in long black morning coat with tails, he arrived at the Inagaki home at ten in the morning, bearing an elaborate wooden tray with the standard bridal payment of 100,000 yen ($277 at the time), of which Segawa took a 10 per cent cut. The Inagakis, as was required of the bride's parents, later gave the couple an array of household goods.

The marriage took place the following February at the Hotel Okura, where Segawa had arranged a special discount through his friend Iwajiro Noda, the man responsible for negotiating the post-war dismantling of the Nomura *zaibatsu* with American officials. Three hundred guests arrived for the elaborate ceremony and Mariko and Terry each had a college professor and their boss at work deliver a speech on their behalf. Minoru Segawa, the man who manipulated the personal and professional lives of key Nomura men with undisguised zeal, fittingly spoke for Terasawa.

18
Hendon and Finchley

Slaving away for Nomura New York, Tadashi Ishida had not taken a vacation in three years. Finally, in July 1963, came the day he had long awaited. Not forgetting to pack his fishing pole, he eagerly loaded his family into the car and drove five hours north to the Adirondacks. Here, on the shore of beautiful Lake George in upper New York state, Ishida looked forward to ten uninterrupted days of pleasure. He drove up to the lodge and, keen to look around, unpacked the car and took his children down to the lake. After helping his children into a rowboat, Ishida slowly rowed out to the middle of the lake. It was the best moment of his life, Ishida recalled many years later. Then suddenly, as he was resting the oars on the side of the boat, the tranquillity was broken by the crackle of a loudspeaker, 'Mr Ishida, Mr Ishida, we have an urgent call for you.' Thinking something tragic had happened, Ishida hastily rowed back. There he found a message to contact his New York office. Calling them, he found the office in confusion. 'Hurry back,' they urged him. 'President Kennedy has just approved a bill taxing American ownership of foreign securities. We don't know what it means.' Ishida put down the phone, packed up the car and immediately drove his family back to New York. A new era of finance had begun.

The bill approved by John F. Kennedy in July 1963, imposing what was known as the interest equalization tax, was an attempt to stem American capital fleeing overseas. By taxing American ownership of foreign securities, Kennedy brought Nomura's New York business – selling Japanese stocks to Americans – to a halt.

Almost overnight the world's financial centre shifted to London. The big four Japanese stockbrokers wasted no time in setting up offices there. If they could not sell Japanese stocks to the Americans they would sell them to the Europeans. Over the years it proved to be one of the most profitable moves Japan's brokers ever made abroad.

Looking back, many British financiers compare the Japanese brokerage houses in the City of London back then to the Korean securities houses there in the 1980s: scruffy, ill-mannered and inexperienced. It was not, however, solely for professional reasons that the British financial community looked down on Japanese brokers in the 1960s. World War II had been over almost twenty years, but the British memory was long and unforgiving. Many senior brokers and bankers had suffered in Japanese prisoner-of-war camps, while others had lost friends and relatives in the Pacific War. A strong cadre of war veterans refused to deal with the Japanese. 'They were still fighting the Second World War,' recalled Tadashi Ishida, who tried to convince the British to buy Japanese new issues in the 1960s. Frequently he could not even get in the door to make presentations. 'The first financiers to forgive the Japanese were the religious men,' observed Edmund Rothschild. Twenty-five years later that hostility would be gone and indeed it would be the British who found it difficult to gain an audience from Japanese institutions.

Chosen to head Nomura's first London office was the dapper, well-mannered Keisuke Egashira, who was determined that both he and Nomura would be accepted by the British. He was enormously successful and became in many ways more British than the British. He rented a home in fashionable Dolphin Square, joined a club with the help of Edmund Rothschild, bought a Daimler and rented offices on Gresham Street, a prestigious address next to the Bank of England.

In many ways Egashira, like Tokushichi Nomura himself, was a master at buying respectability. More importantly, Egashira had led the first Japanese raid on European finance. Decades of unrelenting assaults on Europe's closed old-boy network would later propel Nomura Securities, and indeed

Japan, to a position of power and prestige. Nomura began by selling Japanese stocks to European stockbrokers. At the next stage, Nomura sold stock to fund managers. And finally, it issued new Japanese equity and debt issues in the primary market.

There were few flowers or congratulatory messages, however, when Nomura opened its London office in March 1964. As in New York, Nomura had almost no friends in London. Undaunted, Egashira began building up his Japanese sales force. His recruits, highly charged domestic salesmen fresh from Tokyo, often speaking no English, found London a dismal and lonely place. In 1964 there were fewer than 2,000 Japanese living in London (two decades later there would be ten times that number). Many Japanese men within Nomura and other securities houses and banks moved to England without their families; those who did bring their families moved to Hendon and Finchley, in north London, where there was a Japanese school for their children. Egashira gave his men £100 a month for living expenses and let them fend for themselves. The Hendon and Finchley area later became known as 'Little Tokyo', but for most of the 1960s the sole Japanese restaurant in London was Akiko, while one run-down club on the Thames embankment served as a recreation centre.

But Nomura men had no time for fun anyway. They got into work at 7.30 every morning to prepare to report executions of Japanese stock purchases to European clients. Nomura did not at that time dare to talk to pension funds and large institutions directly, but instead serviced British brokers and merchant banks who gave them orders. One salesman, Tatsuhiko Yagishita, recalled placing telephone calls to Tokyo. The operator usually took half an hour to place the call and, once connected, the Nomura men kept the line open, placing orders. The salesmen hated sending telexes or cables. 'Tokyo frequently lost or misplaced our client orders,' said Yagishita, 'so we had to invent execution prices for clients. We made and lost a lot of money that way.'

After spending the morning calling European clients, the salesmen rushed over to the local pub for a steak sandwich, a great luxury for the Japanese. The bitter, which was all that the pub served to wash the steak down, was a problem, being a heavier and more intoxicating drink than they were used to. After a while things improved when the barman, feeling sorry for the Nomura men, began to refrigerate the beer.

After lunch it was back to work until nine or ten in the evening – an unheard-of work span for their British colleagues even during the bull market of the 1980s. Since there was only one Japanese restaurant, the Nomura men usually journeyed to the seamier streets of Soho in the West End where they ate Indian and Chinese food which reminded them a little of home. (Yagishita said that he never really knew what the British Empire meant until he came to London: ' I could not believe my eyes when I moved here,' he recalled with a certain wide-eyed innocence. 'After seeing so many Indians, I finally knew what "sovereign" meant.') After dinner, a designated salesman toted home the telex roll of orders that had been transmitted to Tokyo. The Tokyo machine always jammed and at two or three in the morning London time, the Tokyo office would awaken the salesman on duty at home to confirm the daily orders.

To these Japanese abroad, keeping up appearances was especially important. So, while Egashira's men beavered away soliciting stockmarket orders, Egashira himself kept up an active social schedule – dining with patrician financiers, clubbing with British nobility, buying old masters and flying to Salzburg to listen to Mozart. In a sense, he was the first Japanese to become accepted by Britain's financial aristocracy. He was befriended by Edmund Rothschild and Sigmund Warburg, who generously gave Nomura a boost by placing orders to buy Japanese shares. Rothschild and Warburg in fact had come to know Tsunao Okumura as early as the autumn of 1962, when Okumura played host to a British delegation in Japan. Through Okumura, both men were introduced to Japan's prime ministers and later were awarded the Order of the Sacred Treasure, First Class, by Emperor Hirohito.

Years later, Edmund Rothschild enjoyed telling the story of meeting Okumura in Tokyo. 'What would you like to see?' asked Okumura. 'I want to go to Beppu,' replied Rothschild. 'You see I am a friend of Ian Fleming and he told me that is where he conceived the book *You Only Live Twice.*' So Okumura and Rothschild flew down to Beppu, a resort town on Kyushu. Only after spending time in Beppu could Rothschild explain to Okumura what an overactive imagination Fleming had: surrounded by beautiful women Fleming had conjured up a castle and moat from the hotel and hot spring, then turned the fish into piranha and the tropical vegetation into poisonous killer-plants.

The last time Rothschild saw Okumura was in 1972 when Okumura was in hospital with lung cancer. Okumura died later that year and as his executor Segawa divided his estate between Okumura's wife and his four mistresses. Segawa even took the paintings off the walls of Mrs Okumura's home. 'You could tell Okumura was honest,' said one member of the Nomura family. 'He did not die a rich man.'

Unfortunately Okumura never saw his international offices blossom. By the early 1970s Nomura in London had seven Japanese and eleven British staff. Then in 1973 came the first oil shock, or 'oil shokku' as the Japanese called it, and Middle Eastern accounts were handled from London. Tadashi Ishida, who had spent so much time in New York, was ordered to begin funnelling Arab petrodollars into Japan, so he travelled down to Kuwait via Beirut to teach the Arabs about Japan.

His first shock was in Beirut airport, in the late afternoon, when suddenly 'all these men in funny white costumes' hit the ground and started bowing. 'I got scared because I was the only one left standing.' Slightly ruffled, Ishida finally made it to Kuwait where he made a presentation to the Kuwait Investment Office (or KIO as it became known), the country's main investment vehicle. He could not believe their ignorance.

'I want to introduce a bond issue for the Asian Development Bank,' began Ishida.

'What is that? Where is their head office?' asked the chairman's secretary.

'It is in Manila,' replied Ishida.

The KIO men were curious and wanted to know more. 'On what continent is Manila?'

'It is in Asia,' Ishida explained.

The KIO were persistent, however. 'Well can you give us a better perspective on where in Asia it is located? For example, how long does it take to drive from Manila to Tokyo by car?'

Ishida's patience paid off and when KIO earmarked tens of millions of dollars for investment in Japan, Nomura were their first call.

PART III
THE RISE TO POWER

19
The Young Rice Crop

There is a saying among small investors, and even among Japanese stockbrokers themselves, that clients who have one million yen to invest in the stockmarket get eaten alive, clients with ten million yen are allowed to make money once, while those with over 100 million yen are always allowed to win. There are no illusions about the stockmarket in Japan. Yet there is always the belief for the gamblers who play it that the odds of making money are fifty-fifty, even if the banker always wins.

By 1990, owing to the unceasing efforts of the *kabuya*, or stock salesmen, Nomura had garnered a staggering five million individual clients, along with 200,000 corporate accounts. Peddled through this colossal network was any flavour-of-the-month financial product, sold door-to-door like Tupperware. Just as the Million Ryo Box helped to impel Nomura to greatness, it was the Japanese brokerage and banking branch networks that made Japan a financial powerhouse. The average household in Japan, beginning with nothing in 1945, had an average of over $60,000 stashed away forty years later, and Nomura, Daiwa, Yamaichi and Nikko Securities took it upon themselves to channel this wealth to other parts of the world.

For Nomura and the other major brokerage houses, recruiting and honing branch salesmen into an assertive sales force is a process as finely timed as the Japan Railways schedule. Any college student without a job by September of his senior year has missed the train. Particularly nerve-racking for students is the paradox that Japanese companies are not allowed formally to visit college campuses before September, but most of them – being unethical in their recruiting practices and ignoring government policy – often have their jobs filled

183

before that date. Nomura Securities is no exception and by May of every year Nomura will have sent out its younger salesmen to bring in the best talent from their alma mater. This illegal strategem is the students' first intimation that life in the business world is not played by the rules. Those few college seniors who wait for the formal company interviews in early September find their honesty unrewarded. They are confronted with the unhappy prospect of either settling for a second-rate firm or, in extreme situations, actually changing jobs later in mid-career, a decision almost unheard of in Japan until the mid-1980s. Even before they become members of the Japanese business community, students are taught that playing by the rules is the path of greatest resistance.

Companies will go to great lengths, at times bordering on the comical, to hire college prospects before the September interview schedule. Students, already sounded out by alumni, usually receive a mysterious phone call in the early summer, telling them to meet a company representative at a coffee shop, from where the student will be led to a rented meeting hall filled with hundreds of other applicants. The cloak and dagger operatives ensure that each student has not been followed and swear them to secrecy. Nomura Securities is notorious in its aggressive tactics and has gone so far as taking its prize Tokyo University prospects, *en masse*, to Hawaii. Such lavish trips are timed to conflict with the official recruitment schedule, effectively keeping strong candidates away from temptation by competitors. Gratuities offered by Japanese firms vary according to the prestige of a graduate's college, so that recruits from less respected colleges are considered fortunate to get a weekend in a cheap resort an hour from Tokyo.

Companies ready to commit to a candidate, which in Nomura's case is after three interviews, extend the student a *naitei*, or pledge of employment. The last date that Nomura and its competitors will hand out a *naitei* is in the second week of September, by which time 90 per cent of Nomura's positions will have been filled. The highly regarded men from

Tokyo University often have three or four *naitei* to choose
from before a firm even comes to campus. For this reason
the Japanese recruiting process is a vicious dogfight for talent,
with no tougher fighters than those from Nomura Securities.

Men within the Japanese personnel departments are the
most feared employees in any firm. Their power is virtually
absolute, especially in Nomura and other brokerage firms,
where they wield extraordinary power throughout a man's
career. Nomura, like most brokers, shifts its staff three times
a year: a management shuffle around December, another
reshuffle in spring for more junior staff and yet another
shift in the summer for any residual or international appoint-
ments. Without warning, and usually once every three years,
the fate of promotion, demotion and relocation is arbitrarily
handed down by Nomura's personnel men. Unlike his Western counterpart, the personnel manager is not an emasculated
attendant, subject to the will of the firm's ranking executives.
He is a decision-maker.

Nomura's personnel department also strikes fear into college seniors. Arrogance is the hallmark of Nomura men in
general but of its recruiters in particular. Politeness and
graciousness are absent in these men, who can be mercurial
in their treatment of potential recruits – especially when they
are rejected.

One student recounted how he was thrown out of a
Nomura office for joining a prominent bank and another
told of how she turned down Nomura only to have a cup
of cold noodle sauce poured over her head.

Some Nomura managers take more drastic forms of
revenge. One young candidate who had been offered a
naitei by both Nomura and Marubeni, a well-known trading
company, decided that Nomura was too aggressive for his
personality and agreed to join Marubeni. He politely went
in to visit Nomura to explain his decision, whereupon the
manager needled him about his choice. 'What firm in Japan
can compare to Nomura? We are the greatest,' crowed the
recruiter, unable to believe the student would work anywhere

else. He pried out the name of the company the student intended joining. Then his language became increasingly abusive and threatening as he tried to persuade the man to join Nomura, but to no avail. Slightly frightened, the student mustered up his courage and told the manager firmly that he wanted to leave the office, got up, and to his surprise was escorted to the lift. Just as the lift doors were closing, the manager growled at the student, 'You have not heard the last of Nomura.' Soon afterwards, the student was notified by Marubeni that his pledge of employment was revoked, a rare act in Japan. He later discovered that Nomura Securities and Marubeni maintained a close brokerage and corporate finance link. One phone call from Nomura to its client had ended his promising career.

After joining Nomura on 1 April, 'the young rice crop' (as they are called by the Japanese) listen to Nomura's president deliver a rallying speech, a heady experience since the trainee will be lucky to glimpse his chieftain again over the ensuing years. As in the rest of corporate Japan, these men are henceforth designated in Nomura by the year of the class in which they joined and the air of seniority pertaining to a class of '81 over a class of '82 graduate will stay with them for ever. This tradition of dating by class is a standard ritual which begins any social or business conversation in Japan. Even Nomura old-timers like Shoshi Kawashima, the chairman of Kokusai Securities who entered Nomura in 1935, refer to men (since put out to pasture) as their 'senior' simply because they joined a year or two earlier.

From the start it is drilled into salesmen that stockbroking is a business of the here and now. On 2 April, after the celebratory speeches and parties, almost all the Nomura trainees are placed out to one of the firm's 131 domestic branches. Most Japanese companies ease the stress of beginning a new job by keeping trainees at their headquarters for a year, but not Nomura. After travelling and moving into Nomura dormitories throughout Japan on day two, the army of young recruits present themselves for inspection on day three, ready for boot camp.

Although work begins immediately for the salesmen, they are eager and the pay, by Japanese standards, is good, thanks to the tradition of Tokushichi Nomura. The starting salary for Nomura men in the 1960s and early 1970s was 30,000 yen, just over $80 a month, which was roughly 10 per cent more than the competition paid – and on top of that the industry paid a bonus equal to about three or four months' salary. By the late 1970s Nomura's starting salary had risen about three times to 100,000 a month and by 1990 to 280,000 yen, almost $2,000 a month. Although the investment houses of Japan are given salary guidelines by the government, Nomura has always found a way of rewarding its sales force in a manner befitting its stature – through more perks or higher bonuses than competitors.

On their first day of work, none of the 'young rice crop' has any customers. They are each given a desk and a telephone and are taught by their *sempai*, or senior, the business of broking. He teaches them how to call potential clients cold. Straight out of college and barely three days into their new job, the anxious Nomura novices are sent out into the streets of Japan to collect a quota of business cards. On the first visit the *sempai* accompanies the raw recruit, but soon the trainees are on their own and are ordered the next day to follow up their visits with phone calls. Most of the trainees become frustrated and embarrassed when discussing the stockmarket and are often ridiculed by the clients they are trying to win over. Day after day for a month the Nomura branch managers underscore the value of experience over textbooks and each day the weary trainees go back to the Nomura dormitory humbled. They know nothing of the stockmarket and each day they are reminded of their total ignorance.

This month of humiliation prepares them for their combined training, which begins on May Day. This programme will continue formally for three years, but informally it never ends. Combined training is much like a military exercise and begins in a specially built live-in training centre, a thirty-minute train ride south of Tokyo in Kamikitazawa. The men cook their own food and bring their own bedding. Lectures frequently last until two or three in the morning and the first battery of lectures and exams are in finance – teaching the future money-earners of the firm about accounting and balance sheet analysis. They are then hit with a barrage of economics and tax study, until finally they are introduced to the products they must sell. During this process each man is moulded to think and live in the Nomura culture, but most importantly to subsume his own personality to become a Nomura man. A Nomura man is indoctrinated to have an arrogant and unerring belief that he is part of a master culture, superior to salesmen in Daiwa and Yamaichi Securities, and his conviction, in turn, convinces the Japanese public.

The great yearly recruitment drive is not only a search to boost the male legions of Nomura's sales staff but a search for the important 'OL', the well-groomed and ever-smiling Office Lady. Nomura has found the 'OL' such a cheap and productive source of labour that the firm actually hires more women than men: 500 two-year and 120 four-year female college graduates were hired in 1987, while only 400 four-year male college graduates were brought in. Although this is down-played, Nomura has almost as many saleswomen as salesmen extracting money from households.

Nomura Securities has always preferred to hire girls straight out of high school or two-year colleges, rather than four-year colleges, to act as sales assistants. Girls with a higher education think too much and, because they are around twenty-two when hired (two years older than most female entrants) and usually leave at twenty-five to get married, are viewed as a poor investment. Ideally, a girl joins Nomura at the age of twenty and she has to be attractive, single and obedient. These flowers of Nomura are picked not only to decorate the firm's branch offices but to allay the fears of housewives handing money over to Nomura. By hiring two-year college girls, Nomura is able to lower its costs since the government requires securities firms to pay all four-year college men and women the same starting salary. The women are usually quickly left behind.

In Nomura, men are men and women are required to serve. This is apparent from the first day of training when the men go to the branch offices to plunge immediately into the task of broking while the women are sent to the company training centre in Kamikitazawa, to be taught the finer points of smiling, walking, bowing, serving tea and answering phones. Then they are handed their blue and white uniform – uniforms being *de rigueur* in every Japanese corporation.

First, in the firm's giant auditorium, the women are given a manual of Nomura's highly confidential rules and regulations, outlining everything from trading regulations for personal accounts (permission is required and everyone must deal through Nomura) to the bonus scheme (paid in June and December of every year). Interesting facts and figures are thrown at the women: 96 per cent of all employees buy Nomura Securities shares and through various Nomura mutual funds the average Nomura worker saves $500 a month (68,000 yen). The tone of the lecture becomes serious as the firm's two unions are described. Everyone joins the employees' union, the Nomura spokesman explains. It has 9,000 members, consisting of everyone except senior managers and low-level personnel, and everyone has $4 a month deducted from his or her salary so that the union can fight against management each spring for a wage rise. The other union, the labour union, the Nomura spokesman inveighs in a deadly tone, is to be avoided. This, he explains, is the Communist Party, consisting of sixteen political activists in the firm manipulated by outside sources. He goes on to imply that their influence can bring down well-meaning employees.

The young female recruits are then broken up into small groups of fifteen and taught by ex-stewardesses of Japan Air Lines how to smile, talk, wear their hair, sit properly and, most important, how to bow. A proper bow of formal introduction in Japan is executed at a 45 degree angle, but in Nomura Securities it is different: first the women must look directly into the clients' eyes, then, maintaining a distance of approximately one metre, place their hands by their thighs and, keeping their back straight, tilt their body 40 degrees. The stewardesses teach them variations – 30 degrees for quick greetings ('this is a business of urgency, so we must be practical,' the instructors emphasize) and 15 degrees when passing seniors in the corridors. The future 'OLs' are then drilled to call executives by their title of *bucho* (general manager) or *kacho* (section manager), addressing only middle managers by their name. 'Executives are at the top of our household, so we must show them respect,' urge the trainers.

Further lessons in the importance of manners in business include learning how to walk, back straight, and sit bolt upright as if wearing a formal kimono. Then comes tea-serving (with both hands and from the right) and the golden rule of tea: 'We are taught to serve men and must never drink tea with them,' explained one OL. 'We must drink in the washroom, not in public.' All telephones in Nomura must be picked up on the first ring. Telephones are the arteries that keep the heart of Nomura beating and no matter how fast the phone is answered, the customary greeting is 'sorry to keep you waiting'. Smiling even on the telephone is important, they are told, for a customer can feel a smile's warmth over the phone. The Japan Air Line hostesses' criticisms of the girls serve as a buffer between them and Nomura: the trainees may make mistakes and be reprimanded harshly without the girls' bridling and associating the stress with Nomura.

Meanwhile, by mid-June the male recruits are back at their branch office. Out they go into the field to meet customers and harvest business cards. They scour phone books and comb through old client lists, passing up no clue that may lead them to a buyer or seller of stock. At noon and in the late afternoon each working day every salesman's name appears on a prominently displayed commission list, detailing the amount of money each has brought into the firm over the past few hours. A few of the more forthright and lucky trainees

190

actually get orders, convincing a sympathetic housewife here or a shopkeeper there to buy some shares, but most of the trainees find their names at the bottom of the list with a zero next to commission income.

There is nothing more shameful in Nomura Securities than receiving no orders. A Nomura man's life centres on his commission figures, which are a measure of his personal merit. Commission income cannot be hidden in Nomura and is the touchstone by which management judges a salesman's worth as a human being. The pressure to generate stockmarket orders is with a salesman every waking hour. Later the trainees realize why the least envied Nomura branch is in Niigata on the north-west coast of Honshu near the Japanese Alps. Niigata is idyllic for skiing, but worthless to the Nomura man who exists solely for his commission income. Here, with clients few and far between, it takes enormous effort in the winter, sealed in by ten-foot drifts, to convince anyone to buy stock.

The next training course, in September, focuses on reading and interpreting the *Nihon Keizai Shimbun* (the *Nikkei*), Japan's exhaustive financial daily, comparable to the *Wall Street Journal* or the *Financial Times*. For an hour each morning the Nomura students read and discuss the paper's 'money page' where news analysts dissect various companies. Each student must prepare his own analysis and forecasts for the company, the instructor choosing at random five people to make a ten-minute presentation. Poor preparation is openly criticized and homework is assigned for Saturday and Sunday. Examinations follow and the class does not move on until everyone has mastered the material – the exact opposite approach to that of many Western educators, whereby the gifted are favoured.

The tempo of work, study, work, increases as more time is spent in the branches. Two weeks later the trainees are back on the street looking for customers and by now each branch manager is looking carefully to see which of them are starting to bring in orders. The pressure is now firmly on and there is little sympathy for non-producers. Those having difficulty finding clients to invest in the market resort to almost any means to prevent an ignominious and public tongue-thrashing by the branch manager. The most common resort is to swallow pride and plead with family members to buy stock. Family orders are not the long-term answer but they provide a day's respite from the pressure of finding another client. Japanese mothers, fathers, uncles and grandfathers usually buy stock once, perhaps twice, but become hardened by the third time their once proud Nomura man comes begging them for an order. Those who struggle, but find it hard to approach family, often buy stock themselves under a fictitious name just to register a trade.

Although pressure may breed ingenuity in some, most salesmen day after day, year after year, use the same tricks to alleviate the stress inflicted by imperious, commission-hungry branch managers. A former executive at a Nomura-related firm recalled his company hiring a retired police chief in the 1960s whose job it was to buy used police vans at a discount. A sales manager loaded everyone aboard, mapped out territory and had his men fan out in a door-to-door campaign. Nobody was allowed to return until they had an order. He recounted the salesmen being under so much stress that they invented 'ghost trades' as they called them, which would not be discovered until it came time to pay for the shares four days later, at which time, the salesman, feigning a hazy memory, could not quite remember the name of the client. The more affluent men set up accounts for themselves under a pseudonym to ward off the anger of the sales manager.

By the first autumn on the job at Nomura, most trainees have no qualms about using such tactics to survive. They are on the street a lot longer this time and their class does not return to the training centre until January, almost into the second year. Now they have two weeks of combined training, for which texts are given out a month and a half beforehand. There is no mercy for the slow. Three groups of sixty are given two weeks of intensive retail marketing lectures followed by examinations. The retail brokers are taught the dos and don'ts of stockbroking in Japan: never sell to old ladies or famous people. Old ladies are lonely and call up four or five times a day just to chat and check their stock prices, wasting precious phone time, while well-known public figures, the Nomura lecturers warn, tend to complain to the press if they have problems with a broker, and adverse publicity is to be avoided at all costs. The winnowing process begins and this time the slow learners are not encouraged but sent back to the branches to take their tests later.

The third year is geared to institutional marketing where the trainees, now full-fledged salesmen, learn how to sell stock to corporations, life insurance companies, banks and trust companies. It is in this third and final year of training that the salesmen learn about other Nomura businesses such as fund management, corporate finance and company research. Nomura men are trained as generalists, a management strategy that plays an integral role in ensuring that everyone remains a team player and no individual builds up so much power that he becomes indispensable. But it is also a strategy that mitigates against creating any real expertise.

The *kabuya* are now real men, soldiers of fortune whose unwritten motto is 'churn and burn'. Everything is done to perpetuate a rough and tumble, Marlboro-man exterior as the *kabuya* learn how to pack an extra shirt in their briefcases, drink whisky and beer into the early morning hours, sleep in a cheap capsule hotel (coffin-like space modules dotted throughout Tokyo and designed for salarymen who miss their last train home), and shave with an electric razor on the trading floor. Every morning before the market opens at nine, the Nomura trading desks are alive with the buzzing of razors.

Nomura has instructed its army of salesmen in the art of persistence, teaching them to cajole anyone with money into believing they too have a chance of getting rich in the stockmarket. Nomura trains the *kabuya* as amateur psychologists adept at reasoning with stubborn individuals or at pushing emotional panic buttons on more vulnerable victims. Over 2,500 Nomura troops knock on doors and make cold calls every day to coax investors into the market. The best performers are then promoted and the ranks replenished the following April with hundreds of new recruits.

20
Soldiers of Fortune

The daily regimes of Japan's 50,000 stockbrokers differ from those of Nomura stockbrokers only in degree. Thousands of single Nomura men live in the firm's antiquated, cement-block dormitories thrown up in most major cities and towns, giving Nomura tactical control over its labour force both night and day. The dormitories sleep between twenty and 200 single men in college-like, single-room accommodation, with shared communal baths, showers and toilets. Living in a college fraternity atmosphere, cleanliness is always a problem. 'You never wanted to be the last in the communal bath water,' recalled Toshio Koyama, a Nomura salesman and long-term dormitory inhabitant. According to Nomura management thinking, anyone spending enough time in the dormitory to worry about living conditions was not knocking on enough doors bringing in commission revenue.

Most of the Nomura sales force wake at 5.45 am to a breakfast of rice balls, miso soup, salad and milk served by the dormitory caretakers, often an elderly couple. Everything is utilitarian, including the food. The rice balls can be bolted down with chopsticks in one hand, while the other hand flips through the *Nikkei* newspaper. Those too late to grab a paper can jump on a tattered communal couch to catch the morning economic news on television, while those sleeping in with severe hangovers will be roused by a woman's voice over the loudspeaker, '6.30, time to get up'.

Nomura's dormitories were built within easy commuting distance of the local branch office, seldom more than a fifteen-minute journey away. Management decided it was best to give their stock-pushers more time to actually sell shares than travel back and forth from work. At 7.15 the first meeting of the day begins to decide the dreaded individual daily commission targets. Nomura earned its infamous punning nickname in Japan, 'Noruma Securities' (noruma means quota), by commanding its salesmen to haul in an average of five million yen a month, close to $30,000. Although this figure varied from office to office and month to month, it was a yardstick by which to measure the troops. Everything was aimed at achieving the almighty quota, including a live broadcast at 8.00 to rally the troops. Nomura branches everywhere, from northern Hokkaido to South-East Asian offices in Singapore, Hong Kong, Bangkok, Jakarta and Kuala Lumpur, listened to reports on overseas markets, economic news, company visit reports, rumours and, the most important item of all, the Nomura stock pick of the day. And it was during this broadcast, which high-lighted Nomura's favoured stocks, that the firm made most of its money. Shortly after eight every morning thousands of Myrmidons faithfully picked up phones and later traipsed through the streets to preach the gospel of Nomura. Initiated in 1967, the daily broadcast became such a potent force in pushing individual stocks while unifying Nomura men that the idea was pirated by Nomura's fierce competitors.

Every Nomura branch manager is under almost unbear-able pressure to meet his monthly commission quota and all commission income is spoken of as a percentage of that quota. Achieving a 65 per cent quota, as occurred in many branches in the months after the 1987 crash, is disgraceful. Recording a 150 per cent quota is admirable, bringing show-ers of praise from headquarters. Nomura's golden branch offices are those located in densely populated, central Tokyo – Ginza, Shinjuku and Toranomon – which have always had the highest absolute revenue to bring in compared to smaller, offbeat branches in Kyushu or Hokkaido. But having to bring in less money than one's sister branches has never eased the pressure, since quotas are relative to one's own performance the previous month. A Nomura manager surpassing his branch quota never cheers for long because headquarters always expect a better performance the following month.

By the end of the 1980s this quota had become a financial ratchet and had made Nomura the titan it is.

A Nomura branch manager who falls behind his daily and weekly quotas becomes a ruthless slave-driver, even in civilized overseas offices. 'One of our Japanese salesmen – a grown man – had his chair taken away from his and was forced to stand throughout the day like a schoolboy. Every day for two months he called his clients until he met his quota,' recalled Paul Smith, an ex-Nomura salesman in London. Nomura policy is based on a simple law of averages: for every ten calls there are five rejections, three or four hesitations and one or two investors willing to purchase stock.

The Nomura sales machine was also driven by women. Throughout Japan, behind their smiling and seemingly unruffled demeanour, many of them had sales quotas to fulfil. Nomura trained the women to answer simple enquiries on stock, bond and investment trusts while the *kabuya* made more important calls to proven accounts or high net-worth prospects. These women numbered over 2,900. In the 1950s these were the part-time housewives recruited to handle Nomura's Ryo 'piggy-banks' and they soon joined the sales staff on a commission basis (the few in the firm to be paid directly by how much they bring in) to loosen the purse strings of other housewives. Every branch soon hired these part-timers to call around for money and even posted some to the specially marked booths in local department stores to entice other women to part with their savings.

Nomura hired good-looking women not only to make money, but as potential wives for their male colleagues, able to empathize with the tremendous pressure endured by them. The personnel department reasoned that the average girl joined Nomura aged twenty and married a Nomura man at age twenty-five. A woman would often take up the cause of a particular salesman, offering comfort and solace, not unmindful of the prospects for marriage. In turn 'Nomura men fell in love with a woman who gave them a warm smile

197

at the end of each evening,' explained one of Nomura's sales staff. Long hours and cramped quarters brought sales assistants and *kabuya* into constant contact and left little time for finding a wife outside Nomura. The firm, in turn, took its role as marriage-maker seriously and the *kabuya*'s immediate boss often acted as the go-between – a sort of modern marriage arranger. Eventually over 40 per cent of all Nomura men take Nomura women as wives.

Finding a husband from the ranks of the well-paid, successful *kabuya* was the goal of most two-year college girls. Salesmen were 'the best catch in Japan outside the Ministry of Finance', according to one. By the late 1980s, there was increasing cachet in marrying a broker, for by then they had begun to achieve a prestige and power that arose from the acceptance of new money in Japan. Interestingly, however, their wealth did not derive from salary and bonus payments but from shareholdings in their own firms. Amazingly, thousands of employees in Japanese securities firms became millionaires. In 1986, when shares in Daiwa Securities raced to a then all-time high of 2,000 yen a share, Yoshitoki Chino, the chairman of Daiwa, Nomura's arch rival, stated, 'Our firm has 500 workers [out of 7,000] with over a million dollars of Daiwa stock.'

Their wealth, salted away in the form of shares by Japanese brokers, especially Nomura men, was startling when considered in absolute dollar terms – especially since few executives under the general manager level earned more than $100,000 before the 1980s. Each major Japanese securities firm was publicly quoted on the Tokyo Stock Exchange and to foster pride in the firm, promote savings and boost the firm's share price, stockbrokers were required by their bosses to buy stock in their own firm. The forty main board directors of Nomura Securities had always been required to hold a minimum 100,000 share block of Nomura Securities. As Nomura's share price rose above 1,000 yen (nearly $4) a share in 1985 and later rocketed to 5,990 yen in April 1987 (nearly $46 a share including the huge upward appreciation of the yen), Nomura was forced to drop this limit to a 33,000 and eventually 10,000 share minimum. Directors holding a minimum 33,000 shareholding at the time of Nomura's explosive rally in April 1987 were each sitting on a $1.3 million gold mine. As old-timers, most of the directors had paid under 300 yen a share for their stock and according to one Nomura family member, eight ex-Nomura directors had holdings of over one million shares, each stake worth nearly $50 million in April 1987. Even more staggering was the 2.5 million share stake held by Minoru Segawa himself in 1980, a holding he later reduced by half.

The senior management of Nomura and the other securities firms were not the only ones enriched by employee stock option programmes. Even the settlement staff, office girls and messenger clerks became wealthy in the Great Bull Market of 1986 and 1987, for under the Nomura monthly savings plan, the company deducted pay from every worker's salary, which was then diverted to buy shares in Nomura Securities itself, with Nomura matching a percentage of each employee's purchase. Large share issues were also extended to staff when Nomura raised money for itself by means of a share offering. In times of market uncertainty, Japan's biggest brokers encouraged their own employees into purchasing a poorly subscribed issue, although this proved a boon for long-suffering *kabuya*, especially in Nomura. As a result of all this, it was not uncommon to discover women in the big four with portfolios exceeding half a million or three quarters of a million dollars. As a perk for managers, Nomura also extended low-interest loans to buy huge lines of Nomura stock offerings, often looking the other way when the time came to pay back the interest.

One such story chronicles the typical rags to riches rise of such a Nomura manager – a man who rose to the crest of the 1980s 'super bull market'. Nobuo Nakazawa, the grandson of a farmer and the son of a medium-level government official, wanted, as he later said, 'to become very rich'. Ignoring the wishes of his father and of his professors, who had arranged interviews with the Mitsubishi Bank, he joined the Nomura class of 1968, immediately buying 200 shares of Nomura Securities at fifty yen a share. Two years later, management spotted Nakazawa and decided to polish his English, sending him off to the University of Wisconsin to study for a master's degree in business. Still in need of pocket money and afraid to go to his father, with some guilt he sold off his Nomura shares; but when he returned to Japan two years later, his MBA degree in hand, he made up for lost time by purchasing as many Nomura shares as he could afford.

Nakazawa was a commodity within Nomura – he could speak and read English – so, like Terasawa and Egashira before him, management posted him to the international division. The next six years were a blur until he was assigned as the number two man to set up a Zurich office. By 1982 he was promoted to number one at Geneva, and there he caught the bull market in full stride, using cash-rich Swiss institutions to absorb huge lines of stock, and helping Japanese firms raise money in the Swiss Franc Euro-market. Returning to Tokyo in 1986 he was made a *bucho*, a full section manager, at the age of thirty-eight, leapfrogging older men, whom he called 'deadwood'. By this time, Nakazawa had accumulated 40,000 shares in Nomura, worth $1.7 million in 1987.

Shortly after his return to Tokyo, Nomura's welfare department, the team that took special care of executives' investments, homes and financial security, advised him to buy land, specifically an 'ideal lot' offered by Nomura Real Estate at a price of $250,000. Nakazawa told them he was low on cash and considered selling off his Nomura shares. 'I had thought of taking a profit in Nomura after it hit 2,000 anyway,' confided Nakazawa, 'but suddenly the welfare department offered me a long-term low-interest loan.' He bought the property and a year later his investment soared to $700,000. In the meantime, his Nomura shares, which the welfare department had discouraged him from selling, had trebled. Shortly thereafter, in one of the biggest shake-ups in management history, Nakazawa was promoted to the main board. At the age of forty-two, he was rich and powerful, the youngest director in the history of the firm.

* * * * *

Life for Japanese salesmen is not made any easier by one of the most frustrating phenomena of urban Japan, mid-afternoon traffic jams, which are partly brought about by the tens of thousands of stockbrokers throughout the country who take to the streets each afternoon after the three o'clock market-close to visit their clients. Armed with small gifts – a box of candy, a chart book, a calendar or a piece of research – a salesman might visit up to twenty-five clients.

From the late 1950s top money-makers in Nomura's major offices were each given the privilege of a car with a driver, who waited at the firm's motor pool after trading shut-down to take the salesman on his appointed rounds. Other salesmen rushed down to the motor pool to be awarded the left-over cars on a first-come-first-served basis – those without either walked, used a taxi service or took a subway to see their customers. The traffic problems meant that Nomura received thousands of parking tickets each year, a headache that Nomura tried to ease by hiring various metropolitan police officials to use their friendships to get these and other minor legal infractions waived.

Nomura also became one of the biggest clients of Japanese taxi services, even in cities outside Tokyo, and bitter fights emerged between rival taxi companies to land the Nomura account. Nippon Taxi and Osaka Taxi claim to work until midnight shuttling Nomura men around. Yamaichi men, they assert, knock off work at six every evening.

Salesmen too burned out, dejected or lazy to see their customers use the few precious late-afternoon hours to drink coffee, see a movie or play pachinko. For them, it was worth avoiding a Nomura-paid taxi service when refused a car at the Nomura pool: 'Nomura drivers have big ears and big mouths,' one ex-salesmen recalled, 'so when you wanted to just watch a movie it was always best to hire an outside taxi company.' Tatsuo Kurita, a middle-level *kacho* at Nomura, observed that 'any afternoon you go out, the coffee shops are filled with Japanese brokers smoking and reading the sports pages.' The best thing to do, he claimed, if you come across a superior as you are coming out of a movie or reading the paper, is to pretend you never noticed him.

The personal touch was always important in the relentless search for orders. Average Japanese households and companies demand some form of humility from a broker before they place an order, but Nomura men would be capable of extremes to extract orders from clients. Mrs Watanabe, the wife of a well-to-do businessman in the Yokohama area who prudently invested her husband's pay cheque in the Japanese bond and stockmarkets, told of one such incident. Like most other housewives, she was called upon several times a week by persistent stockbrokers and she sparingly gave six or seven orders every year to the brokers she liked. Her husband used the promise of his wife's orders to elicit favours from young stockbrokers, whom he had wash the family car in the summer and shovel snow from the path in winter before letting them in the house.

One morning a Kokusai Securities salesman politely told Mrs Watanabe over tea of Kokusai's belief that shares in Nippon Steel were in for a rise. After his intelligent and impressive speech, he thanked Mrs Watanabe and left. Later that day a young salesman from Nomura Securities knocked, came in for tea and presented Mrs Watanabe with a similar story on Nippon Steel. She thanked him and said that she would think the matter over before reaching a conclusion. Suddenly the Nomura man broke down in tears.

'What's wrong?' she asked.

The Nomura man finally blubbered, 'My boss has told me not to return until I get an order. I've tried but it's no use, nobody will buy stock from me.'

'There, there,' said Mrs Watanabe, trying to comfort him.

'Here, I will buy stock from you. When you get back to the office please buy me 10,000 shares of Nippon Steel.'

The Nomura man composed himself and sheepishly left Mrs Watanabe and returned to the office, able for once to leave by 7 pm.

Stockbroking has always had its hazards as Ken'ichi Fukuhara, a retail broker in Nomura, discovered in 1977. He had persistently called on a wealthy shopkeeper with no success, when suddenly he was invited for lunch. This was Fukuhara's big chance. The shopkeeper served up a plate of freshly sliced blowfish, a delicacy in Japan, but poisonous if not prepared by a trained chef.

'Here, help yourself,' he told Fukuhara. 'I cut it myself.'

To refuse the blowfish would mean offending his host and never receiving a stockmarket order. To accept meant facing possible death. Thinking quickly, Fukuhara decided he would just have time to get to the hospital for treatment in the hour or so it takes for blowfish poison to work its effects and, under the watchful eye of his host, he smiled and ate the finely carved pieces of blowfish. Only after the meal did the shopkeeper burst out laughing, telling Fukuhara how he had had it prepared by a proper chef ahead of time. 'For your courage,' he told Fukuhara, 'I will do business with you from this day on.'

Once a salesman convinced a client to purchase shares, however, he had also to convince them to leave the shares in the possession of Nomura Securities. It was here that Nomura made a financial killing, for it earned almost one per cent (including commission for stocks and bonds it bought and sold) for every financial instrument held deep within its vaults. However, Japanese clients did not see the matter in the same way as American retail investors. Americans willingly would leave the stock they purchased in the care of their brokerage house to perform such routine tasks as collecting dividends. Always suspicious of brokers, the Japanese preferred to keep their share certificates in hand after paying for them, squirrelling them away at home or in a bank. Nomura, however, hit upon a brilliant ploy to encourage salesmen to persuade individual clients to hand over stock certificates. It invented the Ten Billion Yen Club, membership of which was given to any salesman who coaxed ten billion yen's worth of assets, nearly $75 million, from his clients. By convincing customers to leave their stocks, bonds and cash with Nomura (who safeguarded the assets and attended to matters such as chasing dividend payments), the firm charged the client a fee. Depending on the type of security held, Nomura could rake in over $750,000 a year for every Ten Billion Yen Club Member, many of whom were paid under $40,000 a year. It turned out to be a gold mine, tightening Nomura's control on the market; at any given time it knew where to find large blocks of stock. At the same time, the glory of club status gave salesmen enormous prestige and once a year its starry-eyed members sat down to eat with the president of Nomura at the Nomura Club, the firm's inner sanctuary on the top floor of its Nihonbashi headquarters.

Nomura's Ten Billion Yen Club did not, however, totally wipe out the Japanese desire to retain physical assets in the safety of their home. When the time came for payment of dividends, which are small in Japan, families could be seen toting their shares down to the company registry to collect their money. This refugee mentality forced retail brokers to deliver contracts personally to a customer on the same day the shares were purchased. Three days later, when settlement came due, the salesman trundled around with a black bag to deliver the share certificates, returning to the firm with a bag full of cash.

An exchange of stock certificates for cash was not the last a client heard of his broker. Once a client borrowed money to purchase shares and the stock price of the shares fell in value, the salesman had to collect additional money for margin requirements. Facing irate investors was one of the most dangerous aspects of being a broker, forcing some Japanese salesmen to put up a margin call from their own salary. Ex-Nomura salesman Ken'ichi Fukuhara recalled visiting an elderly customer, a World War I veteran, to collect margin money after the client's stock had plummeted in value. He was confronted by a furious old man waving a samurai sword who chased him through the garden into the street. He had to return later and crawl over the ground picking up the 1,000 yen notes the client had strewn over the garden.

Nomura advises its men to apologize for and not staunchly defend stock turned sour, nor to defuse irate clients. It is advice to be heeded, for extreme client problems have occasionally ended in violence and even murder. The story of Fujio Kawada (one of the few figures in this book whose name has been altered), Nomura's Shinjuku branch manager, is a particularly distasteful example. Kawada's success in selling stock was partly due to his connections with certain underworld figures – more generally called the *yakuza* – for which Shinjuku was famous. Kawada heard in early 1985 that Yamanouchi Pharmaceutical, one of Japan's largest drug companies, had discovered a miracle drug for cancer, so he passed the news on to his clients.

The cure, according to Kawada's own informant within Nomura Securities, would make world headlines when announced, but until that time privileged clientele would be able to buy into Yamanouchi. Such discoveries were unconfirmed, but Japanese investors loved buying stock on such stories, dreaming of an instant market kill. Fresh in the minds of investors was the story of Ono Pharmaceutical, which tripled in early 1984, shooting up from 5,000 yen a share to 15,000 in a few months on rumours of a new diabetes drug.

Kawada was by no means the first in the firm with the Yamanouchi story. Even within Nomura Securities there had always been a hierarchy for the dissemination of profitable information – controlled by the firm's powerful, and often very wealthy, trading manager. First to be told were the senior executives, who bought stock in the names of relatives or friends, then came the politicians, who filled their campaign coffers, then the valued institutions such as Nippon Life

Insurance and those institutions to whom Nomura owed a favour. And so it went on, from life insurance companies, banks, Japanese companies, foreign brokers to, finally, the hard-pressed individual salesmen.

Occasionally the order was transposed but seldom were Nomura's chieftains or Japan's politicians displaced from their natural position. Kawada was a retail salesman and, although retail men were often the last to hear stories, he had, he thought, enough large accounts to get information early.

Yamanouchi Pharmaceutical had actually been rising since the summer of 1984, more than doubling from a low of 1,100 to 2,760 by the year end, and it was in January 1985 when the stock hit 3,500 that Kawada began getting excited. There seemed no question that Yamanouchi was a 10,000 yen stock and so Kawada pushed it, convinced that he was on to the story early. Around the same time, the rest of Nomura began actively pushing Yamanouchi – out came written reports, calls started pouring in from clients, headlines were made. Shortly Yamanouchi hit 4,000 and it was somewhere in this range when Kawada convinced his *yakuza* account to purchase a huge block of shares. By February 1985 Yamanouchi hit 4,450 and Kawada was a god.

Then the worst happened – what the Japanese called the '*biotech shokku*'. Rumours began circulating about the harmful side-effects of the new drug and investors dumped Yamanouchi and the other drug companies. The share price of Yamanouchi dropped like a rock, falling below 3,000 in April. Kawada's client became surly but for months Kawada was able to hold the ruffians at bay. 'Don't worry,' he said, trying to soothe the gangsters, 'Nomura will bail us out.' And so it went on, with Yamanouchi losing ground day after day, and falling that summer below 2,700. In the autumn the entire stockmarket plunged as the newly introduced Japanese government bond futures collapsed. Although Yamanouchi's share price held firm, the *yakuza* member was now convinced there was no way of recouping the losses – one third of their investment had been chopped away. The thug cornered Kawada and beat him into a coma. He died shortly afterwards and Nomura sadly announced the death of Fujio Kawada, the victim of a long-term illness.

Murders and suicides, though rare, are a gruesome aspect of the broking game, the violent extension of an investment gone wrong, but much more common is the investor complaint. Most of the time, Nomura has successfully muffled the disgruntled cries of investors, and out-of-court settlements are usually reached before a complaint reaches the media. Nomura and the other big brokers have the pull of being among the largest advertisers in Japan, so the media generally try to avoid any hint of scandal within the big four. Stifling investor complaints is, however, sometimes impossible and with the wisdom of Katsuhiko Sori, Nomura's in-house legal counsel, the firm realized that lawsuits brought by investors 'were the cost of doing business'. Those investors seeking vindication of stockmarket losses through legal redress have their day in court and Nomura is prepared to fight them. At any one time Nomura has between ten and twenty lawsuits in progress, usually from investors seeking less than a million dollars. This is hardly a disturbing number compared to American or British investment houses, which may have dozens of angry investors clamouring for tens of millions of dollars at any one time.

The Japanese, however, have traditionally disdained confrontation. Brokerage firms did not need full-time in-house lawyers (up to 1986 Daiwa Securities relied on one elderly legal adviser) until they began to set up operations overseas. Nomura's law department was started in 1963 for tax purposes but expanded in 1965 after the Yamaichi crisis in which small investors became more forthright in demanding compensation for market losses. Those who have crossed the legal divide and taken Nomura to court tend to be aggressive and at times dishonest. 'The closest thing to a man, next to his life, is his money,' Keisuke Egashira was fond of saying. 'Money compels man to do anything.'

One hopeful customer of Nomura bought 100,000 shares

of the Nankai Spinning Company at 1,000 yen a share in the spring of 1985, then took a business trip to Hong Kong. When he returned to Tokyo the price of Nankai Spinning had plunged and he quickly called up the broker demanding to know at what price he had sold his Nankai shares. The baffled Nomura salesman reminded his client that his instructions ordered Nomura to sell at over 1,000 yen a share. But the customer screamed his insistence that he had given strict instructions to sell at market price on a certain date. His demand for reimbursement fell on deaf ears. Nomura knew they were being taken for a ride. When finally the client took Nomura to court the price of Nankai had halved to 500 yen a share and he was staring at a 50 million yen ($208,000) loss. The judge's verdict was swift and confident: no Nomura salesman would ever pass up the chance to earn a commission if asked to do so; they work too hard to give up a free order. The client lost.

It is not always so simple. In the winter of 1984, a wealthy Indian living in Tokyo, Dhana Singh Bains, opened a stock-trading account with the Nomura Shinjuku branch. This quickly turned into a trading nightmare. Bains spoke English but little Japanese and the Nomura salesman, Kensuje Yamada, spoke even less English than Bains did Japanese. According to Bains, Yamada started churning his account – a common ploy – and, without the permission of Bains, bought shares of Mitsubishi Oil, a poorly managed oil refiner that speculators periodically bought on takeover rumours. After Mitsubishi Oil shares headed south on the Tokyo Stock Exchange, Bains received a trading statement from Nomura showing a loss of 50 million yen.

The furious client demanded to see Yamada's manager, Haruhiko Moriyama, who promptly visited the Bains household to try to settle the trading dispute before the media got hold of the story. However, Mrs Bains secretly tape-recorded the interview on a machine concealed in her oven, during which she disingenuously asked what was going to happen to the shares Nomura had bought without telling them.

Moriyama replied that Nomura would return them and, perhaps taking the smile on Mrs Bains' face as conciliatory, hammered another nail in the Nomura coffin by admitting that unauthorized trading, like that indulged in by Yamada, was not of course to be condoned and assured Mrs Bains that Yamada would be punished. After Moriyama left, Mrs Bains rushed the tape to her lawyers, who used it as evidence. The court awarded the Bains family $112,000 in damages.

21
The Castaways

Only the strongest, most battle-hardened Nomura men remained within Nomura Securities for their entire career. The rest were destined to a life of banishment. Kokusai Securities was a brokerage firm shaped by such cast-offs – men too old or too weak, men branded political refugees from battles lost or relegated to a life of stockbroking obscurity, left on the Nomura Securities mountainside to die. 'Sad, disturbing, but true,' a retired Nomura man hesitatingly admitted of his friends at Kokusai.

Rather than wallow in self-pity, however, these 'outcasts' of Nomura made Kokusai Securities the fifth largest brokerage house in Japan. In the short five-year span between 1982 and 1987, they forged one of the greatest unsung success stories in modern-day finance.

Kokusai was formed by a merger of two of Nomura's affiliated companies, Yachiyo and Koa Securities, into the Nomura Trust Sales Company, the nation's leading collector of pooled funds for stockmarket investment. This was in 1981, a year before world financial markets emerged from the slump induced by high oil prices, high interest rates and high inflation. Japan seemed to be heading into a recession and doom and gloom pervaded. The economy, which had grown so rapidly in 1980, halved its growth by 1983. The Japanese stockmarket was marking time and had in fact peaked in August 1981 just above 8,000, a level that would not be seen for another year and a half. Everybody was too busy wallowing in pessimism to recognize that Wall Street had bottomed in August 1982. Then three months later, in October 1982, the Japanese stockmarket took off, sensing an optimistic future for the Japanese economy and that Wall Street was about to go into overdrive.

Until that time, however, nobody was interested in buying stocks from Nomura Securities, or from any other securities company. Japanese individuals were more concerned about paying their heating bill and eking out small wage concessions from their employers than in buying stocks in a declining market. They had seen all this before. Every time world oil prices rose, the Japanese consumer paid the price. Japan had no oil reserves of its own and to fuel its economic machine it imported 99 per cent of its oil, mostly from the Middle East. When oil prices had quadrupled in 1973, rocketing from $3 to $12 a barrel, the Japanese stockmarket went into a tailspin as the economy nose-dived. Life was just returning to normal in 1979 when the Shah of Iran was deposed, destabilizing the Middle East. Within months the oil price was over $40 a barrel, a fresh nightmare for the Japanese, especially for the stockbrokers of less respected firms like Yachiyo and Koa, whose clients went into hiding.

Yet every time the stockmarket declined, Nomura Securities found its market share increased. Investors who did trade in times of market uncertainty flocked to the security of a name they readily associated with market pre-eminence. By 1981, Nomura accounted for one in every six trades on the Tokyo Stock Exchange, a 15 per cent market share. This bothered the Ministry of Finance, who called in Setsuya Tabuchi, the firm's president. The problem, they explained, was one of oligopoly: the big brokers were getting bigger while the smaller ones were dying out. What Japan lacked, they told him, were more fully integrated securities houses, firms that not only bought and sold stock, but also traded bonds, underwrote new issues and wrote research. The solution, they told Tabuchi, was to form another securities company, thereby increasing competition for the big four and providing the market with more liquidity. Here was a mandate to start another firm.

'Nomura Securities executives were overjoyed at this command to start another brokerage house,' revealed Shoshi Kawashima in 1987, five years after becoming Kokusai

Securities' first president. Nomura management wanted to increase their share of daily stockmarket volume to 18 or 20 per cent but no matter how hard they pressed the sales force, the firm kept hitting a natural ceiling of 15 per cent. Nomura's chiefs, frightened that their growth had peaked, called a meeting in 1981. They compared their situation with that of Kirin Brewery, the nation's largest alcoholic-drink producer, which, in 1980, towered over its competition with a 60 per cent market share. Executives at Kirin had come up with a clever marketing strategy of selling whisky under different brand names, after which Kirin's market share had rocketed. Nomura executives took great interest in Kirin's successful market ploy. Nomura salesmen, they reasoned, had already permeated every nook and cranny of Japan, and Nomura was already the top broker to almost every financial institution. The Ministry of Finance ultimatum now gave Nomura the opportunity to expand, while appearing to be financial altruists. Like Kirin, Nomura would create a new brand name. They called it Kokusai Securities.

Forming Kokusai was a stroke of good luck. Not only did Nomura appease the Ministry of Finance, but it increased its influence over the average investor by gaining control over the client base of Yachiyo and Koa which was much more speculative than that of Nomura and especially fickle during downswings in the market. Yachiyo Securities had been around the Tokyo area since 1948, with headquarters in Nihonbashi, a few blocks from the Tokyo Stock Exchange. It was a quiet brokerage house by Japanese standards; 'not as speculative as most,' said Shuzo Nagata, a Kokusai director. Although Yachiyo sold stock, it was known for its expertise in bond trading and was run nominally by a conservative ex-board member of Nomura Securities, a retiring man who presided over the firm's branch network with less vigour than his counterpart at Koa Securities.

The men who worked at Koa Securities were more in the tradition of nineteenth-century rice traders or as John Doyle, an ex-Kokusai trader, remarked, 'They were more like underworld figures than stockbrokers.' For the most part, Koa's sales and trading force was made up of loud and ill-mannered ruffians, uneducated in the ways of fundamental stock analysis. Koa Securities did not have the branch network that Yachiyo had. They sold stock by the seat of their pants, by rumour, charts and inside tips, and had a reputation on the street for being highly speculative.

Setsuya Tabuchi upgraded the status of Yachiyo and Koa by merging them with the successful Nomura Investment Trust Sales department, to form Kokusai. The Investment Trust Sales Company was known and trusted by housewives around Japan and it had a branch network complete with salesmen and offices that could be converted almost immediately into a full service brokerage house. The presence of trained salesmen, Tabuchi thought, would improve the image of Koa and instil a more forceful attitude within the Yachiyo sales force. Moreover, the word 'Kokusai' means 'international', but also sounds like 'government bond', thus appealing to the attuned Western standards of the Japanese.

There was another advantage, too, in starting Kokusai: it enabled Tabuchi to 'bury' aged or unwanted Nomura executives. 'Nomura only kept key men in the fast lane of the main company,' observed Yoshio Terasawa, a main board director who was himself purged in 1987. 'All the others were farmed out to the subsidiaries, Kokusai being the largest.' Tabuchi reasoned that by exiling immobile managers he could breathe life into those younger Nomura men anxious to climb within his own firm, while giving Nomura outcasts a chance to make their name elsewhere. Instead of banishing unwanted men to minor subsidiaries like Nomura Tourist, Tabuchi now offered senior managers lucrative retirement packages to leave Nomura and join Kokusai, with the incentive of a chunk of stock in Kokusai ahead of its planned listing on the Tokyo Stock Exchange in 1987.

Then, in one of the most methodical reshuffles in Japanese corporate history, Nomura president Tabuchi plucked one experienced, but not necessarily (in his view) stellar man from

THE HOUSE OF NOMURA

each of Nomura's research, settlement, personnel, sales, trading and corporate finance divisions and handed them main board memberships of Kokusai. As a final gesture, Tabuchi guaranteed Kokusai its independence, although he made sure that Nomura, with affiliates and friends, held a controlling interest, with nearly 51 per cent of Kokusai stock.

Kokusai is a study in the anatomy of Japanese power. Consumed by the ambition to transact 20 per cent of all Japanese stockmarket bargains, Nomura Securities was not interested in the profits Kokusai passed on to Nomura as a parent company. This obsession for market share rather than profitability was the distinctive difference between the Japanese and the Americans or Europeans, who are always concerned to claim profits from their subsidiaries. 'Control was all-important,' stated Masao Kumon, a Kokusai director. 'Kokusai was used by Nomura as its legs and hands in the market. Nomura received only a paltry dividend from Kokusai each year.'

Control was also partly exercised through the weekly Monday morning meeting, the *Sagami-kai*, where a member of Kokusai's trading and sales team met with other Nomura affiliates to decide on sales strategy for the Nomura group of companies. Here it was relayed which stocks and which sectors they were going to push. Kokusai was the most important of Nomura's affiliated securities houses, which included the smaller firms World, Itogin, Takagi and Ichiyoshi Securities, and the loosely affiliated Taisei and Nichiei Securities, as well as Sanyo Securities, an independent firm run by the Tsuchiya family. The meeting constituted an important element of power and harmony, helping crystallize Nomura's stockmarket share above 20 per cent. Of even greater interest was Nomura's Thursday meeting, called the *Mokuyo-kai*, where Nomura itself highlighted a few select stocks that it intended to push. Buying ahead of the group's stock recommendations became a recurring source of income.

Although castaways, the Kokusai men were imbued with

214

allegiance to Nomura and Tabuchi reinforced this by appointing one of the longest surviving Nomura men to head his new firm: Shoshi Kawashima, from Nomura class of 1935. Kawashima was a member of the prestigious, if somewhat antiquarian, Nomura Old Boys Society, which met once a month on the seventh floor of the Nomura headquarters and at which only the chairmen and senior advisers of Nomura's most important subsidiaries were allowed, and from which even President Yoshihisa Tabuchi was excluded. It was Kawashima whom Segawa had sent out to open Nomura's New York office in 1953 and on his return he had managed the foreign department. Then in 1964 Kawashima had been purged by a man a year his senior, Masao Nagasawa, Nomura class of 1934, and sent down to Osaka. Because of the deference accorded seniority, irrespective of whether the elders were less skilled or, in Nagasawa's case, 'rude and uncaring about other humans in the firm', Kawashima had no choice but to obey his higher-ranking officer, even after thirty years in his job. Not until 1987 did even Nomura Securities, the quickest at breaking down traditional barriers, promote younger, more able class members ahead of seniors. The posting to Osaka was a slap in the face, for, although Osaka had been the pre-war home of Nomura and Kawashima was managing director, since the war the firm's power base had been in Tokyo. In Osaka, one played a waiting game until posted elsewhere.

Kawashima was finally transferred in 1972 to the Investment Trust Sales Company in Tokyo, as its president. This was another hardship post and the hardest time of his career. Salesmen hated selling investment trusts in this period, just after the first oil shock when the stockmarket plummeted day after day. Nomura promised housewives and small shop-owners a guaranteed 10 per cent annual return for buying Nomura's investment trust, which Nomura then invested, along with other people's money, into the market. There was no way Nomura could honour its commitment to paying 10 per cent returns and the salesmen were told after six months to call on the client again and persuade them to switch into a new, more promising fund. 'We sold trusts to clients, then the trust price would fall,' recalled one salesman. 'We sold stock to clients and the stock would fall. Clients would come into the office to visit salesmen and the salesmen would hide, or worse, erase the correct stock prices we kept on a blackboard, marking them up just to keep the client happy.'

Kawashima presided over this unhappy lot but did not give up. Where other senior executives shied away from putting their own money into Nomura's funds, Kawashima believed in his own product and invested in the Nomura fund, for which he earned the respect of his colleagues. Later, when chairman of Kokusai, Kawashima still proudly clung to his title of president of the mutual fund marketing team. Kokusai to him was an offshoot of the department he had built, a department that funnelled the savings of Japanese families all over Japan into the stockmarket. Despite Nomura's control in holding over 50 per cent of Kokusai's shares, he declared: 'We are no longer a baby being nurtured by our parent since our stock exchange listing in May of 1987. We are independent.'

Nomura encouraged this belief in Kokusai as an autonomous company, for a spirit of independence was necessary to generate excitement and orders. Kokusai employees were permitted to cheer in the competitive arena when they outshone Nomura in a stock or bond transaction, and encouraged to forget that Nomura could dissolve the entire Kokusai board of directors at will and throw every employee out on the street.

The unsightly, former Yachiyo Securities building in Nihonbashi, only feet away from an ugly concrete expressway, became Kokusai's headquarters, a maze of low-ceilinged, grey-painted departments, ranging from settlement clerks on the lower floors (they needed to hand-deliver stock certificates and had no time to wait for a lift) to the directors' offices on the tattered sixth floor, with the noisiest being the fourth-floor trading area, kept lively by the presence of three main-board directors without offices on the sixth floor.

Outside, a grimy layer of exhaust soot covers the buildings and street, where a few retired back-office men, now serving as drivers, pass their time polishing the multi-coloured Nissan Cedrics waiting to whisk away Kokusai directors. The latter tend to be issued second-hand cars or, at best, Nissan models one line down from the black Cedrics driven by their distinguished cousins at Nomura. Black is the colour choice of powerbrokers in Japan, especially for Nomura men, and somehow it is understood by Kokusai directors that, as *arrivistes*, they had best not overstep their bounds.

Around the corner from Kokusai, down one of the many unnamed side streets and leading towards Nomura's head office and the Tokyo Stock Exchange a few blocks away, are dozens of traditional, family-run restaurants. At lunch-time the area swarms with office ladies and salarymen, most of them with Kokusai and Nomura pins on their upper left lapel, and in the evenings the sound of mah-jong tiles can be heard from the speciality mah-jong bars where Kokusai managers stop off to drink whisky and beer, and do a little gambling before going home.

During the euphoric stockmarket rise that began in 1982, Kokusai found itself well positioned for the bull market, with a branch network of sixty-five offices and a 500-man sales force that sold stocks, bonds and mutual funds. Bond trading profits and mutual fund commissions each brought in about 11 billion yen (roughly $40 million) during the first year of Kokusai's existence up to October 1982 and by the time Japanese institutional participation pushed the Japanese stockmarket to record levels in the mid-1980s, Japan's go-go years, the equity sales, bond trading and mutual fund sales were each pulling in over $140 million a year.

Despite the striking success of mutual fund sales, which were generated primarily by women at Kokusai, the real glory – for men – was in stock trading and equity sales.

Kokusai's inspiration came from a fierce-looking man by

217

the name of Zen'ichi Toyoda who earned a nickname as the 'Tyson of Kabutocho'. A fascinating anecdote in Nomura history was Toyoda's selection as Nomura president in 1978 by his reigning peers. As if to highlight Toyoda's ferocity, the Ministry of Finance vetoed Toyoda as president (calling him too aggressive) and instead approved Setsuya Tabuchi.

The reputation of brokers in Japan suddenly took a quantum leap in the mid-1980s. Money meant status and there was plenty of money to be made on the Tokyo stockmarket. Selling stock became the macho profession and young college graduates around the country were eager to join brokerage firms. Stockbroking turned into a remarkable success story for Kokusai: commission income from buying and selling shares for clients on the Tokyo Stock Exchange soared from 10 billion yen to over 50 billion yen. Kokusai became a money-making machine, increasing its net profit in five years by almost twenty times, from 1.2 billion yen in 1982 to over 20 billion in 1987, when it was ranked as the seventy-fifth most profitable company and the fifth largest broker in Japan. In May 1987 Kokusai's directors became multimillionaires, as Kokusai's own stock began trading on the second section of the Tokyo Stock Exchange: it opened at a price of $38.50, four or five times the level at which most employees had been given stock or loaned low-interest money with which to buy stock.

22
The Apache

In 1978 Masanori Ito, nicknamed the 'Apache' for his dark, warlike features, took control of Nomura's overseas business. Within five years he was to bring international money rolling into Nomura war chests and put the international team in the black – but it was to be at a terrible price. Within the same years, the Apache, by applying tough sales tactics to overseas branch offices, would take a hatchet to every competent internationalist Nomura had ever hired. He destroyed Nomura's international reputation.

Nomura International had come a long way since setting up a small outpost in New York in 1953: by 1978 it had offices in London, Hong Kong, Amsterdam, Singapore, Frankfurt, Toronto and Geneva. Three of its greatest ambassadors were the amiable Yoshio Terasawa, known as Mr America, the urbane Keisuke Egashira, known as Mr Europe, and the avuncular Yukio Aida, to whom both reported. Known as the 'troika', they combined a friendliness, sophistication and comfort that the firm's overseas clientele came to admire, and under these three elegant emissaries, Nomura International had become the gentleman among Japanese brokers.

Part of Ito's dissatisfaction was that the Nomura overseas offices had grown soft under the undemanding Aida. They had lost sight of profitability. Moreover, Ito feared that Egashira and Terasawa were more Western than they were Japanese and indeed, after spending most of the 1970s changing places as head of New York and London, the two men had taken on Western airs. Ito would have none of their diplomacy and, as one ex-internationalist put it, 'It was time for Nomura to start churning stock abroad as the domestic sales force did it back home.' First Ito shoved Aida aside, then in 1979 he sent Egashira to London and the following year Terasawa to New York, a blow to both men since both secretly aspired to the presidency, and Tokyo was where they needed to be to garner power.

None the less, London suited Egashira's lifestyle and he knew it well, having headed Nomura's first London operation in 1964. Now he resumed his familiar lifestyle, with his tailor-made suits and his tastefully decorated and art-filled home in Dolphin Square. 'He knew the best restaurants and adored French food,' recalled John Quinn, a prominent fund manager who once worked under him. 'Seldom a night went by when he did not dine somewhere of note.' But while Egashira's London social life was resplendent, his career lapsed until he became no more than a Nomura figurehead. He resented interlopers into his London fiefdom, especially Ito. Egashira mingled with London's financial luminaries, and to him Ito was no more than a glorified salesman unable to speak the Queen's English. As the early 1980s progressed, Egashira's colleagues noticed him spending less and less time in the office. 'Attending concerts in Salzburg was his favourite pastime,' claimed an associate. 'I would call his secretary and she would say, "He is away on business and will be back in two weeks".'

The Apache cared only about making money for the firm, regardless of the friendships it cost Nomura. Egashira came to compare Nomura under Ito to a global bear, big and powerful, like the post-war Soviet Union, lumbering through the international forest, pawing at will. Before Ito arrived, Nomura had made its money by gently recommending stocks to its client base, but those days were now gone. The sales managers in London and New York did not report to Egashira or Terasawa, but directly to Ito himself in Tokyo. Talking among colleagues was forbidden, and reading and writing on the job were outlawed. The chief salesmen under Ito berated their staff constantly and took away the chairs of those who failed to meet commission quotas. 'One sales-man named Tanaka was yelled at and humiliated every day,' recalled Paul Smith, an ex-Nomura London salesman. 'After a few months he had to be hospitalized with a huge stress-related growth on the side of his neck.'

Ito was himself assertive to the point of abrasiveness. An arrogant but charismatic personality, big and rough in appearance, he was described by friends and enemies as something out of a western movie – hence his nickname. Even Egashira admitted that 'Ito was without a doubt the strongest personality in Nomura Securities'. But the charisma that had been so successful in Japan faltered overseas, despite an eight-year stint in the United States, and his halting, monosyllabic English won him few friends in international finance.

Masanori Ito had begun his career with Nomura in the Hiroshima branch. In 1948, three years after the atom bomb, he began peddling stock, an almost impossible task since food was still being rationed and few Japanese had any money. Instead, Ito sold kitchen utensils and lottery tickets door-to-door for Nomura. It was a grim time both for Japan and for Ito. He was, however, an outstanding salesman and secured his future within the Nomura power structure by aligning himself with Minoru Segawa. 'If Segawa liked you, luck was eliminated in rising to the top. All you had to do was just work hard,' admitted Yoshio Terasawa, whose illustrious career was, of course, also sponsored by Segawa.

Segawa favoured Ito partly because his pushy, aggressive and unpretentious behaviour reminded Segawa of himself and partly because both men had begun by selling stock in Hiroshima. There was another, compelling reason for Segawa's continued support. In 1954 one of Nomura's prized individual clients had lost massive amounts of money in the stockmarket and Segawa, to help atone, persuaded Ito to marry the client's daughter. The arrangement clearly put Segawa in debt to Ito and it was just a question of time before the favour would be repaid.

Carrying around a Segawa line of credit did not, however, immediately help Ito and his 1960s postings were marred by failure. He was posted to Osaka, then Hawaii ('a managerial backstep and no more than a tourist bureau', according to one internationalist) and on to San Francisco. Only after Ito requested a transfer back to the power base in Nomura Tokyo did things start to go his way. He was put in charge of marketing for domestic stock and bond products and after taking firm control over the marketing duties that created glossy Nomura brochures, he strengthened his power base by asserting control over the salesmen. With probably more nicknames than anyone inside Nomura, he became known as the 'Emperor'. Then, as if taking over all Nomura's domestic activity were not enough, in 1978 he called in his favour with Segawa and asked to be made head of the international side. Segawa could not refuse, and the Apache's conquest was complete.

Segawa acquiesced because while he had been away on business in 1978, Setsuya Tabuchi had been installed as the new president of the firm, while Kiichiro Kitaura, president from 1968 to 1978, had become chairman. The president of a Japanese company holds most of the power while the chairman is essentially a figurehead. It had been a polite way of telling Segawa his tenure as chairman was now over. He was bumped up to senior adviser. Segawa was outraged and wanted at least to ensure his own men were in control of Nomura's domestic and international business.

Ito's blundering heavy tactics, however, ruined the ambassadorial goodwill Nomura had built over the years. Once in Germany, at a meeting with high-level German bankers, he forcefully blamed them for the country's economic woes. An associate recalled him saying: 'German labour unions and trade problems are of your own making. Your country is dead.' He also had no time for the yearly summit with Merrill Lynch, initiated by Egashira, which in 1974 had brought together Donald Regan, William Schreyer and Minoru Segawa. The summit had become a traditional forum for America's and Japan's number one brokerage houses to swap ideas. Ito scrapped it once he was in office.

Although not popular with Westerners, Ito was startlingly successful at boosting Nomura's overseas profitability. In

1978, he formed a worldwide trading network out of Tokyo and told his overseas offices to wake Tokyo traders at any time of night if they needed to complete a deal. This was new to the salesmen in America and Europe, who, in the days of Aida, had no trading support from head office. But Ito carried aggression to an extreme and insisted his overseas teams apply a Japanese retail mentality to sell stock. He bought up huge blocks of stock on the Tokyo Stock Exchange and allocated chunks to each overseas office. Salesmen were told they had until the next morning to offload them. His was a numbers game that ended in harsh reproach when shares were unsold. 'You have failed,' he yelled at salesmen. Colleagues vividly recall him pointing a finger at Tokyo brokers and telling them 'Do not come into my sight again until you have sold all your shares.'

By 1982 Egashira wanted out. Life in London was strained. He was under unremitting pressure from the domestic team in Tokyo, and he was tired of reporting to Ito, whose aggressive mentality in European markets had destroyed every bridge he had built. In Egashira's world everyone needed friends and Nomura existed in harmony with the financial community. In Ito's world there existed only Nomura – the Japanese theme of *noma*, meaning 'volume', which came at the expense of the client and of the employees' private lives. Keisuke Egashira was fifty years old and had spent eighteen of his twenty-eight years in Nomura outside Japan, between London and New York. He carefully weighed the distinctions of the countries to which he had been assigned but Japan was his homeland, where his roots were, where his children, now out of school, were settling down. He had to get back before it was too late. 'Once I made the decision to move back to Tokyo, the idea of working in the Nomura home office atmosphere made no sense. I did not fit. I did not know anything of our domestic operations, which were still the main thrust of the firm. Without a footing in the domestic business, I felt I could not move above managing director, posing a serious problem to my future.' Ironically, Egashira the internationalist had become known as an isolationist within his own parochial firm; he was now too Western for Nomura.

While on business in Saudi Arabia with President Setsuya Tabuchi, Egashira found his chance to explain his position. A sandstorm had closed the airport and the two were holed up in their Riyadh hotel. 'When I go back to head office I will be too specialized. I will be handicapped,' he told Tabuchi. 'But Nomura, being Nomura, will not fire me. Instead I will have a high remuneration, a company car and expense account. Unless properly motivated, I cannot accept my monthly salary. Perhaps my role is coming to an end.' Forever the diplomat, Egashira, rather than mentioning his antipathy to Ito, spoke of the changing international business environment. New skills and technology were needed and perhaps it was time to change the crew. Tabuchi, seeing that Egashira had made up his mind, was understanding, slightly more understanding than Egashira had expected, and even offered financial backing for him to start up his own company. 'My concern is to see everyone, especially board members, happy.' There, in a Riyadh hotel room, Egashira terminated his Nomura career. A few months later he became the right-hand man of one of the world's richest men, Seiji Tsutsumi, and was appointed president of Seibu International, Japan's *avant garde* leisure and department store group.

Over two years earlier, in the spring of 1980, Minoru Segawa had asked to see Yoshio Terasawa. Almost twenty years earlier he had suggested a marriage partner for his young protege and ten years earlier he had sent Terasawa off to New York. Segawa, now seventy-four years old and the retired chairman of Nomura, was still seen as the king of Japanese stockbroking, the intimate of Japanese prime ministers, Diet members and hundreds of Japanese company presidents. Fifty-year-old Terasawa was slightly apprehensive despite the years of friendship between them. Segawa began by gently recounting Terasawa's experiences in New York as president of Nomura Securities International from 1970 to

1975. Then he came out with what he wanted of Terasawa: 'Why don't you consider going back to the States where we have so much to accomplish?'

Terasawa thought Segawa was joking. For the past five years he had been running Nomura's international finance division in Tokyo and had been promoted to a main board director; it was a nice life, with a driver and padded expense account. It was unheard of for a managing director and main board member, especially one who had served abroad already, to pull up stakes from the home office. Executive stockbroking promotions were based on working near the source of power in Tokyo, assuring men such as Terasawa a succession from managing director to executive managing director and finally to executive vice president with a chance of becoming president. He began to object but behind Segawa's polite tone he felt an unspoken command and simply listened to his senior.

'You will be pushed up by your juniors in Tokyo and down by your seniors. It is too bureaucratic here, why not be number one abroad instead of number ten in Japan?' Segawa guaranteed Terasawa complete autonomy in running the American office and emphasized Nomura's desire to get a New York Stock Exchange seat and a primary dealership for US government bonds. Segawa wanted an answer from Terasawa by the following week.

Before he left Terasawa asked, 'How long will I have to live there?'

'Until you die,' answered Segawa.

Terasawa was shocked and confused but realized he had no choice. When Segawa requested him to run the New York office, it was a veiled command from President Setsuya Tabuchi.

For Terasawa, a devout family man, there was no question of leaving his wife and four children behind in Japan as many Japanese businessmen posted overseas felt obliged to do, often because taking children out of the cut-throat Japanese school system stifled their future. Terasawa went

225

home expecting the children to be dismayed, but instead they were overjoyed. The oldest girl, Akiko, was fifteen and already fluent in English, and remembered clearly the family's earlier days in New York. The hard part, the children told their father, had been coming home to Japan from New York in 1975 speaking only kitchen Japanese. Haruko was thirteen, Kuniko twelve and Seido, their only son, nine years old and all were having some difficulties in school. Now, with the chance to go back to New York to see old friends, things seemed happier. Terasawa's wife Mariko was keen and a few days later Segawa's offer was accepted. Again, from behind the scenes, Ito had silently wielded his third hatchet.

Behind Terasawa's appointment lay the vision of Setsuya Tabuchi, who saw that expansion for Nomura meant exploring opportunities outside Japan, not merely in the already saturated Japanese market. Since the fifties, Nomura had relentlessly added fifteen offices throughout the world, but until Ito and the 1980s these were mere listening posts and never brought any significant money into the group. (The only exception had been the London office, which recycled Arab petrodollars into the stockmarket during the 1973 and 1979 oil shocks.) The answer to growth lay not just in expanding overseas but expanding into areas other than the securities business. Translating Tabuchi's vision into reality meant that Nomura's international machine would have to crank into overdrive.

23
Ivy League and Oxbridge

While Nomura's men adjusted to the Apache's new regime overseas, Ito had also decided that international success required American and European talent to complement his Japanese sales staff. By plucking Ivy League and Oxbridge men right from college, the ever-shrewd Apache reasoned, he could bring them to Tokyo and mould them in his own hard-hearted image, then send them out into the world as true Nomura men. They would provide a feeder system for Ito's burgeoning overseas offices. In the past, Nomura managers in London, Hong Kong and New York hired foreign talent on an informal, ad hoc basis. If they needed a British, Chinese or American stock salesman or bond trader, the local office simply budgeted for an extra body. Now things would be different: Nomura would hire students straight out of America's and England's finest universities to shape their minds and control their lives. One trainee later compared the programme to a factory that stamped out high-quality blank tapes on which Nomura were going to record. The occasional tape was defective or had to be erased but there were always more back at the factory. Everything about recruiting and stockbroking was a numbers game.

Nomura hired a middle-aged preppy named Jack Wallace to scour the United States for recruits, paying him $80,000 a year to interview college seniors and put together the Nomura class of 1982. As part of the East Coast old boys' network, Wallace fitted the basic criterion of Nomura's hiring policy: he had graduated from an Ivy League school, in this case Columbia, an important symbol to status-conscious Japanese; however in his Brooks Brothers suits and gleaming penny loafers, Wallace dressed in a fashion the Japanese felt was appropriate to represent their fully fledged investment house. Nomura needed a front man, someone with whom Wall Street could identify.

Twenty-eight graduates from America and England were hired in 1982 and flown to Tokyo – with consequences not foreseen by Ito and his understudy, Hitoshi Tonomura, a Nomura general manager assigned as overseer to the group. Immediately the trainees rebelled. They were used to Western comforts and lifestyle, and were horrified when shown the antiquated Nomura concrete cell-block dormitory in Funabashi, forty minutes north of the Nomura headquarters. The rooms were tiny and they had to take an elevator to the basement to take a shower or to jump in the communal bath. The food was to them barely edible. 'Who could possibly eat fish or rice with a raw egg on top for breakfast?' asked one of the trainees of Tonomura, who told them it was the same food eaten by Nomura's domestic salesmen, some of whom had been living in Funabashi for years. The trainees fought for cornflakes and won.

The programme turned into a cross-cultural battle as relations between Nomura and the trainees went from bad to worse. To the Japanese the newcomers had no social graces: they forgot to scrub themselves before jumping into the pure waters of the communal bath and their practical jokes led to broken furniture lying about the Funabashi barracks, which had been turned into a fraternity house. The two dozen men saw their trip to Japan as a holiday. 'None of us had even heard of Nomura before we joined,' admitted John Feree, one of the trainees from a later class. 'We just wanted to see Japan and once there wanted to travel, drink and chase women.' Nomura imposed a 10 pm curfew on the Funabashi dormitory to try to control these unruly young men anxious to visit the discos and watering holes of Roppongi and the back-street strip joints of Shinjuku. Tonomura listened to their rancorous complaints about conditions that any average salaryman took for granted, though there were particular problems: taxi drivers were reluctant to pick up foreigners, whom they perceived as unruly and unintelligible aliens. One student, after finally jumping in front of a cab, paid out seventy dollars for the ride to Funabashi only to discover the dormitory locked until six the next morning.

Although the trainees took the trip lightly, they were being paid $18,500 a year to attend daily lectures, write an occasional report, visit companies and sit on the sales desk. Each day they commuted by the crowded Tozai subway line into the Nomura head office in Nihonbashi. Sitting through the dry daily lectures given by Nomura's research department on economics, automobiles, chemicals or electronics was little sacrifice for what they considered to be an exotic holiday in Japan. Commercial bank training programmes on Wall Street were not paying much more than Nomura's base pay – $22,000 or $24,000 a year at most – while tight-fisted British companies seldom paid more than $10,000 a year. Moreover, although Nomura, unlike say Morgan Stanley or Goldman Sachs, was not a 'name' firm on Wall Street with which to impress peers, it did mean acquiring basic knowledge of Japanese finance, which held status.

Some of the American men from business school felt they should immediately take their rightful place in Nomura's management structure, but to Nomura these MBA graduates were yearlings whose two years of postgraduate work represented nothing but a piece of paper. Nobody was ever given his first management post in a Japanese securities firm until he had sweated for seven years. Trainees were expected to listen, work and remain silent. To be faced by inexperienced, ambitious young men talking back to managers and telling Nomura how to run its business was certainly not what was expected and in fact, one by one, the trainees from the class of 1982 left Nomura until, by 1985, none remained.

For Nomura, the experiment with Western trainees went a little better the next year. Steve Brunner was typical of the students Jack Wallace recruited to enter Nomura's class of 1983. A senior at Brown, an outstanding athlete and Phi Beta Kappa, he had been flipping through job descriptions in the career-planning department when he came across a firm that offered a trip to Japan, all expenses paid. Like most Americans, he had never heard of Nomura Securities, but he had always wanted to travel.

When Wallace arrived at the Brown campus in Providence, Rhode Island, at the end of March 1983, representing the last of the companies to interview on campus, he found very few students interested in Nomura, but he was impressed by Brunner and invited him to a second interview at Nomura's Wall Street headquarters. Here Brunner was to meet two other Nomura men; if approved, he would have still a third interview with fifteen of their colleagues. Brunner, who had memorized the yen/dollar exchange rate before his second interview, tried to steer the discussion to bonds, a subject he had briefly studied. He passed muster with these two Japanese, an investment banker who looked preoccupied and said practically nothing, and an amiable manager who seemed to speak as if from a script.

Round three proved more disconcerting, since Brunner had not expected to find himself facing fifteen straight-faced Japanese across a huge oak table. One that caught his eye was the stubby chain smoker seated at the end, whose feet, not reaching the floor, were swinging underneath his chair. This was Harunobu Aono, the manager in charge of trading but, more important, and unknown to Brunner, the manager of Nomura's baseball team. When asked about his interests, Brunner talked about the New York Mets. He had played football in college but enjoyed baseball as a youth, and on being asked 'Do you play baseball?' replied in earnest, 'I love baseball.' The Nomura men, aware that their baseball season would begin in only a few months, scanned this blond-haired, sturdy American. Brunner was hired.

The class of 1983 began work in July and eagerly awaited their autumn trip to Japan. The highlight of the summer took place in August with the baseball game for the highly coveted Nippon Cup. Each summer Japanese expatriates in New York strung together baseball teams from their banks, trading companies, sushi bars and brokerage houses for serious ball park competition and, as in Japan where companies such as National Electronics and Nippon Ham hire men for the firm's highly competitive intramural sports teams, so in New York the Japanese firms scout for talent.

This year Nomura had two secret weapons: it had recruited a top-flight Harvard pitcher named Brad Bauer, who swept the quarter and semifinals of the Nippon Cup, and a Puerto Rican messenger with a blistering fastball. On a clear Sunday morning at the St John's University stadium in Queens, the entire Nomura New York office gathered to watch their team play Enka Restaurant in the finals of the Nippon Cup. Aono, the squat head of trading, doubled as the team manager, while New York Chairman Yoshio Terasawa and the other fans drank themselves into roaring appreciation. Enka never had a chance against the pitching of Nomura's hired talent and after the victory everyone circled around Aono and threw him high into the air.

The young American trainees became instant heroes and with a big grin, Terasawa came up to Brunner, who had been celebrating heavily, and handed him the keys to his Cadillac. 'Steve, you drive.' Brunner recalled later that 'I could hardly walk and the chairman of my new company, a big honcho on Wall Street, even more drunk than I was, tells me to drive us all home to his apartment on Fifth Avenue.' Back at Terasawa's apartment, the festivities continued, and the ebullient Terasawa called his Tokyo office,where it was Monday, to announce the great news. He then rang up all the New York managers and told them to meet for dinner and a night of *karaoke* – or group – singing.

Most of the managers who had been at the game were sleeping off their stupor while others were spending a quiet Sunday evening with their families, but all of them showed up. The evening ended with Terasawa again handing Brunner the Cadillac keys: 'Good night, Steve. You drive my car home, I am taking a taxi.' The next day at work Brunner had just finished his turn throwing up in the men's room when a call came through from Terasawa, himself sounding slightly queasy. 'Steve, where did you park my car?' Brunner drew a blank, forgetting that he had driven all over New York trying to find Terasawa's parking garage. Confidently he took a guess, 'I left it in your garage with the keys in it.' Terasawa, who had obviously been in no condition to check that morning, replied, 'Oh, okay. Thanks.' Fortunately Brunner was right.

In Tokyo, after the previous year's fiasco with the Western trainees, the Apache had decided to call on Shoko Araki, an attractive middle-aged Japanese woman who had once lived in the United States. She became Nomura's cultural mediator for the class of 1983 and was an ideal choice. Shoko Araki had been a radio announcer in her early twenties in her native Sapporo. She had studied at San Francisco State University and Stanford as a research scholar in intercultural training, becoming a radio announcer in the Bay area before moving back to Japan in 1978 to broadcast on the national radio programme, Radio Japan, while continuing to advise companies on intercultural relations. She worked for Procter and Gamble in Japan, teaching Japanese men, and their wives, how to adapt to life in a foreign company and had earned the respect and trust of both men and women because of her intelligence, soft tone and warmth.

That autumn, with thirty-five students, the largest foreign class Nomura would ever have, Shoko started bridging the cultural abyss that separated Nomura and its restless young businessmen. The class of ambitious, athletic and slightly arrogant men which included the American contingent fresh from the victory in the Nippon Cup, came instantly under Shoko's spell. She taught them about working in a Japanese environment where they would be considered, if they were even considered at all, to be mere striplings. It was the Japanese way, she told them; do not fight it, accept it. She taught them not to be so ready to express their views and intentions as Americans tended to; the British, masters of reticence, were more adept here. Non-verbal communication was as important within Nomura as it was in Japan as a whole, so she taught them how to use body language, certain hand gestures, facial movements and silence to express their views in a more effective manner than a blustery bellow.

Her classes gave opportunities to vent the frustrations of the freshmen and to air the grievances of management. One manager, upset by the way the slovenly trainees left their cups and dishes lying around the Nomura classroom, showed them by silent example how to clean the room, believing that now he had lowered himself without complaining, the trainees would be humiliated and would clean up after themselves. The next day the manager visited the classroom only to find the room again scattered with litter and no sign of remorse on the part of the trainees. 'They were in fact laughing and telling jokes even as I walked into the room,' he told Shoko. 'They did not even notice me.' Shoko calmed him down and explained that active expressions of silence went unnoticed by the foreigners because they acted on verbal communication. No malice or disrespect was intended.

Shoko then politely lectured the group about the incident, trying to convey a deeper understanding of the meaning of silence and of tea in Japan. 'One cannot force people to speak in Japan and tea has always been a form of communication to us. You are in Japan now and must use all different forms of the Japanese language.' She recounted that when she returned from America to work at the national radio station, she was in an office entirely staffed by men. At the customary Japanese afternoon tea break, knowing that women in Japanese society were not allowed to drink tea alone, and not being part of any group, she had walked over and poured out twelve cups of tea for the office men. She never stood on the fact that she had a post-graduate degree from the United States and more media experience than any of them. 'It would have done me no good to have proclaimed the woman's rights I learned in the States. This is Japan and in Japan a woman, regardless of intelligence or professional capability, pours the tea.'

She also told them how to take advantage of roles in society and to throw out Western conceptions of how men and women were supposed to act in the 1980s. Japan still had roles for its men and women. Japanese housewives had enormous power since they controlled the family budget and children's education. She explained to the young men how Japanese women perceived relationships, a topic of keen interest, telling them that one of her Japanese girlfriends had become attached to a Westerner after a first date, assuming that since he had kissed her she was under an obligation to marry him. 'Kissing is taken very seriously by the Japanese woman and you should be careful not to lead them on.' The men in the classroom sniggered at such naivete but they did begin paying a little more attention to their mating rituals. Shoko's teachings had an impact.

Shoko Araki's training was such a success that Nomura asked her back the following year. The class of 1984 spent a lot more time in the classroom attending lectures headed by Harunobu Aono of Nippon Cup fame, who had since been transferred back to Tokyo. Each week was broken up on Wednesday by company visits when the group piled into a bus and, led by their Japanese chaperon, Shigeru Takeyama, met with management of two companies quoted on the Tokyo Stock Exchange.

One particular visit, to the Sapporo Brewery plant in Ebisu in central Tokyo, was especially memorable. Sapporo Breweries gave the fraternal group a tour of its plant and generously offered them all the beer they could drink, an offer that Takeyama readily accepted. At the end of a riotous morning, Sapporo supplied 150 cans of wine for the two-hour-long bus ride to Fuchu City for their next appointment, with Tokyo Electron, a manufacturer of semiconductor production equipment.

By the time the bus rolled into Fuchu City most of the students had drunk ten large mugs of beer and five or six cans of wine. The Tokyo Electron spokesman was not amused when he met this group. The tour required everyone to put on surgical masks and slippers to prevent dust from circulating in the ultra-sensitive manufacturing rooms where instruments made delicate incisions, but the Nomura group became increasingly riotous, throwing slippers and masks around.

Later that day Tokyo Electron informed Nomura's management it would no longer accept visitors from Nomura Securities. Management apologized profusely, blaming the problem on reprehensible foreign behaviour. The class of 1984 was told that they would be shipped home if a similar outbreak ever occurred again.

Nomura would, however, never have to ship anyone home. By 1985 most of the Nomura trainees left of their own accord. Many of the recruits were using Nomura to learn about Japan before jumping to another job, and others without such intentions suddenly found themselves able to command astronomical salaries as Westerners versed in the Japanese stockmarket. Stockbrokers who understood Japan were to become the darlings of finance in the mid-1980s, and Nomura would be the prime target of Western firms trying to build up Japanese equity sales teams. The Nomura trainees of 1982 and 1983 were in many ways the first in a foreign wave of talent that would go on to make their name in Japanese finance. They were happy making $1,541.66 per month at Nomura until they discovered friends earning similar figures per week at Western firms. By 1988 every foreign Nomura trainee could dictate his terms, and most went on to earn six figures, often over $250,000 a year.

24
Expansion in New York

The superstar salesman to whom the trainees reported once they returned to New York was a remarkable thirty-three-year-old named Yoshitaka Kitao. An amusing man with large black glasses, short hair and a padded double chin, he loved food, and the large belly that protruded over his belt, his salesmen claimed, came from his fondness for beer and potatoes. Kitao sold Japanese stock with a ferocity that came from working under the Apache. He earned the firm $580,000 in commissions each month, roughly $7 million a year. Only two other Japanese on Wall Street pulled in that kind of money, Kitao's counterparts at Nikko and Daiwa Securities. For his sales prowess Kitao was rewarded with $175,000 a year before taxes, high earnings for any Japanese who was not a director in any Japanese firm. He received perks that separated him from other Japanese expatriate salarymen, such as an apartment in a high-rise at York and 83rd Street on the Upper East Side. Most other Nomura men had to commute for over an hour from the Japanese ghettoes in Riverside or New Jersey. Kitao simply drove the company Toyota fifteen minutes down the FDR Drive to Nomura's office at the tip of Manhattan, where he was provided with a parking space at a rent not much less than that of a suburban apartment.

The headquarters of Nomura Securities International, the command centre of Nomura's American operations, occupy the 37th and 38th floors of the shimmering glass building known as the Continental Center. The offices are splendid compared to the cluttered and battered Nomura world head-quarters in Tokyo's Nihonbashi district. A waterfall splashes in the gilded, high-reaching main lobby, while security guards look upon every entrant as guilty until proved innocent. The brown-panelled Nomura reception area on the 38th floor leads to offices with deep-pile carpeting, and nearby a fashionable custom-built staircase with an elegant chandelier hanging above it descends to the 37th floor. In appearance, at least, Nomura has decided to be an American company doing business on Wall Street and so, playing the game, its offices exude opulence. Such extravagance was financed by Kitao's activities.

The old guard, such as the Apache, could point to Kitao to justify their use of Japanese domestic sales tactics bringing in the bucks overseas. Posted to New York as the head of sales to hawk Japanese stocks, Kitao was the embodiment of Nomura's foot-soldier salesmen back home in Japan. To men like Ito, Kitao was retail broking at its best – to Kitao's American subordinates, at its worst. He told salesmen they were never to leave their desks unless they were visiting clients and they should always be on the phone. One day when he jokingly tied Steve Brunner's wrist to the telephone with a piece of string, Brunner recalled thinking, 'Something told me there was a lot of truth in the jest.'

Kitao's lifeline to promotion, his umbilical cord to Tokyo management sitting 7,000 miles away, was the lifeline that tied all Nomura salesmen to their future: commission. Commission equalled glory. To Nomura, Kitao was no more than another salesman in another branch that was called New York. He could have been in Hiroshima or Osaka, Yokohama or Sapporo.

The large commission-generating accounts such as Fidelity, Cititrust, Prudential and Dupont were serviced by Kitao himself. He distributed the remaining first- and second-tier accounts to the other Japanese salesmen. Large American accounts were never called on by Americans. It made no difference that most of Nomura's Japanese salesmen in New York spoke stammering English and that an American could disseminate Nomura's ideas more effectively to his own countrymen. Once a Japanese was cut off from big accounts overseas, he died. He would not therefore consign himself to obscurity by handing the large accounts to Americans, even if it would have meant more commission for Nomura. Let the Americans struggle.

The frustrated American trainees were left with the scraps. As a result those American salesmen deriving the firm's income in yen securities, such as Japanese stocks, were paid relatively low salaries that 'bordered on wages', as a disgruntled salesman remarked. He had been content to join Nomura to earn over $18,000 a year but now, several years into a bull market on Wall Street, was watching everyone else pull in six figures. 'Those guys selling dollar stocks and bonds to investors were making two or three times what we made. Nomura treated anyone selling Japanese stocks as an appendage of the domestic sales network, while those selling products unfamiliar to Nomura such as American stocks and bonds were treated and paid well.' The disparity grew as the American stock and bond departments became more profitable. Something had to change.

John Feree, a scholarly graduate of Wharton, fascinated by Japan, aligned himself with Kitao to survive in Nomura New York. Kitao allocated every trade he could to his own name. He wanted power back in Tokyo and nothing else mattered, but occasionally he helped those he favoured by allocating an unsolicited buy order to their name. Feree was painfully aware that Americans were given unprofitable third-tier accounts, which he said often meant calling stodgy mid-western pension fund accounts who had problems finding Japan on a map. Feree was on the bottom limb of the giant Nomura tree and hoped that by helping Kitao shake the tree, some of its fruit would find its way on to his lap. This approach had its hazards.

Kitao, knowing Feree was from a wealthy oil family in Texas, exploited that connection by taking him on a marketing trip down south. Feree personally owned 5 per cent of a major oil company listed on the New York Stock Exchange and his stake had been worth over $50 million on paper during the boom years of the early 1980s, but later fell to less than $1 million. His family were stalwart Republicans, his mother chairwoman of the Republican Committee in Texas, deep in George Bush country. Kitao did not understand any of these social nuances. He only cared about the pedigree of Feree because of the increased revenue it promised for Nomura. He arranged for Feree to meet him in San Antonio for a client breakfast meeting, but the American missed a connecting flight and called up Kitao from Houston to say he could not make San Antonio by the morning. Kitao replied, 'John, when I your age nothing stood in path of what I wanted. Time no concern. You take bus to San Antonio tonight.' Humbled, Feree endured a miserable bus journey and arrived in San Antonio at 3.30 am to find his hotel reservation cancelled. From a lobby phone he woke up Kitao, who called him upstairs and announced, 'John, you sleep with me tonight so we save on hotel room.' Three hours later they got up for a breakfast meeting and then flew back to Houston.

Nomura usually had at least one chance to convince even sceptical institutions that they should buy Japanese stocks. One of the hardest accounts to crack on Wall Street was that of Steinhardt Partners. Steinhardt was a highly successful hedge fund, a pool of money run by its founder Michael Steinhardt, who sought huge gains in return for a percentage of the reward. Hedge funds were not registered with the Securities and Exchange Commission and their managers were known as gunslingers on Wall Street, playing the highest leveraged instruments available and frequently putting their own money on the line. The Japanese stockmarket to them was a gambling casino and qualified as a highly leveraged game. Most hedge funds survived no more than five years, but Steinhardt Partners was a shining exception, having been in existence since the 1960s.

Kitao set up a meeting with Steinhardt and appealed to Steinhardt's love of high-paying gambles by telling him of a winner Nomura wanted him to buy stock in – Asahi Chemical, which, according to Nomura's information, had

239

just discovered a wonder drug to cure cancer. Steinhardt readily placed an order through Nomura for a million shares on the Tokyo Stock Exchange, buying them at 700 yen each. Within a week they had rocketed to 815 and Steinhardt sold the shares through Nomura for a 16 per cent profit. Kitao, meanwhile, had become the hero of the office: he had done the impossible and had dealt for Steinhardt. Nomura New York had arrived.

Steinhardt pushed Kitao into recommending another stock and, brimming with confidence, Kitao bought him a huge block of shares in the Honda Motor Company, a sure winner. But unknown to Nomura New York, on that same day the Nomura auto analyst on tour in Europe had sent a secret telex to Nomura Tokyo informing them that Honda would not achieve its profit forecast for the fiscal year. According to a salesman close to Kitao, as New York slept that evening, Nomura Tokyo quietly sold shares from their investment trust and then warned their large clients of the looming problem. The price began falling on the Tokyo Stock Exchange. By the time the London market opened, the price of Honda had fallen even further in over-the-counter trading and when the price opened on the New York Stock Exchange, the share was down 4 per cent. Steinhardt called Kitao and demanded an explanation. Kitao had no answer and not until the following day did he discover that his own analyst had issued an official sell recommendation. When the price of Honda had plummeted 12 per cent from the level at which Steinhardt had bought, Steinhardt closed the account and Kitao went from hero to goat.

Though Kitao was a master at hopping from one American institution to the next, the days of the Apache's influence were coming to an end. It was still 1984, still a year until a younger, more diplomatic man, Yoshihisa Tabuchi (no relation to Setsuya Tabuchi), would take over the presidency of Nomura, but change was in the air. Tokyo management was becoming upset over foreign accounts lost to commission-hungry salesmen. Tokyo wanted respect and it was willing to buy it. The man chosen was a short, well-dressed and self-assured American bond trader by the name of Robin Koskinen, who over the next few years would single-handedly reforge Nomura's name on the street and do it without ever touching the stockmarket.

A graduate in English literature from Colgate, Koskinen had entered Bankers Trust in 1972, moved to the Bank of Boston in 1976 and then to Blythe Eastman Dillon in 1978, until it was absorbed by Paine Webber in 1979. A year later he had joined Eagle Income Management. In the summer of 1984 he was headhunted by Nomura, and hired by Yoshio Terasawa to head Nomura's United States government bond trading team. Nomura Tokyo had realized in the early 1980s the importance of US treasuries and took a keen interest in Koskinen's success because it represented a future revenue stream; Japanese investors wanted the higher yield that American bonds offered – as much as 4 per cent higher than bonds in Japan. Nomura Tokyo bought US bonds in New York and, depending on market conditions, passed them on to Tokyo clients at a profit.

A practical man with vision, Koskinen was the perfect manager. Unlike most bond traders he was neither egocentric nor threatened by the idea of surrounding himself with talent. The first thing he did on arrival at Nomura was to replace the outmoded dealing equipment – a hodgepodge of dealing screens sitting randomly atop desks. Traders had even been using abacuses. Not one for cultural nuance, the no-nonsense Koskinen got rid of the wooden beads and put personal computers, previously non-existent, on nearly every desk. Skimping on equipment was not an option in bond trading. Brokerage firms needed to react with precision to political and economic news, making lightning-quick decisions to buy or sell millions of dollars.

One Nomura colleague thought that Koskinen's greatest strength was his patience, an essential trait bearing in mind the numerous and often frustrating Japanese meetings he had to attend. Everything was done through consensus and

Koskinen let the Japanese 'win the countless little victories, knowing all along he would win the war', according to one of his close colleagues. With a compulsive attention to detail that bothered some of his colleagues, he saved Nomura hundreds of thousands, if not millions, of dollars. He examined the back office, the last place most managers wished to venture, but it was here amidst the ill-educated Puerto Rican and black settlement clerks that Koskinen knew much of the money was made and lost on Wall Street. The longer it took Nomura to process a trade between buyer and seller, the more money it lost on interest payments.

Bond transactions were substantially larger than stock deals and involved millions of dollars on which Nomura made a razor-thin margin, a sixteenth of one percentage point at best. Before Koskinen's arrival Nomura was not even discovering unsettled trade problems until a day after they were supposed to be settled. According to Koskinen, Nomura settled all bond trades inefficiently through Bankers Trust via Morgan Guaranty and was losing a fortune in interest payments, so he switched all Nomura's bond settlement to Security Pacific, who guaranteed timely settlement. Once he had brought Nomura up to speed operationally, it was time to pull ahead of the market, and for this he needed experienced bond traders. To launch trainees into the world's most cut-throat market was out of the question.

Bond traders had become expensive since the New York financial markets had awakened in the summer of 1982. When Koskinen entered the market for talent in 1985, a bond trader with five years' experience who was not taking home a $200,000 salary was considered a failure, and good, not necessarily spectacular, traders were making over a million dollars a year. The Dow Jones Industrial Average had risen over 30 per cent between 1982 and the beginning of 1985, and bond prices had risen even more quickly, 40 per cent since interest rates had peaked in late 1982. Finesse was required to lure big-name players from Wall Street, and Koskinen painted for candidates a picture of working for the largest securities firm in the world with a historic opportunity to pioneer its entry into the largest marketplace in the world, the US treasury market. Hindered by a low budget, he could offer seasoned traders only a quarter of their salary at major Wall Street firms but he was able to outline a team pool system whereby a percentage of all profits would be split. The salaries were low but there was no limit to the bonus. Nomura management, usually opposed to profit-sharing schemes, granted Koskinen this concession.

Koskinen began picking off the competition one by one, first coaxing head trader Tom Griven from his comfortable perch as executive vice president at Drexel Burnham Lambert in January 1985. Larry Isabel, the national sales manager at Bankers Trust, was his next big acquisition in August 1985, followed by Andy O'Flagherty, a senior vice president at Dean Witter Reynolds, in October. He then hired a former assistant secretary of the Treasury as the Nomura sales manager and, finally, snatched his fifth heavyweight, the chief economic officer at Harris Trust Bank of Chicago. By the end of 1985 Nomura, which had done no business in US bonds in 1984, accounted for more volume than the average primary dealer. Now Koskinen was gunning for a primary membership, a highly sensitive affair given the trade friction between Japan and America.

A primary dealership allowed Nomura to bid for US treasury bonds, thus to be among the very few bond dealers allowed to put their hand into the national pocketbook. When Nomura applied for membership in September 1985, it was unwittingly the last company to go through the formal process of sending letters to all other members announcing its intention. Koskinen then paid courtesy calls on the members, most of whom he recalls as being gracious towards Nomura entering the ring as the first Japanese primary dealer, although Drexel Burnham Lambert, whose chairman was irked that Koskinen had pinched one of his stars, was opposed.

Salomon Brothers announced its public support of Nomura

since it was demanding a Tokyo Stock Exchange membership and access to the Japanese bond market, but privately, according to Koskinen, did everything it could to thwart Nomura. One Salomon executive remembered that in 1975 Masanori Ito had sent three men from the Nomura Research Institute to learn about bond computer trading systems in the Salomon bond department. According to Shoichi Kadokawa in his 1985 book *Why 'Finance' is Nomura*, the men wanted more than the limited access they were given to Salomon's confidential manuals. These outlined everything Nomura needed to know about bond trading. They wooed the woman controlling the manuals and, after presenting her with an expensive pearl brooch, persuaded her to lend them out overnight. The three men stayed up all night photocopying the ten volumes and returned them to Salomon the next morning, saving Nomura at least a year of painstaking research and leaving Salomon with a nasty memory.

Under Koskinen, Nomura built one of the world's premier bond-trading operations. Sensationalists would claim that it kept the United States government in business. Without Nomura, they said, America would be bankrupt. It was a slight exaggeration, of course, since the other Japanese brokers, especially Daiwa, were heavy bond purchasers. Nonetheless, Koskinen became the conduit for much of Japan's wealth, channelling it into the high-yielding sanctuary of US bonds. The one-way flow of funds from Japan to America through most of the mid-1980s certainly supported United States government-backed bonds and American investors became understandably nervous whenever the Japanese were reluctant to purchase their bonds, since the Japanese accounted for nearly 30 per cent of US government bond purchases from 1985 to 1987. With a short flight of imagination it was easy to see how any lapse at Nomura or Daiwa posed a national security risk to America. If the Japanese stopped buying bonds then America had significantly less money to run the country – interest rates would rise in an attempt to lure buyers. Meanwhile, higher rates would rupture the stockmarket and choke off economic expansion, sending unemployment soaring.

25
Crisis in New York

For a short time the striking success of Nomura's American bond traders masked the near-demise of the company's New York office. In 1985 it was ripped apart by petty squabbles and warring fiefdoms within the upper management. The problem began when Nomura decided to compete with the big Wall Street houses by selling American stocks to Americans but failed so miserably that the entire New York office almost collapsed.

Nomura first thought it could tackle the big boys on Wall Street in the early 1980s. In fact it was Yoshio Terasawa's idea. Terry ('Just call me Terry' he would tell people on first meeting them, a rarity for Japanese, who usually liked to be addressed formally) was a forward thinker, a power broker whose social skills had enabled him to survive within Nomura without making enemies. On Wall Street the Americans loved him because he looked, and played, the part of a chairman. Well connected and sociable, he had a certain athletic grace that complemented his broad, smiling, tanned face, while his grey-streaked black hair lent a distinguished air, accented by his well-tailored grey suits and button-down shirts. One colleague commented that 'Terry's presence was that of someone six feet tall but it was not until you observed him the second or third time you noticed how short he really was'.

Although Terry's dream of becoming president of Nomura Securities had ended when he was shipped off to New York in 1980, his tenure in the States differed from that of most other Japanese expatriate executives in lasting, as Segawa had pointed out, 'until you die'. This left him with autonomy, independence from Tokyo and an added confidence. While other Japanese in New York were haunted by their head office and busy preparing a power base for the return home to Japan, Terasawa had nowhere to return to and, with no downside career risk and nobody to impress, he became quite aggressive compared to other Japanese businessmen. With the piles of cash that his fellow countrymen were sitting on back home, Terry thought that it was only a matter of time before the Japanese funnelled their money into New York. Therefore Nomura would begin bidding for chunks of corporate America on behalf of Japan.

First he set about buying a New York Stock Exchange seat, and achieved his goal in 1981, becoming the first Japanese to do so (only individuals, acting on behalf of corporations, could buy a membership). He then searched Wall Street for someone to build Nomura's American trading and sales team, and in 1984 appointed a *nisei*, or second-generation Japanese, named Norm Ohtaka, an experienced, middle-aged man who lorded over traders responsible for trading every imaginable foreign stock – Japanese to British, Australian to Dutch. Ohtaka had begun his career at Nikko Securities in 1963 and had the distinction of having started more overseas trading desks than anyone in the financial world, moving to Drexel Burnham Lambert, then to First Boston and finally Shearson. But to the Japanese within Nomura, Ohtaka was perceived as an anomaly, more a threat than an experienced leader. He was an outsider brought into an operation above Nomura men who had spent their lives in the company. Moreover, as an ex-colleague commented, 'From the beginning, the Japanese thought Ohtaka too Western and the Americans thought him too Japanese.'

Ohtaka, however, was no stranger to Nomura politics. In 1977 Keisuke Egashira had tried to hire him. Though Ohtaka admired Egashira, he had refused to join Nomura because he disliked the power struggle between the domestic and international teams. With hindsight, he thought his decision to spend the seven years elsewhere was correct: 'The internationalists were all purged by Ito and the outright victory by the domestics hindered the growth of Nomura.' Not everyone agreed with Ohtaka's view that

Ito damaged Nomura: 'Only the internationalists believe Nomura suffered,' said a former Nomura manager. 'I was one of the men who hated Ito's methods, but we were a minority.' By 1984 the damage done by the domestic team was being repaired as overseas and international talent in Nomura began to regroup itself. Ohtaka saw an opportunity to become a leader of a new team when he joined Nomura New York in July 1984. He was promised that management would rectify changes made during the previous power struggle, which meant giving Ohtaka a mandate to spend whatever money he needed to build an equity trading team.

Ohtaka laid out a pragmatic blueprint. First he needed help from other Nomura departments, namely research and sales, while his team would worry about providing stock at competitive prices. The problem, he soon discovered, was the division of responsibility between trading, sales and research, which was more acute in a Japanese than an American company. To make matters worse, there was dissent within his own trading group over his responsibility. The biggest problem Ohtaka faced, however, was hiring talented Americans on the meagre pay scale Nomura offered. And he needed Americans because few Japanese in the firm were sufficiently conversant with English to persuade America's biggest money managers to deal in the Japanese market, let alone the US market.

It soon became apparent that the New York office under chairman Terasawa, 'a respected figure on Wall Street with little power in Nomura', did not have the political muscle to put through the budget Ohtaka needed to hire talent. He had overestimated Nomura Tokyo's dedication to the US market. Although the New York office had recovered from the international purge of the late 1970s, it did not yet have the power base in Tokyo to expand by committing the firm's capital. Management wanted to see the dollars rolling in before they allocated big money to New York.

Such circumspect logic baffled Ohtaka, who knew a firm could not produce money without talent, nor talent without money. He was forced to concentrate what little money he had on building up the American trading team. As far as Ohtaka was concerned, the Japanese trading team could run itself. 'Instead of hiring talent of the calibre of eight on a scale of one to ten, I found myself hiring green traders and salesmen of a calibre of two or at most three.' He thought that by training these men he could make enough money, once profits started coming in, to hire skilled traders.

Meanwhile, a Japanese resistance group, which resented Ohtaka's profile, power and earnings, was building up within the firm. It was spearheaded by 'Andy' Saito, who was in charge of all equity sales at Nomura New York and loosely third in the power structure after Chairman Terasawa and President Akira Shimizu. A casually dressed, rough-talking manager, Saito had worked his way up the retail ranks. He was tough on subordinates, 'as bad to the Americans as he was to the Japanese', said one Japanese manager; and John Quinn, one of the few men who liked working under Saito, recalled his preoccupation with making money: 'Everything was how much did we make, how much did we make.'

Terasawa, like most chairmen of Japanese companies, was seldom in the office and delegated full responsibility to Shimizu, to the irritation of Saito, who wanted total control of the New York office. Since his Japanese and American equity departments accounted for 45 per cent of Nomura New York's profits, Saito felt he had some right to power and he endeavoured to thwart every directive from his boss, Shimizu. Shimizu, meanwhile, was putting his efforts into the new bond side of the business and mistakenly leaving the daily management of the New York office to his covert enemy.

Saito was able to play on the weakness of Shimizu's position in Tokyo, where Shimizu's rapid switch of allegiance from Aida to Ito in the late 1970s now left him exposed, and this rebounded on Ohtaka: 'Being the new guy I had no connections in Tokyo and relied upon Shimizu, who I slowly realized had no contacts at the home office.' Meanwhile Saito had the attention of Tabuchi Senior, who was still president, and undermined Shimuzu on every important management decision Shimizu made. Saito's young salesmen were encouraged not to listen to Shimizu; 'Saito promised them the moon in return for their backing,' said Ohtaka.

Shimizu, under daily pressure from the lack of support received from his superiors overseas, realized that there was a move to oust him from the international department or, worse, from the firm. While Saito was away for three months during the autumn of 1985, on a McKinsey management training course, Shimizu had Saito recalled to Tokyo. Kitao, a great trader but hopeless manager, tried to fill the power vacuum left by Saito.

With the day-to-day tension in the office, morale hit a low in the late summer of 1985. Nomura New York was split between those in the Shimizu/Ohtaka faction and those in the Saito faction, whose leader had just left them for three months and who were further confused that autumn when they heard that their messiah was leaving for good. Who would deliver all the promises they had been given? Who would transform their allegiance into promotion and money? Meanwhile Kitao, as senior salesman, tried to force himself on both camps. Then Ohtaka and his traders began squabbling.

The spirit of the American salesmen trying to peddle Japanese stocks from New York was broken as they found themselves treated as 'mere telephone operators', as if they were an extension of Nomura's domestic Japanese sales force. Tensions rose when the Nomura Investment Management Company decided to issue a US dollar-based mutual fund to fulfil America's desire to invest in Japan. New York salesmen were ordered by Nomura Tokyo to dig up $40 million from investors.

The assets of this mutual fund were primarily stocks listed on the Tokyo Stock Exchange. Nomura wanted fast results and gave each salesman a monthly quota of $500,000 to meet, reckoning that with twenty salesmen it would take four months to reach the $40 million target. Every Friday the salesmen convened to discuss progress, meetings which became gradually more heated as they realized that Nomura would not even achieve its $25 million breakeven point for the fund by the autumn.

Most large institutions already familiar with Japan had no interest in Nomura investing their money since they could buy and sell stocks themselves *through* Nomura. Big pension funds were prospective targets but they were cautious decision makers. Nomura had bought client lists from companies that provided names of high net worth individuals scattered throughout the United States but the lists were unreliable and salesmen were put in embarrassing situations, calling on people long since deceased or relocated. It was a frustrating numbers game, where every tenth phone call ended in abuse. As pressure increased to sell the fund, salesmen were told to forget about calling their regular clients on the Japanese stockmarket: 'Sell the fund.' What had been an effective office of twenty institutional salesmen in the first half of 1985 was reduced to a disgruntled, rebellious retail sales force.

Meanwhile, Kitao was under enormous pressure from Tokyo to push the salesmen. Steve Brunner recalled one meeting where he was berated by a Japanese salesman for not selling the fund: 'Brunner, you suck, you are a shitty salesman, why are you a broker?' Brunner, normally not one to back down from a fight, realized that the salesman had cracked under the pressure and so said nothing; in fact he was doing the same amount of business as the other Americans and brought in $300,000 of net commission to Nomura in 1985. Public abuse was problem enough for the thick-skinned Americans; but for the Japanese ridicule from a superior in front of peers was a terrible degradation. As the weekly targets were invariably missed, excuses were invented: 'The client went out of town suddenly' or ' I cannot get in touch with them' and absenteeism increased, tempers flared and frustrations mounted. By December 1985 the fund had raised only $26 million and was months behind schedule, and most Americans had decided by bonus time on 6 December that they would find another job.

Ohtaka thought of the mutual fund as only one in a series of failed campaigns (which included a computer sales drive) to promote products not yet ready for their market. He recognized that the political battle between Saito and Shimizu had taken its toll but he thought, wrongly, that the bonuses to be paid at the beginning of December would help inspire the American traders and salesmen. The Americans working under Ohtaka on US equity thought him niggardly on bonuses, though they were making four times more than the Japanese stock salesmen. Americans everywhere except in the bond department were feeling insecure. Two sets of meetings were held each day, a company-wide meeting followed by an exclusive Japanese meeting, further widening the gap between East and West. Americans felt excluded from all management decisions, since it was obvious their meeting was to inform rather than to discuss. The American bond traders seemed immune from the internal strife, while their counterparts selling Japanese stocks were in despair: all they got were the small accounts and the market-sensitive information was withheld. Questions sent by fax in English to the Nomura International Research and Advisory Department in Tokyo were answered in Japanese and had to be translated back into English.

The chief figure in revolt against Ohtaka after the bonus decisions was the Nomura head position trader, Billy King. Position traders, relatively minor players in Japanese firms since the big money was earned from commission, were the backbone of many Wall Street brokerage houses, buying and selling stock for the firm's own account to generate profit. King had wanted a guaranteed $125,000, including bonus, to join Nomura in 1984. Ohtaka had persuaded him to take a percentage of the commission he brought in, telling King, rightly, that he would make more money. During the spring and summer of 1985 King brought home monthly paychecks averaging $16,000 a month and most of the salesmen who watched him trade called him brilliant.

In 1985 as a whole, King brought Nomura $2 million in revenue and was paid close to $200,000; Ohtaka felt there was no need to compensate him with a bonus since his monthly paycheck fairly reflected his work. But King wanted a bonus and moreover felt constrained by his cautious boss, wanting more autonomy to trade. Ohtaka had too much responsibility and was afraid of letting King loose: 'He was still immature in many ways.'

Ohtaka also had difficulties with Joan McCullough, a senior sales trader whom he hired to work under King. Her job was to call on large American institutions to ferret out business. A fiery Irish blonde from New Jersey, who had worked her way up to being a name on Wall Street through sheer temerity, she had been guaranteed a pay-out of $200,000 by Ohtaka with a promise of more money if she exceeded her revenue target. The Japanese, wary of Billy King's aggressive trading style, were at first totally flummoxed by the bawdy antics and outbursts of foul language of McCullough. Despite this, within a month she was a big hit in the New York and Tokyo offices. Accustomed to a grand lifestyle, she was outraged when Ohtaka paid her no bonus on the grounds that her sales trading profits fell far short of her goal for the year. McCullough blamed her failure on the substandard research Nomura was producing on the US market and, though Ohtaka paid her the entire $200,000 promised, she still wanted a bonus.

The disgruntled King, who had long been a disciple of Saito, and was now without a standard bearer, went off to a traders' convention in Chicago, overstayed by a day and booked himself into a palatial suite of rooms. Ohtaka, discovering the cost of the suite, had a fight with King over the phone, which ended with King shouting every kind of obscenity at his boss. Ohtaka, after calling a Nomura in-house counsel to discuss the procedure, sacked him.

As soon as he was fired King called McCullough to orchestrate a boycott in his support and the *Wall Street Journal* was informed of their walkout. 'Once insubordination takes place in a brokerage firm the standard procedure is to fire all the leaders in order to protect the integrity of the operation,' claimed Ohtaka. Nomura, however, did not play by the rules simply because it did not know the rules, nor did it back Ohtaka's sacking of King. The *Wall Street Journal* article, sympathetic to the traders' walkout, had an immense impact on Nomura management in Tokyo. Like all Japanese, they had a particular aversion to bad press. Ohtaka was made the scapegoat for the situation in New York and, although Shimizu tried to help him, he was unable to do so. In the end, Nomura kept both King and McCullough.

At the Nomura New York Christmas party of 1985 Andy Saito told the Christmas revellers a story. It was the tale of the success of Matsushita Electric Industrial, the world's leading consumer electronics company. Saito followed this with the story of Matsushita's competitor, Philips Electronics of Holland, which, he said, was a relative failure. 'The reason for Philips' problems is that it does not have a tight grip on its overseas offices. That is why Matsushita is a world leader, it rules its overseas offices and gives them little autonomy. Remember, Nomura will always be a Japanese firm run by Japanese.' The party took on a sombre tone as everyone present took Saito's comments as a bad omen for Nomura New York. Saito was heading back to the Tokyo headquarters and wanted to scare the Americans. He succeeded but not in the way he had hoped. Within two months five of the salesmen selling Japanese stock to Americans had left.

By March 1986, Ohtaka too had left, hired by the blue-chip research house Donaldson, Lufkin & Jenrette, to head up his fifth foreign equity trading department.

PART IV
THE AGE OF BROKING

26
The Lone Wolf

As tensions mounted in the New York office during the summer of 1985, back in Japan a government minister named Toshio Komoto was about to lose everything he had spent the last fifty years building: he had received a telephone call from his stockbroker telling him that shares of Sanko Steamship Company, the firm he had founded in 1934, had just been suspended from trading on the floor of the Tokyo Stock Exchange. The Exchange had learned that Sanko's three main banks, at the instigation of Daiwa Bank, had refused to grant the company additional loans to keep it afloat. Komoto had already known his bankers' decision – what infuriated him was that stockbrokers had been selling Sanko shares in advance of the public announcement, sending Sanko's stock price into one of the worst tailspins in Japanese stockmarket history. He had been dealt a devastating blow. Komoto held nearly 5 per cent of Sanko's outstanding shares, 34 million shares that in 1973 had been worth 2500 yen, or nearly $8, apiece and were now to fall to one yen a share, less than half a cent each. The stock exchange finally ended Komoto's public humiliation by delisting Sanko's shares on 14 November 1985, capping one of the most dramatic sagas in Japanese corporate history. Komoto's wealth had been estimated at half a billion dollars at its peak in 1972, but that wealth had vanished and with it one of the world's largest shipping companies.

On the surface the story of Sanko was of one man's undoing, but the Sanko saga went deeper, into the hidden world of Japan's master influence-peddler – a man who held sway over the banking community because of his bureaucratic power and played the stockmarket for corporate and political gains. Toshio Komoto perfected the art of aggressive stock trading in the late 1960s and early 1970s at a time when the nation's markets were languishing in the wake of the collapse of Yamaichi Securities. Single-handedly he brought about a new age of broking which would ultimately result in banks losing their financial muscle to brokers – and in Nomura's success.

What made the Sanko Steamship saga so fascinating in 1985 was that financial collapses of Sanko's magnitude were almost unheard of in a country where the government took such an active role in nurturing and sustaining corporate Japan. The demise of Komoto's company was spectacular because Komoto had been a key figure in orchestrating the very policy that was supposed to protect companies such as his. In the fifty years it took him to build Sanko Steamship, Komoto had achieved the remarkable distinction of becoming both a corporate leader and a leading politician. He had been appointed by prime ministers to head the Ministry of Posts and Telecommunications, with responsibility for the largest pool of savings funds in the world – over $250 billion – and then the Ministry of International Trade and Industry (MITI), the centre of Japan Inc. Komoto's other political achievements were no less impressive: he had served in the House of Representatives since 1949 and run for prime minister against Yasuhiro Nakasone in 1982. Later he served as head of the Economic Planning Agency, which guided Japan's economic policy.

Everything about Toshio Komoto, even as a twenty-three-year-old law student at Nippon University, bespoke ambition. It was that same year, 1934, that Komoto founded a partnership called the Sanko Steamship Company with his brother-in-law, and three years later he became its president. This small Osaka shipping company carried military goods between Japan and its two occupied colonies in Korea and China. Shipping was a highly leveraged business and young entrepreneurs like Komoto required heavy bank financing to buy steamships. Raising money was, however, difficult, for banks favoured the creditworthy *zaibatsu* shipping concerns and most of the major banks had their money tied up in their own group shipping companies – Mitsubishi Bank in the Nippon Yusen Kaisha, known as NYK Line, Mitsui Bank in the Mitsui Line and the Sumitomo Bank in the Osaka Steamship Company. Komoto was rejected by every bank he approached in Osaka, including the Nomura Bank, but he was persistent and came in to visit Nomura's bank managers day after day. It was Komoto's renegade spirit and burning confidence that finally convinced Nomura's bankers to back his proposal, grant him the working capital to buy his steamships and agree to become Sanko's main banker. Nomura also took a stake in Sanko Steamship, since the Nomura *zaibatsu* did not have a shipping affiliate of its own and Tokushichi Nomura reasoned that it could finance Sanko's tramp steamers in return for a guarantee of space aboard the ships. The Nomura group chartered Sanko Steamship vessels to transport bagged coffee, refined rubber and palm oil and minerals from Nomura plantations, refineries and mines in South-East Asia to Japan. But the chaos of war destroyed any plans the Nomura group had for Sanko to become its shipping arm: Tokushichi and Yoshitaro Nomura died, the Nomura group was dissolved and the Nomura Bank renamed, so that Sanko Steamship by the late 1940s was just another borrower of the Daiwa Bank.

Komoto's relative rise in corporate and political Japan began a few years after World War II. Kansai residents in western Japan admired Komoto's independent and rebellious nature and in 1949 elected him to the Japanese Diet as a representative from Hyogo prefecture, an agricultural district west of Kyoto and Osaka. They saw in him a flair for the free enterprise so admired by Osaka men and they saw his natural disdain for government – and was it not the government who had just brought war down upon the nation?

Komoto listed Sanko Steamship shares on the Tokyo and Osaka Stock Exchange in 1949 and wisely distributed the publicly quoted shares among friendly banking institutions, including Nomura Bank (now called the Daiwa Bank), all of whom he later asked for money. How could any bank holding shares in the personal company of a member of the Diet refuse him a loan? He then expanded his brokerage and underwriting contacts and appointed Yamaichi, Nikko and Osaka-based Oi Securities (later renamed Wako Securities) to advise him on financial matters, diversifying away from the Nomura group. He cultivated bankers and brokers with equal ardour, knowing that bank loans and equity capital raised on the stockmarket were the key to expanding Sanko and enhancing his personal wealth. Komoto had become a somebody in the chaotic and socially levelling aftermath of war, and though he was not yet a contender in the upper echelons of Japan's corporate and political hierarchy, his stature and wealth were rising.

His notoriety as a renegade was publicized in 1964 when sixty-nine of Japan's seventy shipping companies were re-formed through government guidance into six major firms. In an act that earned him the nickname of the 'lone wolf' of the shipping business, Komoto refused to include Sanko in the restructuring and Japanese shipping became the 'big six' and Sanko. Komoto was now the obtrusive nail in the Japanese woodwork and most felt it was just a matter of time before the hammer came down on him. But Sanko Steamship grew even without the government subsidies handed to the other six firms. From 1965 until 1975 he increased the size of his fleet one hundred times, while conservative shippers like the NYK Line increased theirs only six times.

The tactics he used to boost Sanko Steamship's profit in the 1960s once again demonstrated a marked irreverence for the way things were done. He became impassioned with the concept of leverage, aggressively buying and selling ships as one would trade rice futures, only with borrowed funds. He no longer relied solely on Daiwa Bank for his operating funds, although the bank remained Sanko's main lender. He borrowed heavily from the Long Term Credit Bank and the Tokai Bank to fund his shipbroking activities until Sanko became known euphemistically in Japan as the 'Sanko Floating Real Estate Company'. In the late 1960s Komoto began to explore a whole new, untapped resource for raising capital and increasing revenues – the Tokyo stockmarket.

Never before had any shipping company and seldom had any other corporation used the stockmarket so aggressively. At first he treated it as a kind of financial playground, where hot tips and speculative forays generated extra pocket money. But as a natural risk-taker, the game soon commanded more and more of his attention and interest, so that by the early 1970s his firm had gained a second, more appropriate nickname within the Japanese financial community: 'Sanko Securities'.

Eventually Komoto saw in the stockmarket an opportunity to increase the share capital of Sanko fourfold by placing shares with third parties and raising $300 million (100 billion yen) for the firm. Before each new share placement Komoto engaged in what was then, and still is, a relatively common arrangement with underwriters: he pushed the price of the stock up to an attractive level in the months before the third party allotment and then, at the time of the financing, issued the shares at the new price. Such tactics not only brought Sanko more money, but, with the promise of a stock run-up, there were additional opportunities to make money by speculating in the shares.

Minoru Segawa, at the helm of Nomura Securities, was naturally in on the Sanko run-up and he in turn whispered to his friends to buy Sanko shares. News of the profits to be made travelled quickly in the stockmarket, making Sanko stock the hottest of the 1970s, even of the post-war era. Security house executives, politicians, salesmen, floor traders, company presidents, institutions and individuals took part in the buying hysteria. 'Everyone was guaranteed to get rich and many did,' recalled Fujio Kodama, the ex-chairman of Wako Securities, who was recommending the shares heavily in 1972. Nobody could have enough Sanko shares and the price soared from 700 yen to 2,560 in 1972, having been only sixty yen a share three years earlier. Komoto's personal net worth from Sanko shares alone was in excess of $250 million and made him one of the world's richest men.

Komoto became acquisitive with his newly earned wealth, and boldly used his funds to buy 41 per cent of the shares of rival Japan Line, the nation's largest shipping company. He later sold the shares back to the company at a huge profit. It was a prime example of Japanese greenmail – buying a stake in a publicly quoted company with the intention of frightening management into buying the shares back at a substantial premium. Such a tactic made Komoto one of the earliest of the post-war corporate executives to see the stockmarket as providing the kind of additional revenues that could stabilize earnings in firms whose primary businesses were subject to debilitating cycles.

Komoto's rise to financial prominence in the early 1970s was part of a wider picture. 'Komoto used his membership in the Diet as a means to procure bank loans so that his seat in the House of Representatives became no more than another aspect of his business,' observed Brian Stewart, a shipping analyst who later wrote a dissertation on Sanko Steamship. But Komoto was always careful to take good care of the residents of Hyogo prefecture who kept him in office and who, as one of them later noted, were granted an excessive number of bridges, highways and schools by the government. Cash became Komoto's weapon to influence politicians and bureaucrats into accepting his leadership. 'Politicians were afraid of Komoto because he knew how to spend money,' said Stewart. He had been appointed by Prime Minister Eisaku Sato in 1969 to preside as minister of posts and telecommunications. When granted the appointment, Komoto felt it only proper to resign from day-to-day command of Sanko Steamship to prevent any talk of conflict of interest, but as Sanko Steamship *was* Komoto, such gestures did little to actually separate his activities and his interests. In some way, no matter what Komoto's political responsibilities, he would always maintain a hand in the running of Sanko.

In 1974 he was appointed by Prime Minister Takeo Miki to

run 'Japan Inc.' as minister of international trade and industry. Japanese scholar Chalmers Johnson compared it to being the head of the Department of Defense in Washington and thought the Ministry of International Trade and Industry was 'without a doubt the greatest concentration of brainpower in Japan .... MITI's jurisdiction ranges from the control of bicycle racing to the setting of electric power rates, but its true defining power is its control of industrial policy.' This policy control was known as administrative guidance. As characterized by *Business Week* in 1973, 'Komoto was the antithesis of the traditional bureaucrat. He had developed the very un-Japanese habit of fighting the government at every turn. The soft-spoken, grey-haired man is clearly contemptuous of the government bureaucracy.' For years he had rejected government subsidies for his own business and had made it a matter of pride to demonstrate that businesses could succeed without government guidance. But now that Komoto was actually running the guidance, this abhorrence became less vehement.

As Komoto became more powerful, it was more difficult for Daiwa Bank and Japan's politicians and bureaucrats to refuse him support on pet projects. His electorate received the benefits of Japanese government spending, his political friends received cash as 'election contributions', while his enemies were in danger of being cut off from government subsidies. But as he became more embroiled in personal financial difficulties, these practices would come to work against him.

The first seeds of the downfall of Toshio Komoto's business empire were sown as early as 1972. In an act of unbridled arrogance, which was hailed at the time as a masterly stroke, Komoto tried to corner the world shipping market. Convinced that he could provide transport for the major oil companies about to open the North Sea oil fields, he negotiated to provide them with low-cost shipping services *before* ordering his tankers. He already owned very large crude carriers (VLCCs) but felt the future was in 80,000-ton tankers that were less costly and more mobile than their gigantic counterparts, and he placed a half-billion-dollar order, the largest peacetime shipbuilding order in history, for fifty-six tankers from Japanese shipyards. There was outrage in the international community that Komoto could offer such low-cost shipping charters, which were made possible, they claimed, because Japanese shipbuilders were subsidized by the government – as of course they were. However, Komoto could not forecast that in the cold winter of 1973 the finance ministers of the world's industrial countries would agree to let exchange rates float freely. Komoto earned all his revenue in dollars, and in 1972 the yen was stable, pegged against the United States dollar, which meant that for every dollar he made on renting his ships he brought in 308 yen. By 1980 he would be bringing in only 210 yen for every dollar he earned, a loss of 31 per cent.

It was an act of hubris to invest half a billion dollars of borrowed money into oil-carrying ships but perhaps Komoto would have succeeded even with the exchange rate problem if it had not been for the Arab-Israeli war and the ensuing oil crisis in the autumn of 1973. The Texas Railway Association had set oil prices for the past forty years, and oil had never been above $3 a barrel. But in 1973, with TRA's power stripped away by the Organization of Petroleum Exporting Countries, oil rocketed to $12 a barrel, and Komoto was in deep trouble.

Demand for Komoto's existing fleet of VLCCs plunged and he desperately tried to extricate himself from his new ship orders and heavy-handedly cancelled a third of them. Meanwhile, consumer and wholesale prices in Japan rocketed and Komoto learned the meaning of inflation the hard way. He had no way of renegotiating his shipping contracts to reflect the rising wages of sailors, insurance costs and port fees. Sanko was having trouble finding oil to fill his ships and he was receiving depreciating dollars to carry what oil he could transport, while facing higher and higher costs.

Sanko Steamship did not, however, go under in the 1970s. Ship financing was always a complex business and with a wheeler-dealer like Komoto at the helm it was impossible to tell exactly what Sanko's financial position was. He baffled financial analysts for years, in the meantime using his political clout to keep money pouring in from the banks. 'The reason Daiwa Bank and the other banks did not reduce their exposure to Sanko Steamship after 1975 was because of Komoto's political connections,' asserted Stewart. Sanko began taking losses in 1978 and was forced to accept government assistance – which also brought with it a plan to completely restructure the company.

In spite of these mounting financial concerns, Komoto's primary attention in 1982 was on his unsuccessful challenge to Yasuhiro Nakasone for the prime ministership of Japan. Redirecting his attention once again to the problems of Sanko, he abandoned the government's restructuring plan and, after posting another loss of 55 billion yen in 1983, tried to corner the world shipping market yet again. This time he ordered 126 bulk all-purpose carriers from Japanese shipyards.

Shipping magnates around the world were both astounded and angry that Komoto was bringing so much capacity on to the world market. 'To be quite frank I am surprised Toshio Komoto is still alive today. I know of quite a few shippers who went under because of him,' remarked one of Komoto's Osaka competitors. The shipping industry did not just fail to pick up in the mid-1980s as Komoto had forecast, but the market for carriers actually deteriorated. It was only his power as minister of the Economic Planning Agency that kept Sanko afloat. (In 1989 Komoto was wooed by the Liberal Democratic Party as a successor to Noboru Takeshita as prime minister, because he was one of the party's few 'clean' members.)

Relations between Daiwa Bank and Komoto were severely strained by the summer of 1985, when Sanko announced losses of $283 million (68 billion yen), bringing its cumulative losses to $700 million (168 billion yen). Komoto began making the rounds to the presidents of his major banks accompanied by one of his best friends, the influential Tokuo Yamashita, from one of Japan's most famous shipping families, founders of the Yamashita-Shinnihon line. Yamashita was a member of the Diet, where he was minister of transportation with jurisdiction over the problems that befell Sanko Steamship. The Japanese media, normally reticent about sensitive political matters, questioned the influence that Komoto as a government politician was wielding to save his own company. Some newspapers claimed that Prime Minister Yasuhiro Nakasone was prepared to bail out Sanko Steamship in return for the backing of Komoto's political faction in the Diet.

Bankers hated publicity and since the Japanese media associated Sanko Steamship with Daiwa Bank, the matter became all the more odious to Daiwa Bank executives. There was never any fear of a banking panic in Japan, the Ministry of Finance simply would not allow it, but in the first half of 1985 Daiwa Bank came as close to creating a stir as any of the nation's twelve commercial banks had since the war. Since its founding as the Osaka-Nomura Bank in 1918, the Daiwa Bank had risen to become the ninth largest commercial bank in Japan, with 200 branches, and the fifteenth largest bank in the world. Moreover, it was the only commercial bank with a trust banking licence. The Japanese thought of it, however, only as a medium-sized bank with particular strength in western Japan around Osaka. It was not in the first tier of banks such as Daiichi-Kangyo Bank (the world's largest) and Sumitomo Bank.

Although Nomura Securities had been spawned by the Osaka-Nomura Bank in 1925, relations between Nomura Securities and Daiwa Bank had been fraught with tension since World War II. At the end of the war Nomura Securities had purchased 3 per cent of Daiwa Bank's outstanding stock, while other affiliates such as Tokyo Mutual Life

Insurance and Osaka Gas had each bought 2.6 per cent of the company. Daiwa Bank and other Nomura Group companies had taken similar stakes in Nomura Securities. The Nomura Group, though chopped up by the Americans, had thus nonetheless remained interconnected by means of shareholdings. Such inter-company share swaps of between 2 and 5 per cent, which generally served to bolster business relations, were a common Japanese occurrence, but in this case they merely masked a clash of two forceful personalities, which would evolve into a major clash of corporate cultures.

The first president of Daiwa Bank after the war was an elite Todai graduate called Takeo Terao, who had begun his professional career as a clerk under Tokushichi Nomura. Terao had two prejudices: he detested the seamy world of stockbroking and was a firm opponent of the nepotism that had prevailed in the pre-war *zaibatsu*. When Motogoro Nomura, Tokushichi's younger brother, was purged as the president of the Nomura Bank in 1945, Terao was happy that the Nomura family, with all its favouritism, was gone from banking and he was deeply opposed to any formation of a new Nomura Group after the American Occupation forces left Japan in 1952. His firm was profitable enough without the aid of a stockbroking firm.

This did not stop Minoru Segawa, the president of Nomura Securities from 1958 until 1968, from trying to coax Daiwa Bank back into the Nomura fold. The abrasive and aggressive Segawa personified everything Terao disdained about stockbrokers, and he found his overtures particularly distasteful. The sour relationship between them deteriorated further with time, but in characteristic fashion the animosity was seldom discussed. In 1987, Kozo Nomura, who acted as a neutral party in the fray, observed: 'The word hatred is too extreme in Japanese society, dislike is more appropriate to describe the feelings between Segawa and Terao.' As corporate entities Nomura and Daiwa Bank remained civil but aloof towards one another. The disdain between the two presidents, however, trickled down through the firms and was reinforced by the different corporate cultures that emerged under each man's leadership. Nomura Securities remained Daiwa Bank's main underwriter but the bank frequently turned instead to Osakaya, later called Cosmo Securities, the post-World War I stockbrokerage legacy of Nomura Shoten.

As problems surrounding Sanko Steamship became more pronounced through the 1970s and 1980s, and as Daiwa Bank's chief executive grew old and securities houses rose to greater prominence, Nomura Securities found its power relative to Daiwa Bank growing. While banks relied on asset accumulation for their growth through a strong loan port-folio, securities firms relied on volume turnover for their prosperity. Securities firms could blossom overnight under the right market conditions, but banks took years to develop a client base. The syndicated loan business was not a high margin industry at the best of times (a quarter percentage point on a $100 million loan was a measly $250,000 return a year) and in the recessionary 1970s and early 1980s, banks such as Daiwa Bank faced hardship. The brokerage business in Japan, unlike America, raked in non-risk, straight commis-sion income while the banks faced huge losses in times of trouble as borrowers defaulted.

The Sanko Steamship debacle of the 1980s rocked Daiwa Bank and forced its board to call on the help of Nomura Securities. In many ways it was symbolic of the age: the financial industry of Japan was undergoing a radical shift with the gradual decline of banking and the rise of broking. By 1985, Daiwa Bank executives were anxious to cut their ties with Sanko Steamship. The bank owned 7.5 per cent of Sanko's outstanding shares, or close to 51 million shares, which had been worth 2,000 yen a share in the early 1970s but were now trading at a tenth of that price. Moreover, the investment community associated Sanko Steamship with Daiwa Bank, damaging its image. Through its principal bro-kers, Osakaya and Nomura Securities, Daiwa Bank had been searching for a buyer for Sanko shares since the early 1980s, but every time they tried to place a block of Sanko stock, the market price mysteriously tumbled ahead of their order. They sold some shares, but remained holding tens of millions.

Sumio Abekawa had taken over the difficult post of president of Daiwa Bank in 1984 and his early tenure took him through some particularly rocky times. Daiwa Bank was also the main banker to a plywood manufacturing company called Eidai Sangyo, a firm to whom it had extended loans in the hope of diversifying the bank's loan portfolio into manufacturing, but it went bankrupt, not long after the bank had been forced to swallow an entire $100 million Eurobond issue launched in 1983, for which Nomura had been the main underwriter. In late 1984 the Fuji Sash company, another borrower, also went into bankruptcy and Abekawa was then faced with Sanko. Abekawa held none of the malevolence towards Nomura Securities that Terao had exhibited, nor was he close friends with Komoto as Terao had been. The moment he stepped into the presidency of Daiwa Bank he urged fellow board members to reconsider its exposure to Sanko. The bank was now in such deep trouble because of $212 million in irrecoverable loans to Sanko that Abekawa had to resort to extraordinary tactics to revive it.

Kozo Nomura was worried about the financial soundness of the bank and arranged for a dinner with the chairman of Daiwa Bank, Susumu Furukawa – a graduate from Kyoto University in 1938, four years after Kozo, and therefore willing to be open with his senior. 'How can Daiwa Bank survive this crisis?' Kozo inquired. Furukawa leaned over and in a conspiratorial whisper replied, 'Nomura-san, do not worry, we have plenty of stock in reserve – paying for Sanko will be no problem.' Although the fifty million shares it held in Sanko Steamship were worthless, Furukawa was referring to an extensive share portfolio Daiwa Bank had built up since World War II on which it had massive unrecognized profits. It was time to realize those gains and Furukawa had Abekawa arrange a meeting with Minoru Segawa, by then the senior adviser to Nomura Securities. Daiwa Bank needed to raise cash by the summer of 1985 and raise it fast.

269

Turning to Nomura Securities had been a difficult decision since one of the largest holdings in the Daiwa Bank portfolio was forty-two million shares in Nomura Securities itself. But what better place to sell shares in Nomura than Nomura Securities?

The meeting between Minoru Segawa of Nomura and Sumio Abekawa of Daiwa in the summer of 1985 was momentous since it reconciled the two firms and gave a tacit understanding that Nomura Securities was now the dominant member of the Nomura group. In fact, before the meeting Daiwa Bank had not even considered itself part of the Nomura group. The discussion between a powerbroker of Segawa's stature – he was now seventy-nine years old – and a fifty-five-year-old bank president was also of symbolic importance given the Japanese respect for seniority, and, with Terao now dead and unable to interfere in Nomura's overtures, Segawa was able to play upon this age difference to gain every advantage for Nomura Securities.

Segawa began by agreeing to help Daiwa Bank's chief quietly find buyers for the huge share portfolio it needed to sell. In return, Segawa wanted Daiwa Bank to retain Nomura as its principal broker on the bank's stockmarket transactions in the future, a request that implied a cutback in relations with Osakaya. (Soon thereafter Daiwa Bank amended its internal dealing policy to allow Nomura to control their stockmarket investments.) Furthermore, Segawa wanted to increase Nomura's shareholding in Daiwa Bank, the implication being that Nomura was now lead member of the group. Shortly afterwards Nomura was seen buying Daiwa Bank shares on the open market with the approval of the bank's senior management.

By September 1985, only two months before Sanko went belly up, Nomura had sold over thirty million shares in Nomura Securities held by Daiwa Bank in its portfolio. These shares were sold to Nomura affiliates. By law, a company in Japan was not allowed to purchase its own shares, so Nomura sold them to Nippon Godo Finance, its venture

270

capital arm, to Nomura Investment Trust, to Nomura Real Estate, and to the dummy company that managed Nomura's buildings, Nomura Land and Building. The balance of the shares was buried with friendly institutions. When the sell programme was complete, Daiwa Bank had raised nearly $150 million from its sale of Nomura shares alone. Only eleven million shares of its former forty-one million share stake in Nomura were left. Symbolically and practically it was a victory for Nomura Securities and a triumph for the brokerage community.

Ironically, after the downfall of two Japanese prime ministers in 1989, it was Komoto, still a Liberal Democratic Party heavyweight, whose name kept appearing as a contender. His followers billed him as 'Mr Clean', but by now the Japanese public knew better and squashed this second bid for the national leadership.

27
The Yomiuri Incident

Nothing epitomized the power of Nomura Securities in Japan more than the 'Yomiuri incident', a classic in the annals of Nomura powerbroking. The story centres on two enormously wealthy men, linked to the Japanese underworld, who attempted to take over the Yomiuri group, one of the world's largest media conglomerates. Only Nomura, at the behest of Prime Minister Yasuhiro Nakasone, could break the takeover attempt.

The first of these men was Eitaro Itoyama, born illegitimate in 1942. The second was his father, a nefarious, self-made business tycoon named Shintaro Sasaki, who had created his first fortune manufacturing light bulbs before the war and in the early 1950s diversified his profits into golf courses and hotels, anticipating that one day the Japanese would begin to work less hard and think of relaxation. A decade later the value of Sasaki's real estate holdings had multiplied many times over. Itoyama grew up under his father's protection and influence but was ashamed of his birth and spent little time in his father's company. The first job he landed was selling used cars. He almost succeeded in his ambition of building his own fortune and making a name for himself independently of his father, but went bankrupt after one of his suppliers defrauded him. Itoyama returned to his father for support and Sasaki, impressed by his son's single-mindedness and ability, welcomed him into the family business, giving him the lead role in a company he had spent most of his life putting together. The New Japan Sightseeing Company specialized in leisure and entertainment. It employed 5,000 people, operated thirty-five branch offices and enjoyed revenues of sixty billion yen. By the early 1970s, Sasaki was getting old and Itoyama seemed the ideal successor to run his company after his death.

272

Sasaki, in his loud pin-striped, three-piece suits, chain-smoking his way from one deal to another, looked every inch the bullying hotelier and entertainment magnate. Indeed his success was due in great part to his ability to negotiate with the underworld. Perhaps his most notorious connection was Ryoichi Sasakawa, a deal-maker who could count himself one of the world's richest men.

Sasakawa had built his fortune initially by dealing in the Manchurian black market during the Second World War. When the war ended he was indicted as a war criminal, partly for his Manchurian activities, partly because of his connections with extreme right-wing societies during the 1930s when he was a well known fascist agitator. Once out of prison Sasakawa built up the new sport of motorboat racing, which formed the basis for what would become one of Japan's largest post-war fortunes, and he directed the profits from public motorboat betting to a charitable organization misleadingly known as the Japan Shipbuilding Foundation, from which he claimed to have given away twelve billion dollars. This was the man whom Sasaki called a friend and, having brought Itoyama into the family business, he completed the circle by marrying Itoyama to Sasakawa's niece.

Itoyama's activities took a fresh turn in 1973, when he wrote a bestselling book entitled *The Monster Way of Doing Business*, an account of the spectacular success that he and Sasaki had in attempting to take over the Nakayama steel works in 1971 and 1972, about the time that Toshio Komoto started running up Sanko's share price. Brimming with stockmarket fever, the Japanese public rushed to buy his book and Itoyama became an overnight sensation. So great was his wave of popularity that before long he ran for a seat in the forthcoming Diet elections.

All was going well until, during his election campaign of 1974, the *Yomiuri Shimbun*, the world's largest circulation newspaper, approached Itoyama with a commission to write another bestseller. Itoyama was flattered but declined. After continued pestering by the *Yomiuri*, who argued that anything from his pen was bound to be a bestseller, he eventually relented and under the stresses of the election campaign wrote one of the most embarrassing flops in publishing history. Out of a print run of 200,000, Itoyama's book sold a paltry 2,000 copies and relations between the *Yomiuri* and Itoyama sank lower as the newspaper pressed him to buy up the unsold books. Then the *Yomiuri* unleashed a series of scathing articles accusing Itoyama of electoral improprieties.

War had been declared, and Itoyama and Sasaki plotted their revenge. But the Yomiuri group was a mighty foe to take on. The *Yomiuri Shimbun* controlled a rambling media, real estate and entertainment empire of twenty-three companies, founded by Matsutaro Shoriki, who was better known as the father of professional baseball and a pioneer of commercial television in Japan. With the support of a wealthy sponsor, he had taken charge of the *Yomiuri* newspaper in 1924 and over the next thirty years had built the Yomiuri group, using the newspaper as the control centre. In 1936 he had founded the Dai Nippon Baseball Club, which later became the Yomiuri Giants, based in Tokyo and Japan's leading baseball team.

When World War II ended, Shoriki had struck up a friendship with Tsunao Okumura, an association which was to cement relations between the Yomiuri group and Nomura Securities for the next three decades. Okumura had just assumed the post-war presidency of Nomura at the age of forty-five and Shoriki regarded him as his special ward, while Okumura looked up to Shoriki for guidance and advice. It was the classic '*oyabun-kobun*', master-servant relationship, which occupied such an important role in Japanese society. Okumura would tell Shoriki of the difficulty of building a securities company when the stockmarket was officially closed and he had a life-and-death obligation to feed his employees. Shoriki could point out in response that Nomura's president had suffered little compared to the indignities that he himself had endured because of the war: imprisoned by the Japanese military, his health ruined, his job, salary and status lost.

After the war, Shoriki staged a comeback and Okumura played a vital role in raising capital for his fledgling companies. Shoriki founded Nippon Television (NTV) in 1952, a private broadcasting company that sparked a huge television boom in Japan, and soon afterwards he appointed Nomura Securities as underwriter to list NTV's shares on the Tokyo Stock Exchange. Then the Nomura group took a sizeable stake in Yomiuri Land, Shoriki's flagship real estate company. Shoriki went on to serve in the House of Representatives from the mid-1950s until 1976 and with his newly acquired political responsibilities handed the reins of Yomiuri's day-to-day operations to Chozaburo Sekine.

It was the success and power of the Yomiuri group that fuelled Itoyama's desire to redress the public humiliation served on him by the *Yomiuri Shimbun* in 1974. It equally rankled his father, Sasaki, that Yomiuri competed for customers with his own golf courses, hotels and commercial centres, especially when, in his view, Yomiuri knew little about the leisure industry. But he could never forgive Shoriki for scooping a prime piece of real estate from under his nose, land that he had intended to develop into a first-class golf course. In 1962 the Tokyu Corporation had offered Sasaki a large plot of land at 500 yen ($1.40) per tsubo (thirty square feet). Sasaki had leapt at the offer, but before the agreement was signed, Shoriki heard of the proposed deal and doubled Sasaki's offer. Fifteen years later the Yomiuri group was sitting on a piece of real estate worth an estimated fifty million yen, or $450,000, per tsubo.

As shrewd businessmen Itoyama and Sasaki were well aware that Yomiuri Land was sitting on a gold mine of property assets, from golf courses to office buildings, which the two partners estimated were worth over 1,200 yen per share, more than five times the actual share price of the company. If Sasaki and Itoyama bought Yomiuri Land shares through the stockmarket, their return after dumping the property assets would be astronomical. The rest of the Yomiuri group companies were similarly undervalued in stockmarket terms, but the means of unlocking their value was blocked by the controlling interests held by the privately owned giant newspaper, the *Yomiuri Shimbun*. That meant Itoyama and his father could not seek control over the Yomiuri companies by the simple device of buying *Yomiuri Shimbun* shares – they were not traded on the stock exchange.

The Yomiuri companies were cross-held and artfully distributed by Nomura Securities in spiderweb fashion, making a takeover doubly difficult. Sasaki described the structure as an 'incestuous web of inefficiency'. Over 40 per cent of Yomiuri Land was scattered among affiliates and friendly parties, including the newspaper, Nippon Television, Nomura Securities and Korakuen Stadium; close to half of NTV was in the hands of the newspaper, Yomiuri Land, Nomura and Yomiuri TV. The list continued: the Yomiuri Giants were owned by Yomiuri Kogyo, a private company, while Yomiuri TV was privately held by *Yomiuri Shimbun*. Korakuen Stadium, now known as the 'Big Egg', the popular Tokyo ballpark and home of the Giants, had an ownership list that read like a Yomiuri company directory. And there were other, personal links within the group: Chozoburo Sekine was married to the daughter of Shoriki; Kosai Kobayashi, head of *Yomiuri Shimbun*, was married to another daughter.

But Sasaki and Itoyama uncovered the Achilles heel of the Yomiuri group and Itoyama's course began to become clear. He realized that although he could not buy directly into the core company, the newspaper, he could secretly accumulate shares in Yomiuri Land, which was listed on the stock market, and thus indirectly put pressure on the group. He saw that Yomiuri Land, though not the controlling company, held many of the group's prime assets. Any attack on the real estate company would threaten the entire group. The newspaper, he felt, was especially vulnerable because it was grossly undervalued and owned by employees who would fear for the stability of their firm. As a main shareholder he could possibly control Yomiuri Land, oust Sekine and demand a board position on the newspaper.

Eitaro Itoyama and Shintaro Sasaki began buying Yomiuri Land shares in 1978 and a year later Sasaki visited Sekine at his Yomiuri office with inquiries about the company's performance. The two rivals, who already held each other in contempt, disagreed violently over the goals of Yomiuri Land, Sekine arguing that the firm should serve society and Sasaki demanding that the president adopt a hard-nosed, commercial approach. Sasaki was aware of the disdain with which Sekine, a Tokyo Law School graduate, treated him and he did not like it. He pointed out that the president of Nakayama Steel had visited him with gifts in 1971 when he was the major shareholder, and an unfriendly one at that. Sekine had not even sent him a New Year card. 'That is no way to treat your owners,' Sasaki told him gruffly.

Yomiuri was in trouble. Itoyama and Sasaki had bought so many shares by the early 1980s that Yomiuri Land was in danger of being suspended from trading on the Tokyo Stock Exchange because of the reduction in the number of freely traded shares. The number of shareholders also threatened to fall below the minimum permissible level and the stock exchange gave Yomiuri Land a year to redress the situation. Faced by such a deep embarrassment, Yomiuri went on the offensive. They publicly accused Itoyama of offering to stop buying shares in return for payment. They set private detectives on the tail of Sasaki and Itoyama, looking for unsavoury details about them or their company that might be exposed to the public. The *Yomiuri Shimbun* was brought into action and accused Itoyama of buying company shares to force the group into buying out his holding at an inflated price. But Itoyama innocently proclaimed he wanted only to become president of the land company.

There was only one man in Japan who could settle the dispute: Minoru Segawa. In 1981 Itoyama consulted Segawa, asking him to find a buyer for his Yomiuri Land stock, presumably, rumour suggested, because he could no longer afford his interest payments. Segawa played the diplomatic role of arbiter. On one side were Sasaki and

Itoyama, not to mention Itoyama's almighty uncle-in-law and motorboat-betting tycoon, Ryoichi Sasakawa. On the other side were the time-honoured Yomiuri group, close friends of Nomura management. Segawa had continued the amicable relations with Yomiuri that his predecessor Okumura had enjoyed. Nomura was not only Yomiuri's main underwriter but a major shareholder in a number of group companies and Segawa himself was one of the Yomiuri Giants' most avid fans, owning a reserved box seat at the Korakuen Stadium (now the Tokyo Dome) and sending a side of beef to the Giants' training camp every year.

In the interest of a cease-fire, Segawa paid a visit to Yomiuri's Sekine, telling him that Itoyama wanted to sell his shares. But Sekine and his advisers hesitated to accept the offer, calculating that Itoyama had borrowed heavily to buy Yomiuri stock and the burden of interest payments would eventually force him to sell. They would let Itoyama sweat for a while.

Yomiuri was less happy, however, about rumours that uncle-in-law Sasakawa, with his almost unlimited financial reserves, had provided support to Itoyama. Now turned philanthropist, Sasakawa would be well worth paying to escape from. Frightened, Yomiuri approached Sasakawa in April 1982 but he denied any complicity in the affair. Itoyama continued to state publicly that he had had approval, but not financial support, from Sasakawa. The rumours continued to fly and finally the Yomiuri group decided to run an appeasing article on Sasakawa and disarm him. On 23 May 1982, the *Yomiuri Shimbun* ran an article on Sasakawa's self-styled philanthropy, complete with photographs, describing his beneficence.

Itoyama claimed that Segawa had invited him to a Japanese inn for an elaborate dinner at which he had asked him to reduce his shareholding so that Yomiuri Land could retain its stock-exchange listing. Itoyama refused and said that he would continue to buy shares. He also insisted that he and his family had financed the entire investment. Sasaki supported his son in the later stages of the operation, but denied greenmail as his motive. Itoyama stated, 'Sasaki and I have a quarter of Yomiuri's shares. He does not care about the share price. He's only interested in assets and profits.'

By 1983, Sasaki and his son had indeed collected 25 per cent, or 18 million out of 71 million shares, of Yomiuri's issued capital. Itoyama would not admit it, but the borrowing costs of revenge were becoming painful and it was clear that he was not going to dislodge the company or take control of the newspaper.

Both sides faced a stalemate. Itoyama could not bear the carrying costs, and the Yomiuri Land's Tokyo Stock Exchange status was under threat. The shadowy presence of the hugely rich Sasakawa was a wild card that Yomiuri could ill afford to ignore. It was then, according to many sources, that Prime Minister Yasuhiro Nakasone (to whose Diet faction Itoyama belonged) personally intervened and brought in Segawa to settle the affair.

Nomura negotiated a settlement, buying Itoyama's entire position in Yomiuri Land worth over twenty billion yen or nearly $87 million. Segawa then had his aides sell the shares among the Yomiuri group and friends, and added to Nomura's already sizeable Yomiuri investments by purchasing Yomiuri shares. The price Itoyama received for his shares was never revealed, but in the summer of 1988 *Forbes* magazine portrayed Itoyama as one of Japan's richest men. He was still a member of the Diet and president of the New Japan Sightseeing Company, which he inherited from his father on his death. At the age of forty-eight, Itoyama was worth $2.5 billion.

Quite apart from Nomura's role, the Yomiuri incident, astonishing though it was, also represented dozens of similar, less spectacular events in the Japanese financial world. So frequent were cases of 'greenmail' through the accumulation of hostile shares in companies by wealthy speculators that they attracted little or no publicity in the Japanese press; but they did dispel the myth of Japanese business as a world where everybody worked together for the good of Japan Inc., and where a contested takeover bid was considered a western phenomenon.

28
The Extortionists

If the Yomiuri story gave only a surface glimpse of behind-the-scenes financial life in Japan, other racketeers were more overt and made no attempt to disguise their identity as they swaggered down seedy back streets in their chalk-stripe suits, black shirts and white ties. Evoking a hackneyed gangster movie, their jackets were purposely undersized to highlight their muscular physiques. Gold chains often hung around their necks and bracelets from their wrists, and most wore their hair in a crew cut or punch perm. More often than not they were missing the top joint of their little finger, amputated as a token of loyalty to their underworld leader. Demanding money, these men plagued and harassed almost every Japanese company, from the mighty house of Nomura to Daiwa Bank, and at times protected other companies such as government-owned firms like Japan Air Lines.

Professional extortionists had been active in Japan since the early days of industrialization in the late nineteenth century. However, only in the early 1960s did organized racketeers begin to assert themselves within public companies, at first as a response to pressure on company management from shareholders with actual problems. The 1960s saw the birth of consumerism in Japan as ingenuous shareholders began speaking out at shareholder meetings, asking for explanations for poor performance or for payment of damages arising from dangerous products. Inspired by Japanese politicians who used underworld figures to hush opposition, Japanese companies hired thugs to bully the consumer groups into silence, in order to minimize the embarrassment of public conflict.

These thugs took payments to gag unhappy shareholders, but also took blackmail money from companies themselves.

By buying a few shares in a company and exercising their rights as shareholders to gain entry to the annual general meeting, they were able to strong-arm management into paying them a 'fee' in exchange for which the *sokaiya* (as they later became known) promised to keep themselves, and everyone else, quiet. It signalled the end of the traditional Japanese company meeting, a restricted affair between the board, the representatives of financial institutions and a few wealthy individuals. The *sokaiya* had become accepted by the boardrooms of corporate Japan.

That lowly gangsters can browbeat the supermen of corporate Japan is a remarkable phenomenon to Westerners, but the Japanese are not, and never have been, like the rest of the world. Companies in the United States and Britain have – or feign to have – an exaggerated respect for shareholders, in particular small investors. Western chairmen might speak patronizingly to them of 'your company', 'your board' and 'your directors', but shareholders only become important to Western companies during a time of crisis such as a hostile takeover attempt.

Senior executives in Japan, on the other hand, make no pretence of running their company for the benefit of small shareholders: they pay a tiny dividend and disclose information only to friends. Management and workers alike refer to the firm as 'our company' and the president and senior management readily state that the business is run for the benefit of the employees. In the West, such sentiments are concealed, not only because they offend the notion of shareholder rights but because they express what companies feel but dare not say. (Later, in Japan, a law was even passed stating that a greenmailer must pay its victim its profits from dealing in the target company's stock. The money was to be paid to the target company, not the shareholders.)

There were also other differences between East and West. In Japan, two-thirds of all publicly quoted companies were tightly held by friendly banks, insurance companies and affiliates whose investment horizon spanned decades rather than the quarterly myopia which prevailed in America. While Western companies disclosed financial information to everybody, Japanese companies revealed details only to their top ten shareholders. In America the slightest item of information about sales, earnings or new products given to one shareholder had to be made public immediately. Japanese companies were under no moral or statutory obligation to do the same.

Neglected by company management, the small investor in Japan did not make his money from dividend payouts but from capital gains. Thanks in part to Nomura's Tsunao Okumura, Japan, unlike Western countries, had never taxed capital gains and for this reason the small investor was more interested in stock price charts than in the capacity of a company to pay increased dividends. As long as a share price went up, the Japanese private investor was happy – and with the stockmarket rising almost continuously since World War II, he usually had a smile on his face.

Annual meetings were a charade. Japan's benign ownership structure provided no incentive to raise questions at shareholders' meetings and the Japanese were anyway reluctant to voice their own opinions, especially in front of those they regarded as their leaders or superiors. Meanwhile, the *sokaiya* greedily sucked the blood of Japan's frightened companies. Payment of hush money became so institutionalized that most firms listed on the Tokyo Stock Exchange appointed a manager of general affairs, responsible for paying off 'registered' gangsters twice-yearly amounts totalling around $4,000 per head. Lines of *sokaiya* formed outside company offices, waiting to be registered on the official payment list, and over time they developed a certain sophistication, researching companies and their directors for financial, political and sexual scandal with which to threaten the management. By the early 1980s their activities were so acknowledged and so conspicuous that public authorities were shamed into action.

In 1982, the Diet passed a law forbidding the payment

of money to the *sokaiya* and the police formed a special task force to crack down on the menace. But even with the law behind them, most companies were able to rid themselves of their parasitic 'advisers' only after paying them substantial retirement fees. The new law sought to limit the presence of *sokaiya* at shareholders' meetings by restricting attendance to those holding more than a certain number of shares. This had some effect and by the middle of 1984, only 1,700 *sokaiya* satisfied the legal requirements, compared with 6,800 active *sokaiya* before 1982. But they were not ready to give up such a lucrative source of income easily.

In their efforts to circumvent the 1982 law, the *sokaiya* set up respectable fronts for their basic business of extortion. Many styled themselves 'research' organizations, publishing news sheets packed with scandals (often with a basis in truth) concerning their target companies. Others set up bogus political societies and solicited donations from their all-too-willing victims, who now avoided the attention of the authorities by making payments overseas or paying inflated prices for subscriptions to the *sokaiya*-backed companies. Instead of ostentatious lines at the company payout windows, the general affairs manager made payments to only a handful of crooks rather than hundreds or even thousands of *sokaiya*. Money was not handed over directly but left in the company's reception area where the director of a research company would collect his reward.

But only the hardened *sokaiya* groups made money. Those with low rankings, i.e., the *sokaiya* incapable of creating a real stir or commotion, had little chance to score a big payoff. As firms became even more selective, they chose one large *sokaiya* group to whom they paid up to $40,000 a year. In return, the larger *sokaiya* scared off the smaller extortionists.

Haruhiko Sakurai, a journalist who for years was forced to write under a pseudonym to protect himself, described the Rondan Doyukai, Japan's best known *sokaiya* group, which had the temerity to list itself in the telephone directory. Its headquarters on the main street of Yamate-dori, a bustling section of Tokyo, had its name emblazoned in large letters across huge plate-glass windows and occupied the first three floors of a nine-storey building.

The Rondan Doyukai were a group of intrepid financial warriors bold enough to have blackmailed even Nomura Securities. 'Everyone knows that in August 1985 the Rondan Doyukai began buying Nomura shares,' explained Sakurai, who claimed that they accumulated 300,000 Nomura Securities shares at a cost of 350 million yen (almost $1.5 million), giving them the right to attend the Nomura Securities' general meeting in December. Brazenly, the Rondan Doyukai called upon the male secretarial assistants of high-ranking Nomura board members, men known as the '*hissho-shitsu*', demanding money to keep order at the shareholders' meeting and to resist the temptation of exposing Nomura's supposed dirty laundry in public.

This special secretarial department of Nomura, common to other securities firms in Japan, was staffed by men of significant power assigned to each high-ranking Nomura board member, who acted as aides-de-camp in everything from travel schedules to pay-offs. The Nomura men were surprised by Rondan Doyukai's offer. Such an explicit threat caused a much greater stir than a normal under-the-table 'research' hand-out. Under the usual procedure, according to Sakurai, the secretaries met with Nomura's legal department before making pay-offs to bogus research organizations such as the Kaga Economic Research Institute, a smaller version of the Rondan Doyukai.

Then the problems began. After hitting a high of 1,300 yen per share at the end of September, Nomura's stock price plummeted, along with the rest of the market. Rondan Doyukai, who had paid 1,200 yen for Nomura shares, began to worry. Worse, in November 1985 the Japanese government bond market plunged and Nomura's share price, the barometer of the Tokyo Stock Exchange, sank to a low of 995 yen. The Rondan Doyukai were sitting on a paper loss equivalent to $300,000, larger than any protection money the group was likely to receive from Nomura. They went to Nomura and suggested that they would like to sell their block of Nomura shares on any rally. In *sokaiya* doublespeak it meant, 'Get your share price up by any means, otherwise we will make a serious nuisance of ourselves at your meeting.' By mid-December Nomura's share price was back to 1,140 yen, and both Nomura and Rondan Doyukai were a lot happier than they had been a few weeks earlier.

Nomura Securities was not Japan's only heavy hitter to tangle with the Rondan Doyukai, and some firms went so far as actually to seek their involvement. In preparation for their general meeting in 1985, Japan Air Lines, then 35 per cent owned by the Japanese government, employed the services of Rondan Doyukai's 'corporate research team', anticipating criticism for its failure to pay a dividend that year. (After a highly publicized airline crash early that year, business had fallen badly.) When the president of Japan Air Lines rose to ask forgiveness for the company's unprofitability, he was greeted with shouts of 'we understand, we understand!' from a crowd of muscular, weather-beaten shareholders at the back of the hall. Afterwards, Japan Air Lines strongly denied the presence of racketeers, but experienced journalists recognized the familiar crew cuts, punch perms, vulgar suits and Rambo-like body builds of the Rondan Doyukai corporate research department.

Like the Rondan Doyukai, the other *sokaiya* groups had turned into shrewd financial operatives, obtaining huge capital backing to purchase the large block of shares necessary to obtain attendance rights at the shareholders' meeting. No small-time racketeers now, the *sokaiya* were supported by a well-oiled extortion machine funded by the illicit proceeds of gambling, prostitution and drug peddling with the full knowledge and tacit consent of the police force. By 1987 there were over 300 *sokaiya* groups operating in Japan, with an active membership role of around 1,700. Two to four representatives showed at each company meeting. Between

1982 and 1986 there were only two arrests arising from illegal payments to *sokaiya*, but, with so few prosecutions, companies and *sokaiya* alike were becoming complacent and in 1986 the police department attempted a crackdown on under-the-table payments, which companies no longer made any attempt to conceal. Among those arrested were employees of some of Japan's most respected companies: Sumitomo Marine and Fire, Nikon, Noritake (the ceramic manufacturer) and Sogo Department Store. Typically, one manager accepted responsibility for the incident, denying that his company had any knowledge of the hush money he was paying out. Police activity intensified to the point where, in June 1987, over 6,000 policemen staked out the premises of 1,067 annual meetings, which were intentionally held on the same day in order to dilute the presence of the *sokaiya*.

The police usually went no further than identifying and prosecuting a few unfortunate paymasters. From time to time, however, they went about their task with unseemly zeal. One instance was the public prosecutor's probe into *sokaiya* payments by Yamaichi Securities on behalf of Mitsubishi Heavy Industries. The probe uncovered a complex web of relationships between gangsters, stockbrokers, public companies and leading politicians; a world which, though sparely documented, was an established way of life in the upper echelons of Japanese society. Mitsubishi Heavy Industries, Japan's leading manufacturer of heavy machines, ships, planes and cars, and the descendant of the company which produced the Mitsubishi Zero fighter plane, had decided to issue convertible bonds to the public in 1986. Nikko Securities, a Mitsubishi group company, had always been the principal investment adviser to the thirty or so Mitsubishi companies and it managed all of Mitsubishi Heavy's domestic offerings of stock, while overseas financings were rotated among Nomura, Daiwa, Nikko and Yamaichi.

Spurred on by a sense of supreme power, Nomura decided in 1985 to wrest control of Mitsubishi's domestic issuing activities from Nikko. To prove its good will towards

Mitsubishi and to enrich clients in the ensuing war, it accumulated Mitsubishi shares between December 1985 and the spring of 1986. This was a vital point in Nomura's strategy since Mitsubishi, and most other companies for that matter, judged a broker's fitness for corporate advisory work by its ability to move its share price. The higher a company's share price in Japan, the higher its status.

After buying up shares for itself, clients and leading politicians, Nomura had the Nomura Research Institute publish a 'strong buy' recommendation on Mitsubishi Heavy shares. Then Nomura's almighty stock department swung into action. Responsible for selling shares to clients through its massive branch network, they urged customers to buy Mitsubishi Heavy. Not until then did Nomura's corporate finance managers approach Mitsubishi, seeking an appointment as the firm's financial adviser. Receiving a non-committal reply, Nomura simply concluded that they had not pushed the share price of Mitsubishi high enough.

The shares rose steadily, hitting 674 yen by the summer of 1986 from a low of 350 yen earlier in the year and Nomura's corporate finance department was pleased with the efforts of their colleagues in the stock department. Such collusion was the mainstay of Nomura's business and in fact of most Japanese brokerage businesses. At the time there were no Chinese walls in Japan like those that legally prevented Americans and Britons from leaking sensitive company information to their equity sales force. On the contrary, in Japan the relationship was notably close and mutually beneficial. The executives of Mitsubishi were impressed. Mitsubishi executives were galvanized by Nomura's talk of Mitsubishi Heavy's gargantuan asset value, their skill in aerospace technology, and defence procurement. As a reward for boosting Mitsubishi's share price, Nomura won the lead management of Mitsubishi's 100 billion yen domestic convertible bond issue in August 1986.

Everyone awaited the new Mitsubishi issue with greedy anticipation. Not only was the stockmarket reaching new highs almost every day, but Nikko Securities, upset at having been nosed out of the issue, began to buy Mitsubishi aggressively as if to show that it was still a force to be reckoned with. It became a dogfight. Nomura had the biggest share of the bond to place with its clients, but the others all had a portion. To be issued at a fixed price of 100, the bond's first traded price promised to exceed 150, yielding an instant paper profit of 50 per cent to everyone lucky enough to get an allocation from one of the underwriters. Some expected a first price of 200. Excitement reached fever pitch, with unofficial, 'grey' market trading reaching 225. In a binge of influence peddling, brokers were handing out bonds on which investors could instantly double their money. The first traded price of Mitsubishi's bond was 235 and rumour had it that Prime Minister Yasuhiro Nakasone and two other members of his cabinet, Shintaru Abe and Noburu Takeshita, had all received a Mitsubishi allocation as campaign contributions from the brokers.

Then Yamaichi got into trouble. The public prosecutor's office discovered that Yamaichi had paid off Mitsubishi's *sokaiya* with Mitsubishi bonds. Such a flagrant violation of the 1982 law could not have happened at a worse time. Cracking down on *sokaiya* payments, the police no longer looked the other way. Documents were subpoenaed, alarming Yamaichi, who told the public prosecutor's office that of course they had sold bonds to the *sokaiya*. Should customers be turned away? Anyway, they said, why don't you look into Nomura's sale of Mitsubishi bonds to the politicians?

To complicate matters, the chairman of Yamaichi let out to a reporter of the weekly magazine *Zaikai* that it was Mitsubishi Heavy who had asked Yamaichi to pay off the *sokaiya*. Unafraid, the reporter printed the story. Yamaichi, Japan's fourth largest brokerage firm, immediately sacked its chairman, not for his flirtations with the *sokaiya* but for his lack of discretion. Tensions inside Yamaichi were running so high that a managing director involved in the incident took his own life.

Then suddenly and without warning the Tokyo Metropolitan Police dropped the case. Yamaichi's accusations about Mitsubishi hand-outs to senior politicians were too dangerous to bring to public attention. Some of the investigators, upset, leaked details of the probe to the press. Yet the press did nothing. The three largest advertisers in the Japanese media were securities companies, automobile manufacturers and cosmetic companies. It was unwise to risk the revenues from several huge advertisers for the sake of a story. There was lingering anxiety that someone would ask questions publicly before the close of the 1987 summer Diet session, implicating Japan's leading politicians with the notorious Mitsubishi Heavy convertible bond issue. Nobody did.

Matters would be different next time, however. When the Recruit scandal broke, a year later, the politicians fell but the securities companies remained protected by the press.

29
The Speculators

The spiralling Japanese real-estate and stock markets produced a new breed of wealth in the 1980s, which was personified in the machismo image of the stockmarket speculator.
Prototypical of this new man was the dashing and smooth
Juniichi Suzuki (as he shall be called here: one of the few
figures in this book whose names have been altered). To
his neighbours, the puzzle about him was that he never
got up to go to work in the morning, although three days
a week he was out of the door early with a leather golf
bag slung over his shoulder and a mobile telephone in his
hand, speeding off in his new, dark-green Jaguar XJ12.
What he played was Japanese power golf at the highest
level but there was one difference between Suzuki and the
politicians, financiers and bureaucrats he played with – he
owned the golf course. When not dressed in the plaids, greens
and yellows of his golfing gear, the dapper Suzuki was fond of
tailored, double-breasted suits with a fluffed-up handkerchief
and matching tie. The evenings were his domain and Suzuki,
followed by his entourage, regularly hosted lavish dinners at
famous tea-houses like Wakabayashi and Fukudaya, where
he entertained Japan's rainmakers – from Diet members to
shady underworld bosses.

The style of the high-riding stockmarket speculators was
coveted by thousands of Japan's *nouveaux riches*. But
membership was select. Only those who had cornered their
first stock or greenmailed their first company had arrived;
anyone without a net worth of fifty million dollars or a
line of credit of $100 million need not apply. Suzuki's
game was different from corporate extortion elsewhere
in the world, especially in America, where greenmail was
legal, a game played by brazen but prominent business-

men. In Japan, those who buy big blocks of shares and try to run up stock prices are thought of as corrupt and collusive, akin to gangsterism. After a stock had been cornered it was common practice to send round a heavy to the company to announce that it had a new director. Funded by a local bank, the company would shortly buy out the threatening shareholder at an exorbitant price and disperse the shares to subsidiaries.

Many of the aspiring speculators in the 1980s were erstwhile real-estate millionaires who, though they may have gone on to become notorious market operators, knew very little about shares on the Tokyo Stock Exchange. 'I hardly know the day-to-day business of the companies I buy,' admitted Suzuki. 'I buy a large block, send the share price for a ride and sell out at a profit.' The bold assumption of most speculators is that they can wield enough financial and political control over the stock they buy that they will never lose money. As Suzuki and his companions discovered, money in Japan did indeed bestow financial and political control.

Like many speculators, Suzuki came from a humble background. His father had been a livestock trader, one ignominious step removed from the trades of butchery and leather tanning which the Japanese labelled as outcast work, and Suzuki had left school at the age of sixteen to sell vegetables. But he was full of ingenious schemes to make money. When he learned that the tobacco farmers he visited had to stay up all night in order to regulate the fire that controlled the smoke and temperature of the tobacco-curing houses, he had the idea of producing a thermostat to do the regulating for them. To his surprise, the thermostats that he began manufacturing were bought in dozens by the well-subsidized farmers and at the age of eighteen Suzuki found himself a wealthy man. By 1968, he had made over two million dollars and, like most big-time speculators, he began buying land and golf courses with his new-found riches. Part one of his career was over — the small-town boy had done well.

Part two of Suzuki's life was more complicated. He

invented another contraption, a water-sprinkling system, which again was such a success that in a year he had stashed away another five million dollars. However, his system rusted after one season, damaging the tobacco crop, and, once the farmers began complaining, Suzuki learned about Japanese politics. The farm lobby was one of Japan's strongest and when complaints started coming in, Suzuki was forced by national politicians to compensate the farmers for their losses. He lost his entire second fortune and part of his first but chalked up a gain of political credit. He claimed to be fortunate to have learned so much by the age of twenty. 'Japan is not like the States. Here I learned that to clear the wall you must keep giving politicians money.' Suzuki's refunds were treated as direct political contributions, an investment that was later repaid many times over.

Suzuki entered the grey world of stock speculation in the early 1970s, inspired by a drive to recoup. He had been watching enviously as the stockmarket's top operators greenmailed corporate Japan in 1971. It was a year of rampant speculation when Sanko Steamship was trying to take over Japan Line, while Eitaro Itoyama was in the midst of cornering Nakayama Steel shares. At the same time, Suzuki's business partner sold him out of one of their golf courses without consulting him and, moreover, sold at what Suzuki suspected was an artificially low price, taking an under-the-table payment as an incentive. Knowing that his ex-partner was also head of a medium-sized industrial company listed on the Tokyo Stock Exchange, Suzuki began buying up shares in it on the exchange, using his own source of funds: exorbitant golf membership deposits at his other courses. Finally he had bought so much that he threatened to gain control of the firm, forcing his enemy to buy out his shares at a huge mark-up.

Such greenmail was nothing new to Japan, but Suzuki was discovering that speculation was not a closed affair. 'Everyone gets a part of the action when you corner a share, especially the politicians,' he complained. In return, the politicians were able to introduce banking contacts to speculators.

Suzuki noticed that ruling Diet members Toshio Komoto and Eitaro Itoyama conducted two of the greatest corporate raids of the early 1970s. These were, however, exceptionally high-profile instances of stockmarket killings channelled into politics. The preferred route was a collusive arrangement among the speculators, politicians and a local bank manager who provided a large line of credit. The speculator risked little or none of his own capital, bought up stock, sold it back to the company at an inflated price and paid back the bank, splitting the ill-made gains among himself and his political friends. The politicians then took receipt of the funds in the name of a third party. Alternatively, the politician could use his own credit channels and set up a brokerage account in a third party name.

Money begot money, and after Suzuki had made his first ten million, he found it easier to make his second. 'I am a self-made man and have never worked for anybody,' Suzuki would proudly tell his friends. Despite this independent streak, after his first speculative deal Suzuki was never able to work alone. Every speculator worked with a group – a team of other wealthy market manipulators who pooled their capital and credit lines to amass the tens or hundreds of millions of dollars needed to corner and support a stock. Nonetheless, Suzuki did not hesitate to call any deal he worked on 'his deal'; they were his ideas which he orchestrated by rounding up the usual investors, politicians, bankers and brokers. One of Suzuki's counterparts was aptly called 'the Sun'; all speculative life emanated from and gravitated around him. Most of the speculators never knew who the other members of their own group were, only the central coordinator. Even the glorified world of speculation had a hierarchy and, as Suzuki pushed, he found himself on top.

Suzuki's stockmarket deals got bigger, his credit lines longer and his pocketbook fatter. To send out a sure sign that he was a major player, Suzuki bought Hawaiian real estate and a piece of land in the fashionable Roppongi district of Tokyo worth over three million dollars. He completely rebuilt his home, decorating it in white Italian marble. Suzuki also backed the candidacy of Mr Fukuda in his bid for the prime ministership, continuing to finance Fukuda's home and family after his term expired.

By 1985-86 Suzuki's greenmail tactics had reached record proportions and he decided to go for a big kill. A friend of his at a famous speculative group named Video Seller owned 15 per cent of the outstanding shares of the family-run Fujiya confectionery company, which had begun as a small bakery in 1938 and had grown into one of the nation's largest food conglomerates. It was common among market operators to accumulate stock and pass it on at a profit to someone who would do the same. Suzuki offered to buy the Video Seller's twenty-million-share block at a price of 300 yen per share. Another friend at Oriental Finance owned a further twenty million shares, which were pledged to Suzuki, and the total percentage now in his control came to 30 per cent.

Reckoning that he needed another twenty-three million shares to gain 51 per cent of the firm, he bought Fujiya shares on the Tokyo Stock Exchange through 1985 and the first half of 1986. The chairman and founder of the company, Goro Fujii, thought Suzuki was trying to bluff his way to a handsome greenmail payment and told him that he could not possibly buy another 20 per cent of Fujiya on the open market. Unknown to family members, however, Suzuki had oiled the palm of Fujii's son, who owned a big chunk of the firm and who began selling secretly to Suzuki. Shares of Fujiya jumped from 1,000 yen in 1985 to over 3,000 yen by the middle of 1986. Trading volume slowly dried up, and the market price bore no resemblance to reality. Even small buy orders shot the price up 5 or 10 per cent in a day. Goro Fujii did not budge until Suzuki presented him with evidence of ownership.

Suzuki threatened to sack the entire board of directors unless Fujiya bought the 51 per cent stake off him at over 1,500 yen a share, which he claimed was fair since he had paid close to 900 yen a share for the block, not including financing costs. To scare Fujii, Suzuki went to Sanyo Securities to ask if they could find a foreign firm to buy the company, a story that not only made its way back to Fujii, as Suzuki intended, but also to some protectionist members of the Diet who told him, said Suzuki, 'enough was enough and to settle this immediately'. Goro Fujii brought in Kyowa Bank, his main bankers, who agreed to put up over $500 million to buy Suzuki out. Goro Fujii knew it was an inflated price (the quoted price on the Tokyo Stock Exchange had risen to an inflated 3,700 a share) and, after haggling, both parties agreed in November to transfer the block at 1,280 per share. Any Japanese individual unfortunate enough to have been holding Fujiya shares watched the price plummet overnight from 2,800 to 1,280 yen per share, once the deal had been consummated. 'The best part of the deal was that I really paid only 720 yen for all my shares,' laughed Suzuki. He walked away with nearly $200 million before political pay-outs, the largest single greenmail in Japan or America. 'I can't think of any single individual who has ever made that much on a deal,' remarked Joe Flom, America's legal takeover guru. And nobody in the Japanese or Western press even knew Suzuki's name: once the anonymity of any stock coordinator such as Suzuki is lost, he is no longer an effective master of the universe and his mantle is passed on.

While Suzuki had been threatening the Fujii family in 1986, a host of other speculator groups had blossomed and had begun setting the tempo of the Tokyo Stock Exchange. Many speculators entering the stockmarket were real estate groups with cash surpluses they wanted to invest, others were out for a quick corporate mugging, while still others wanted to line the pockets of their favourite politician. It was a heady time for the Japanese market as it raced to new highs. Prices roared ahead as these groups bought up steel and heavily capitalized shares and then passed on latent asset rumours to branch offices of major securities firms. Then suddenly, in August 1986, Nomura Securities put an end to the frenzied buying.

The Japanese bull market of 1986 was a rare instance of Nomura Securities losing control of the stockmarket, a control it had exerted since 1965. As Suzuki stated, 'Nomura knows everything in the market, but does not necessarily interfere in every manipulation. It has its ways of manipulating Japan.' Nomura's role was to settle market feuds. Nonetheless, Nomura Securities still had the best speculative contacts. As if to emphasize this, a well-known and embarrassing photograph taken in 1986 showed Prime Minister Yasuhiro Nakasone playing golf with Yoshihisa Tabuchi, the president of Nomura Securities, and with the head of Korin Sangyo, one of the most potent political and stockmarket speculative groups in Japan.

When Nomura did aid groups like Korin Sangyo it was with extreme secrecy. In such an event, Nomura's corporate strategy and services department would find a buyer for a threatening block of stock, a task carried out by Minoru Segawa in the 1960s and 1970s. After he had been bumped up from chairman to senior adviser to Nomura in 1978, his successors played down the firm's role in 'fixing' corporate deals in Japan and, like many American investment houses, they institutionalized greenmail, called it corporate finance, and tried not to tarnish the Nomura name by actively seeking out that sort of business.

What angered Nomura executives in the summer of 1986 was the low-quality of buy orders that began taking over the market. Nomura was losing business to smaller, less reputable houses. Speculation bred disruption. Once the speculative, aggregate market share rose above 10 per cent, as it did in 1986, Nomura muscled in and cut off the source of funds to the stockmarket, thus wittingly precipitating a fall in the market itself. The swift, severe and highly effective means by which it strangled the market was through an obscure, unlisted finance company named Kaneoka, whose business it was to lend money for real-estate and stockmarket investment.

Founded in 1958 by Nobukera Kaneoka, the company

began by taking over the bills due to be paid to manufacturers, paying the manufacturer an immediate cash percentage,
say 80 or 90 per cent, of the worth of a bill, then collecting
the total for itself. Some bills carried a heavier risk than others
and Kaneoka dealt with bad credit risks by hiring thugs to use
threats or force to collect money. Sometimes an office raid
yielded furniture and valuables that paid off the debtor's
bill. By 1986 Kaneoka was making money by borrowing
short-term funds from the money market and lending them
out to speculators at high rates of interest.

Nomura picked out Kaneoka because it was at the top of
a financial pyramid with long lines of credit from Japanese
banks which enabled it to lend out to other finance companies with less clout. A firm with under 200 workers, Kaneoka
was able to fund the exuberance of the world's largest
stockmarket from its head offices in the heart of Tokyo. Yet
few Japanese had ever heard of it. Moneylending has always
been a secretive business and no billboards announced its
presence. Kaneoka did not cater to the consumer but rather
to property wheeler-dealers and market operators in need of
tens of millions of dollars. Most business was done over the
phone with known market players. 'We can lend millions of
dollars in under an hour,' bragged Kaneoka's spokesman, Mr
Yajima, an ex-Sanyo Securities man. 'A bank takes up to a
month to make a credit decision.'

When Nomura executives approached Koji Kaneoka, the
founder's son and president of the firm, in the summer of
1986 they made him a simple offer: shut down all credit for
speculative purposes and Nomura will get Kaneoka's shares
listed on the stockmarket. It was a potent offer, for Koji
Kaneoka had long yearned for the prestige a public listing
would give his family.

Like Suzuki, Kaneoka was a striking example of Japan's
new rich and had been able to get his hands on huge lines
of cash for speculative purposes; moreover, he had come to
control the flow of credit to other speculators. He did not
need to take Kaneoka public in order to raise money: in fact,

the total market capitalization of Kaneoka after it eventually did go public was a paltry $126 million. Friends were in awe of how much money he invested in the Japanese stockmarket. 'I have seen Koji Kaneoka sell over a billion dollars of leveraged stock in a two-day period,' swore one observer, in shock at the sheer size of his stock portfolio. 'On that particular sale, he recognized over a quarter-billion-dollar profit.' To the mega-rich Kaneoka, Nomura's offer had a richer appeal than mere money.

When Kaneoka pulled the financial plug for Nomura in early August, the ensuing three months became tough in the Japanese stockmarket. The 'investment groups' Kaneoka had financed, no longer able to carry their huge stock inventories, dumped shares to raise cash and stock prices plunged. The first to take a nosedive were vulnerable shares that had been cornered, but by mid-August the carnage had spread to entire sectors and finally the whole market. Meanwhile the Ministry of Finance looked away as Nomura strong-armed the upstart groups. Earlier in the year the Ministry had sent round its own investigative teams to raid speculative groups in order to quell rampant stock price inflation; it did not prosecute the groups, but simply warned them to calm down the market. By the summer of 1986, however, the market had been beyond its control. As one stockmarket analyst noted, 'It was hard to stuff the genie back in the bottle, so Nomura took over.'

By mid-October, Nomura had reasserted its domination over the Tokyo Stock Exchange. The uncontrolled fires which had burned earlier that year had been stamped out. Nomura's market share rose to over 18 per cent as it sold the safe theme of asset value throughout its branch network. Sensing the end was near, on 23 October the Nikkei 225 average bottomed out and began heading north again. Kaneoka was given the go-ahead to release cash to the dozens of finance companies it supplied. Although the speculator started coming back to the market, the small investor to whom Nomura sold stock played a more cautious game. They had been stung and stayed closely by Nomura's side.

Having met Nomura's conditions of their underwriting, in November Kaneoka shares were listed on the over-the-counter market, where listings were given to firms to whom Japan's brokers owed a debt or where a favour could be called in later. The OTC market was filled with over a hundred companies of a quality and size too small to list on the Tokyo Stock Exchange – a diminutive phone market that mirrored the successful NASDAQ in America, where over 3,000 companies were listed. Nomura, however, promised to upgrade Kaneoka to the second section of the Tokyo Stock Exchange and in the meantime, Nomura and Sanyo Securities wrote up several buy recommendations on the firm, touting Kaneoka shares to their branch networks. The Ministry of Finance was happy at the return of a stable market and Nomura was happy to regain control of its client base. Kaneoka was the happiest of all because Koji Kaneoka could now think of himself and his firm as respectable members of Japanese society.

30
A Modern Empire

Barely two weeks after the Great Crash in the autumn of 1987, Nomura Securities startled the Japanese financial world with one of the most revolutionary management shake-ups in post-war Japanese history. Eight of Nomura's forty main board directors were forced into retirement, while 800 managers and staff were reshuffled, a move that shook the very roots of Japan's seniority system, where clambering up the corporate pyramid had been a function of time, patience and endurance. Nomura Securities named two directors to the main board who were in their early forties, youngsters by Japanese standards, where the average age of a main board director was fifty-six. With one reshuffle of the Nomura corporate deck, all that changed. Age no longer played a part in deciding managerial futures. The fastest climbers were to be the firm's rainmakers, the men who brought in the most revenue.

Nomura Securities then made another breathtaking, but less heralded, announcement: salesmen were to be awarded bonuses in line with the money they made for Nomura. This was inspiring news to the sales force, especially middle-ranking *kabuya* adept at churning client accounts. Previously, members of each Nomura class advanced *en masse* through management ranks, but now production salesmen could skip ahead of what they called 'old dogs' – the middle managers who idled their working day by reading the paper, making a few calls, drinking coffee and commuting home. Never in Japanese history had money been so blatantly brandished as a means of advancement.

Yoshio Terasawa and Koichi Minaguchi, the two executive vice presidents who formed half of the mighty inner circle below the president, resigned from their posts with golden handshakes. It was rumoured that both men received close to a million and a half dollars in severance pay, tax free, after serving for years in half-million-dollar-a-year jobs. Large handouts were, however, common perks at Nomura. 'A Nomura man will never forsake his board membership for higher pay elsewhere,' asserted Hisashi Moriya, a former Nomura board member who left to join Merrill Lynch for more autonomy as a Merrill vice-chairman. 'Nobody has more benefits than Nomura.' Senior Nomura executives estimated that Setsuya Tabuchi alone would receive close to one billion yen in severance payments, equivalent to seven million dollars at the time of the restructuring when he relinquished his chairmanship.

There was disappointment but not disgrace in the reshuffle. Terasawa, the man who brought Wall Street to Japan, spent his last months in office writing two books about his tenure in Nomura before being nudged out of his plush Nihonbashi offices to take up a senior position with the World Bank. With their premier international ambassador (known as 'Mr Nice Guy' throughout the financial world) ousted, Nomura made it quite clear that it was making room in its line-up for younger super-stars. Koichi Minaguchi, who had been Nomura's conduit to the Ministry of Finance, resigned to regroup the Nomura Research Department, the world's largest commercial think-tank (which had just acquired the Nomura Computer Company, one of the nation's leading software companies). He replaced the man known in Japan as the 'brain of Nakasone', Yukitsugu Nakagawa, whose retirement, Nomura executives reasoned, seemed appropriate with the passing of Yasuhiro Nakasone as prime minister.

Nomura did not prune senior managers simply to let super-salesmen take their place. The restructuring was a well-conceived plan to shape the Nomura empire into a combine to match its pre-war glory. 'By tightening control over its subsidiaries and affiliates,' said Kozo Nomura, Tokushichi's nephew, 'Nomura Securities is reforming a *zaibatsu*.' However, it was unlike the pre-war *zaibatsu* where entrepreneurs flourished. This was the era of the corporate *zaibatsu*.

By forcibly retiring main board members when they reached the age of sixty, Nomura was able to farm some of them out as presidents of other Nomura subsidiaries. In fact, Nomura paid hefty premiums to implant such high-ranking talent in less desirable posts. The fourth most powerful man in Nomura, Takashi Takano, resigned as executive managing director, reputedly with nearly $600,000 in severance pay, and went to preside over Nomura Real Estate, Japan's fifth largest property developer. As the former head of Nomura's equity sales division, he was ideally suited to boost sales at Nomura Real Estate as a prelude to one day listing the firm's shares on the Tokyo Stock Exchange.

At the same time a pair of directors resigned to take charge of World Securities and Takagi Securities, two of Nomura's satellite brokers. And so the list went on. The new jobs were high-paying, came with limousines, chauffeurs, expense accounts that could easily be padded, fawning underlings and pretty secretaries – everything to which the directors were accustomed. Furthermore, most of these postings came with the title of president, with the prospect of five or six years to what was in effect their second retirement, when each would receive another lump-sum severance payment – 'the price Nomura paid to satisfy its generals', as one retiring executive called it.

There was no concern about how Nomura Securities would fund the departure of its senior members, or its future bonuses to stellar salesmen. The firm had earned close to four billion dollars before taxes in the full year to September 1987. Two weeks after President Yoshihisa Tabuchi tore apart and rebuilt the House of Nomura (and exactly one month after the Great Crash), he was able to announce that Nomura had become the most profitable company in Japan.

The Japanese media feasted on the Nomura earnings story, comparing Nomura's rise to the relative decline of the Toyota Motor Company. Trumpeted in every newspaper was the cry that the Age of Broking had arrived while the Age of Industry and Manufacturing had peaked. The Japanese had long equated finance with elitism, especially in the immediate post-war era when the nation's industry was funded by banking loans. The gradual power shift from the Ministry of International Trade and Industry to the Ministry of Finance had been completed by the late 1970s – but through the prowess of bankers, not brokers.

Now, though, the Japanese faced a problem – the possible social upheaval caused by the new wealth generated through the stock and property markets. Well-educated men and women sought to join Nomura Securities in the mid-1980s, not for the prestige that Nomura offered but for money – and, as Tokushichi Nomura had discovered, prestige ultimately followed money. By the autumn of 1987 the once scorned stockbroker was at long last looked upon with envy by the average salaryman. Not only did Nomura pay higher than most other Japanese firms, but there was a cachet in being associated with the stockmarket. It was as if Japan, as a nation, had decided during the Great Bull Market of 1986 and 1987 that money was now a refined topic of conversation.

Nonetheless, there was unease among Japan's working class. While corporate Japan was becoming phenomenally rich, practically none of the money was trickling down to the working man. Close to 90 per cent of all Japanese listed companies had employee stock ownership plans, but few companies distributed more than one per cent of their stock and when they did, it was to themselves or friends. Nomura was one of the few firms to lend money to managers, salesmen and office ladies to buy shares. Overall, in a stockmarket worth over three trillion dollars, only twenty billion dollars' worth of shares – or slightly more than one half of one per cent – were owned by Japanese workers. Somebody was getting rich and it was not the worker.

The brokerage community, corporate chieftains, politicians, bureaucrats and favoured friends were those who prospered, separated from the salaryman not only by money but by an elite network of personal and social ties, fostered on golf courses, in tea-houses and board rooms.

However, the Recruit scandal of 1988-89 was an unparalleled example of influence peddling and signalled the end of an era in which brokers such as Nomura dispensed lavish financial favours.

Recruit, a Japanese employment agency, had offered shares in its unlisted property company to over 155 legislators, bureaucrats and businessmen between 1984 and 1986. When the shares were listed in 1986, they soared and everyone involved made huge profits. Shares had been handed out hundreds of times throughout the post-war years but this time a city reporter – rather than the political desk, which would have squashed it – on the liberal newspaper *Asahi Shimbun* got hold of the story and doggedly pursued it through 1988. By 1989 an entire list of Recruit stock recipients was uncovered, toppling the prime minister, a finance minister, two justice ministers, a deputy prime minister, the opposition chairman and the chairman of Nippon Telephone and Telegraph.

The Recruit scandal, uncommon only in its magnitude, posed a potentially serious problem for the future of Nomura Securities. Clearly, the money-politics era was gone – an era when Nomura's presidents and Japan's prime ministers had a mutual understanding that the securities markets would be unencumbered by heavy legislation and taxation. That understanding no longer existed.

This was the first post-war fracture in Japan's old-boy network. It was a sign from the people of Japan that they had had enough.

Appendix 1
Nomura Family Tree

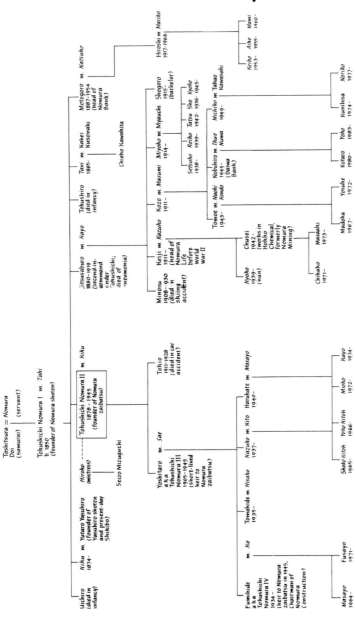

The Nomura Family Tree

Note: *Italics denote female names*

Appendix 2
The House of Nomura –
Corporate Make-up

The House of Nomura

THE NOMURA SECURITIES CO, LTD

(subsidiary companies under direct control of Nomura Securities, wholly owned unless otherwise stated)

FINANCE / SERVICES

The Nomura Securities Company

World's largest stockbroker
Ownership: Toyo Trust & Banking 2.6%

Nomura Securities Investment Management

Japan's largest money manager

Nomura Securities Investment Trust Management

Japan's largest unit trust manager

Nomura Research Institute

World's largest commercially-owned think tank, Japan's second largest software firm, incorporating Nomura Computer

Nomura Wasserstein Perella

Japanese mergers and acquisitions specialist
Ownership: Wasserstein Perella 20%

JAFCO

Venture capital subsidiary

Nomura Land & Building

Management company for Nomura properties; holding company for long-term and short-term Nomura investments unable legally to be held by Nomura Securities

NOMURA GROUP

(affiliated companies – many with historical links to the Nomura zaibatsu – over which Nomura has direct or indirect control, owned by Nomura Group with minority shareholders as stated)

Daiwa Bank

Japan's ninth largest commercial bank
Ownership: Nomura Securities 2.9%
Tokio Mutual Life 2.7%
Osaka Gas 2.6%

Toyo Trust & Banking

Japan's fifth largest trust bank
Ownership: Nomura Securities 4.9%
Nomura Land & Building 2.5%

Dai-Tokyo Fire & Marine

Japan's fifth largest non-life insurance company
Ownership: Nomura Land & Building 4.9%
Nomura Securities 4.8%
Toyo Trust and Banking 3.7%

Tokio Mutual Life Insurance

known as Nomura Life before WWII, technically owned by policyholders

Kokusai Securities

Japan's fifth largest securities house
Ownership: Nomura Securities Investment Management 16.0%
Nomura Research Institute 8.3%
Nomura Land & Building 6.2%
Nomura Securities 4.9%
Daiwa Bank 2.9%

Osaka Securities Finance

Major securities finance company for Nomura Investments
Ownership: Nomura Land & Building 12.0%
Nomura Securities 5.0%
Daiwa Bank 4.1%

MAJOR SHAREHOLDINGS

(over which Nomura has indirect control or power; Nomura's shareholding is stated)

Sanyo Securities

Japan's sixth largest securities firm
Ownership: Nomura Land & Building 5.5%
Nomura Securities 2.9%

Ichiyoshi, Taisei, Nichiei Securities

Wasserstein Perella

American mergers and acquisitions powerhouse
Ownership: Nomura Securities 20%

308

APPENDIX 2

Nomura Tourist Bureau

Travel agency for Nomura Securities and affiliates

Nomura Card Services

Itojin, World and Tsuragi Securities

Cosmo Securities

Medium-sized Osaka-based broker
Ownership: Daiwa Bank 4.9%

Osaka Gas

Japan's second largest gas supplier
Ownership: Daiwa Bank 4.9%
Tokio Mutual Life 2.2%

Yomiuri Land

Central company of one of world's largest leisure companies
Ownership: Nomura Securities 4.9%

REAL ESTATE/
CONSTRUCTION

Nomura Real Estate Development

Japan's fifth largest real-estate broker

Nomura Industrial Construction

Nippon Television Network

Part of Yomiuri Group; major TV station
Ownership: Nomura Securities 4.5%

Standard Shoes

Chuyo Shirts

Sugimura Warehouse

Ownership: Nomura Land & Building 27.9%
Toyo Trust & Banking 13.2%
Nomura Securities 5.0%
Daiwa Bank 5.0%

TRADING/
MANUFACTURING/
MISCELLANEOUS

Nomura Microscience

Nomura Trading

Shikibo

Osaka-based spinning company
Ownership: Daiwa Bank 4.9%
Osaka Securities Finance 4.1%
Tokio Mutual Life 4.9%

Hokko Chemical

Japan's third largest agrochemical manufacturer
Ownership: Tokio Mutual Life 7.4%
Nomura Construction 7.2%
Nomura Securities 4.9%
Daiwa Bank 4.9%

Meiji Leather

Japan's third largest tannery
Ownership: Tokio Mutual Life 9.9%
Nomura Land & Building 5.0%
Nomura Securities 5.0%
Daiwa Bank 5.0%
Nomura Trading 5.0%

APPENDIX 3
Holdings of the Nomura *Zaibatsu*

It has been said of the great pre-war *zaibatsu* families that never in the industrial history of mankind had so few controlled so much. Today, that control – that power – takes a different form. The landed families of Japan – names like Mitsui, Iwasaki, Yasuda and Nomura – hold much less sway over corporate Japan. But their legacy survives. Japan is ruled today through the banking, broking and insurance arms of former *zaibatsu* houses.

The same names remain but the ownership of Japan's companies has passed from family to institution. Where once family cross-holdings existed, now more potent and equally self-interested institutional cross-holdings rule.

The following is a list of shareholdings held by Nomura group firms in Tokyo Stock Exchange first section companies, Japan's equivalent of the New York Stock Exchange.

All figures represent percentage shareholdings.

Nomura Securities was founded on Christmas Day, 1925. Although it did not become the largest stockbroker in Japan until the early 1960s it was the first firm with a research department and the first to sell stock directly to the masses. Though Nomura's shareholdings may not appear large in comparison to the holdings of Daiwa Bank and Toyo Trust & Banking, it must be remembered that the Ministry of Finance frowns upon corporations, other than banks and insurance companies, becoming holding companies. Nomura will often use Japan and Osaka Securities Finance to park stock in a nominee account.

Chiba Bank, one of Japan's largest regional banks, 2.1
Dai-Tokyo Fire & Marine, sixth largest non-life firm, 4.8

held by Nomura Securities, 4.9 by Nomura Land & Building
Daiwa Bank, ninth largest commercial bank, 2.9
Daiwa Danchi, prefab house builder, 3.4 held by Nomura Securities, 3.7 by Nomura Land & Building
Hokko Chemical, third largest agrichemical company, 4.9
Japan Securities Finance, largest market lender, 3.3
Kokusai Securities, fifth largest broker, 50 held by Nomura affiliates
Nippon Television, major network, 4.5
Nissan Construction, 2
Sanyo Securities, sixth largest broker, 2.9 held by Nomura Securities, 5.5 by Nomura Land & Building
Sekisui Jushi, resin processor, 2.3
Sogo Department Store, 4.1
Toyo Denki Seizo, electrical manufacturing, 2.3
Toyo Trust & Banking, fifth largest trust bank, 4.9 held by Nomura Securities, 2.9 by Nomura Land & Building
Yomiuri Land, 4.9

The Dai-Tokyo Fire & Marine Insurance Company, Japan's sixth largest non-life insurance company, and a loosely affiliated Nomura satellite, was established in 1918.

Daiichi Cement, 5.9
Daikyo, condominium builder, 3.8
Inageya, supermarket, 4.8
Izutsuya, department store, 2.7
Kitanippon Sogo Bank, 2.1
Naigai, sock maker, 3.5
Nippon Gas, 3
Osaki Electric, meters, 3.3
Tokai, LPG distributor, 6.3
Tokyo Nissan Auto, 4

The Tokio Mutual Life Insurance Company was called Nomura Life Insurance before World War II. After the war, the Japanese authorities, with American guidance, took ownership of life insurance companies out of the hands of private owners and put it in the hands of the policyholders themselves. From the policyholders, representatives are elected to run the firm. Many of the older representatives retain connections with the Nomura group. Its listed holdings are not extensive:

Hokko Chemical, agrichemical producer, 7.4
Daiei, chain store, 1.5

Osaka Gas is the second largest gas company in Japan. In 1925, Tokushichi Nomura rescued the firm from predators when the trust of its American owner decided to sell their stake. Nomura owned nearly half the firm by World War II, a stake that was later sold off to the public. Osaka Gas still retains a 2.6 stake in Daiwa Bank.

The Nomura Industrial Construction Company is the Nomura family firm, the only remnant to survive the dismemberment of the *zaibatsu*. The main shareholders are its president, Fumihide Nomura, and Keiji, Kozo and Tomohide Nomura (see Appendix 1) with a small stake held by both Nomura Securities and the Daiwa Bank. It has a 7.2 stake holding in Hokko Chemical, a real-estate portfolio and over one million shares in Nomura Securities. The stake in Nomura Securities was worth nearly $70 million at the peak of Nomura's share price in the bull market of 1987.

Daiwa Bank is the ninth largest commercial bank in Japan. Founded by Tokushichi Nomura in 1918 as the Osaka-Nomura Bank, it changed its name to the Nomura Bank in 1927 and finally to its present name in 1948. Unlike American banks, which are not allowed to own shares in firms to which they lend money, it is Japanese practice to purchase a strategic shareholding in a corporate borrower. The breadth of Daiwa Bank's shareholdings is staggering:

Akai, consumer electronics, 2.7

Araya, bicycle parts, 4.1
Asanuma, construction, 4.7
C. Itoh Fuel, 2.6
Chino, instruments, 2.3
Chugai Ro, furnace maker, 5
Chugoku Electrical Construction, 3.9
Chujitsuya, supermarket, 3.3
Cosmo Securities, 4.9
Dai Nippon Screen, 4.7
Daifuku, equipment maker, 2.2
Daiichi Jitsugyo, trading house, 4.5
Daisan Sogo Bank, 3.9
Daishinpan, credit company, 4.9
Dowa Fire & Marine, 3.4
Fuji Kosan, oil refiner, 4.6
Fuji Photo, 2.7
Fujitec, elevators, 4.6
Fukutoku Sogo Bank, 4.9
Furukawa Mining, 2.3
Fuso Pharmaceutical, 2.9
Gunze, raw silk, 4.2
Haseko, construction, 4.8
Heiwa Real Estate, 1.7
Hitachi Seiki, machine tools, 2.9
Hitachi Zosen, engineering, 2.3
Hokko Chemical, 4.9
Intec, software, 2.4
Ishihara Sangyo, titanium dioxide, 4.7
Iwatani, gas trading, 6
Janome Sewing Machine, 2.5
Japan Aviation, 2.4
Jusco, supermarket, 3.7
Kanegafuchi Chemical, 5.4
Kansai Electric Power, 2.6
Kao, household products, 3.3
Kawasaki Steel, 3.3
Kawashi, steel trader, 2

Kinki Nippon Railway, 2.5
Kinki Sogo Bank, 4.8
Kobori Juken, home builder, 4.9
Kokusai Kogyo, aerial survey, 3.8
Konami, software, 4
Kubota, farm equipment, 3.3
Kuraray, synthetic fibres, 4.4
Kureha, chemicals, 4.9
Kurimoto, cast iron pipes, 4.9
Kyokuro, fishery, 4.9
Marimoto, construction, 5
Maruichi Steel, largest welded steel pipe maker, 3.4
Matsushita Refrigeration, 6.8
Meisei Industrial, thermal insulation, 4.9
Minolta, camera maker, 4
Mitsubishi Metal, smelter, 3.6
Mitsubishi Mining & Cement, 2.1
Mitsubishi Rayon, acrylic fibres, 4.4
Mitsubishi Warehouse, 2.1
Musashino Bank, 4.9
Mutow, catalogue marketer, 3.2
National Securities, 4.1
Nichiboshin, short-term lender, 4.9
Nichido Fire & Marine, 4.7
Nichiei, contractor, 3.3
Nichimo, condominium builder, 5.1
Nippon Conveyor, 2
Nippon Housing Loan, 3.8
Nippon Koei, consulting, 2.5
Nippon Metal, stainless pipe, 5
Nippon Shokubai, chemicals, 4.6
Nippon Soda, caustic soda, 5
Nippon Synthetic Chemicals, 4.6
Nishi-Nippon Bank, eleventh largest regional bank, 4.9
Nissin Food, noodles, 3.3
Nisso Iwai, sixth largest trading house, 3.6
Okasan Securities, medium-sized broker, 2.7

Okomura, construction, 4.7
Osaka Cement, 4.1
Osaka Gas, second largest gas company, 4.9
Osaka Kiko, machine maker, 5
Rohm, integrated circuit maker, 3.4
Saeki Kensetsu, dredging, 5
Sakai Heavy, road paving machinery, 2.4
Sanyo Electric Railroad, 4.7
Sato Shoji, metal trader, 4.9
Sekisui Chemical, prefab houses, 3.6
Sekisui House, largest home builder, 3.3
Sekisui Jushi, resins, 3.6
Sekisui Plastics, foam plastic, 3
Sharp, consumer electronics, 4.3
Shikibo, spinning, 4.9
Shimano, bicycle parts, 4.9
Sogo Department Store, 3.5
Sumitomo Electric Wire, 2.5
Takara Standard, kitchen equipment, 4.4
Takashimaya, Japan's oldest department store, 4.4
Tateho Chemical, 4
Tatsuta Wire & Cable, 4.9
Toa Doro Kogyo, road paver, 4.1
Toa Spinning, 3.8
Tokai Senko, cloth printer, 4.4
Torishima Pump, 4.9
Totoku Electric, CRT displays, 4.6
Toyobo, textiles, 2
Toyoda Gosei, rubber parts, 2.6
Toyota Motor Company, 2.3
Towa Real Estate, 4.3
Yamazen, trading house, 4.8
Yodogawa Steel, 4.9
Yoshimoto Kogyo, theatres, 4.9

Toyo Trust and Banking was founded in 1959 by Nomura Securities' securities management division, Sanwa Bank and the Bank of Kobe – all three from the Osaka-Kobe area. Notably, Toyo Trust has a stake in almost every major pharmaceutical company in Japan, a tradition in keeping with Osaka's history as a centre for medicinal remedies. Toyo Trust also has significant holdings in almost every major electronics and high tech firm in Japan. At the time of Toyo's birth in 1959 it was Yamaichi, not Nomura, who acted as financial adviser to blue chip firms such as the textile, mining and trading companies. Electronics firms were high growth, high risk and, at the time, low class clients. But it was this client base that Nomura and Toyo Trust and Banking won over.

Advantest, instrument maker, 2.1
Alps, component maker, 3.6
Amada, machinery maker, 2.7
Anritsu, appliance maker, 5
Asahi Breweries, 1.9
Asahi Denka, chemicals, 2.2
Asahi Organic Chemical, 2.8
Bando Chemical, 3.5
Cosmo Oil, 2.7
Dai Nippon Pharmaceutical, 3.2
Daicel, acetic acid, 3.5
Daihatsu Motor, minicars, 2.6
Daiichi Katei Denki, electronics chain store, 3.5
Daiichi Seiyaku, pharmaceuticals, 2.6
Daikin, air conditioners, 2.6
Daikyo, condominiums, 3.8
Daishinpan, consumer credit, 4.9
Dai-Tokyo Fire & Marine, 3.7
Daiwa House, home builder, 2.5
Denki Kagaku, chemicals, 2.4
Ezaki Glico, confectioner, 3.4
France Bed, 3.5
Fuji Photo Film, 2.9
Fujisawa, pharmaceutical, 5.8

Fujitsu, Japan's largest computer maker, 2.5
Futaba, world's largest fluorescent tube maker, 3.6
Green Cross, pharmaceutical, 2.8
Haseko, construction, 3.4
Heiwa Real Estate, 1.5
Hirose, connectors, 2.8
Hisaki, machines, 5.1
Hitachi, Japan's largest electric machinery maker, 2.8
Hitachi Cable, 2.5
Hitachi Credit, consumer finance, 4.4
Hitachi Metals, 2.2
House Foods, spices, 2.1
Hoya, optical glass, 7.2
Ikegami, broadcasting equipment, 3.4
Intec, software, 3.6
Isetan, department store, 2
Iwantani, gas trading, 6
Iwatsu, telecommunications, 5.5
Joshin Denki, electronics chain store, 3.5
Jujo Paper, Japan's third largest paper manufacturer, 2.4
Jusco, supermarket, 2.8
Keisei Electric Railway, 2.4
Koa Fire & Marine, 2.6
Kokusai Electric, testing machines, 3.8
Komatsu, world's second largest maker of construction
equipment, 3.1
Konica, copier and camera maker, 2.8
Kyocera, ceramics, 2.9
Lion, household goods, 2.1
Marui, department store, 2.2
MCI, industrial electronics, 3.2
Meidensha, heavy machinery, 2.1
Mitsubishi Gas & Chemical, 2.1
Mitsubishi Metal, smelting, 3.6
Mitsubishi Warehouse, 2.1
Mitsuboshi Belting, industrial belts, 5
Mitsui Real Estate, Japan's largest real-estate company, 3.8

Raito Kogyo, civil engineering, 6.3
Rinnai, largest gas appliance maker, 2.3
Sanken, 2.1
Sankyo, Japan's second largest drug company, 3.4
Secom, security systems, 3.4
Sekaicho Rubber, shoes, 4.3
Sekisui House, largest home builder, 2.4
Sekisui Chemical, prefab houses, 2.4
Sekisui Plastics, 2.6
Shikibo, textiles, 4.9
Shimadzu, precision, 2.1
Shin Meiwa, dump trucks, 2.2
Shinetsu, silicon wafers, 3.4
Shionogi, pharmaceuticals, 2.4
Shokusan Jutaku, wooden house builder, 2.8
Sony, 2.7
Sumitomo Cement, 2.7
Sumitomo Metal Mining, 2.8
TDK, tapemaker, 4.3
Taiyo Yuden, ferrites, 2.2
Takeda, Japan's largest drug company, 2.4
Teijin, polyester, 5.6
Teikoku Oil, 3.4
Tobu Railway, 2.2
Toho Rayon, 2.6
Tokuyama Soda, caustic soda producer, 5.5
Tokyo Broadcasting System, 3.4
Tokyo Electric Power, world's largest power company, 1.6
Tokyo Seimitsu, semiconductors, 2.9
Tokyu Railway, 2.2
Toppan Printing, 2.4
Toray, synthetic fibre maker, 2.6
Toshiba Ceramics, quartz producer, 2.4
Tosoh, chemicals, 2
Towa Real Estate, 4.3
Toyo Construction, civil engineering, 5.3
Toyo Ink, 6

Toyo Linoleum, 4.7
Toyo Telecommunications, 4.7
Toyo Tire & Rubber, 2.6
Toyoda Machine, 2.9
Tsubakimoto Chain, 3.1
Tsugami, machine tools, 2.1
Tsukishima Kikai, oil tanks, 5
Yamamura Glass, bottle maker, 2.1
Yamanouchi, pharmaceuticals, 4.6
Yasakawa Electric, 3
Yodogawa Steel, 4.9
Yokogawa Bridge, largest bridge builder, 2
Yoshitomi, pharmaceuticals, 4.4

Appendix 4
The Presidents of Nomura Securities

Otogo Kataoka	25 December 1925–17 December 1944
Seizo Iida	30 September 1941–13 August 1947
Tsunao Okumura	15 April 1948–1 June 1959
Minoru Segawa	1 June 1959–21 November 1968
Kiichiro Kitaura	21 November 1968–18 October 1978
Setsuya Tabuchi	18 October 1978–20 December 1985
Yoshihisa Tabuchi	20 December 1985–

Appendix 5
Periods of Modern Japanese History

Tokugawa	1603-1867
Meiji	1868-1912
Taisho	1912-1926
Showa	1926-1989
Heisei	1989-

Appendix 6
The Yen

The yen is the modern Japanese unit of money. In the early 1870s, Yl was equal to about US$1. By 1897, the yen had devalued to Y2 to the US dollar. From then until 1931, the exchange rate remained fairly constant (except in the early 1920s devaluation). For the rest of the 1930s the yen remained at about Y4 per US dollar. In 1949 the yen was set at Y360 to the US dollar and remained there until 1971. It was then revalued at Y308 to the dollar until February 1973, when it became freely floating.

(*Source*: Kunio Yoshihara, *Sogoshosha*, Oxford University Press, Tokyo, 1982)

Select English Bibliography

Abegglen, James C., and Stalk, George Jr., *Kaisha: The Japanese Corporation*, Basic Books, Inc., New York, 1985.

Abegglen, James C., *Management and Worker*, Kodansha International Ltd, Tokyo, 1973.

Adams, T.F.M., and Hoshii, Iwao, *A Financial History of the New Japan*, Kodansha International Ltd, Tokyo, 1972.

Allen, G.C., *A Short Economic History of Modern Japan: 1867-1937*, George Allen and Unwin Ltd, London, 1946.

Bisson, T.A., *Zaibatsu Dissolution in Japan*, University of California Press, Berkeley, 1954.

Caves, Richard E., *Multinational Enterprise and Economic Analysis*, Cambridge University Press, Cambridge, 1982.

Clark, Rodney, *The Japanese Company*, Yale University Press, New Haven and London, 1979.

Daems, Herman, *The Holding Company and Corporate Control*, Martinus Nijhoff Social Science Division of Leiden, Boston, 1978.

Dodwell Marketing Consultants, *Industrial Groupings in Japan*, Dodwell Marketing Consultants, Tokyo, 1975.

Doi, Takeo, *The Anatomy of Dependence* (translated by John Bester), Kodansha International Ltd, Tokyo and New York, 1973.

Drucker, Peter, *Innovation and Entrepreneurship: Practice and Principles*, Harper and Row, New York, 1985.

Elliott, T. I. (trans.), *The One Hundred Year History of Mitsui & Co. Ltd., 1876-1976*, Mitsui & Company, Tokyo, 1977.

Gibney, Frank, *Japan, the Fragile Superpower*, New American Library, New York, 1975.

Hadley, Eleanor M., *Anti-Trust in Japan*, Princeton University Press, Princeton, 1970.

Halliday, Jon, *A Political History of Japanese Capitalism*, Monthly Review Press, 1975.

Hirschman, Albert O., *The Strategy of Economic Development*, Yale University Press, New Haven and London, 1958.

Hirschmeier, Johannes, and Yui, Tsunehiko, *The Development of Japanese Business 1600-1973*, George Allen and Unwin Ltd, London, 1975.

Hirschmeier, Johannes, *The Origins of Entrepreneurship in Meiji Japan*, Harvard University Press, Cambridge, Massachusetts, 1964.

Inouye, Junnosuke, *Problems of the Japanese Exchange*, Robert Maclehose & Co., Glasgow, 1931.

Jansen, Marius B., *Japan and China: From War to Peace, 1894-1972*, Rand McNally College Publishing Co., Chicago, 1975.

Johnson, Chalmers A., *MITI and the Japanese Miracle: The Growth of Industrial Policy, 1925-1975*, Stanford University Press, Stanford, 1982.

Kojima, Kiyoshi, and Ozawa, Terutomo, *Japan's General Trading Companies: Merchants of Economic Development*, OECD, Paris, 1984.

Lockwood, William W., *The Economic Development of Japan: Growth and Structural Change 1868-1938*, Princeton University Press, Princeton, 1954.

Lockwood, William W. (ed.), *The State and Economic Enterprise in Japan*, Princeton University Press, Princeton, 1965.

Marshall, Byron, *Capitalism and Nationalism in Prewar Japan: The Ideology of the Business Elite, 1868-1938*, Princeton University Press, Princeton, 1954.

Mitsubishi Economic Research Institute, *Mitsubishi Enterprises*, Mitsubishi Economic Research Institute, Tokyo, 1955.

The Mitsui Bank, *The Mitsui Bank: A History of the First One Hundred Years*, The Mitsui Bank, Tokyo, 1976.

Nakane, Chie, *Japanese Society*, Weidenfeld and Nicolson, London, 1970.

The Nomura Securities Company, Beyond the Ivied Mountain, Nomura Securities, Tokyo, 1986.

Oka, Yoshitake, *Konoe Fumimaro*, University of Tokyo Press, Tokyo, 1983.

Okimoto, Daniel, *Between MITI and the Market*, Stanford University Press, Stanford, 1986.

Ozawa, Terutomo, *Multinationalism - Japanese Style: The Political Economy of Outward Dependency*, Princeton University Press, Princeton, 1979.

Pacific Basin Reports, *Japanese Financial/Industrial Combines, 1972 Handbook*, Pacific Basin Reports, San Francisco, 1972.

Pepper, Thomas and Merit Janow, Jimmy W. Wheeler, *The Competition: Dealing with Japan*, Praeger Publishing, New York, 1985.

Phipatseritham, Krirkkiat, and Yoshihara, Kunio, *Business Groups in Thailand*, Research Notes and Discussion Papers no. 41, Institute of South-East Asian Studies, Singapore, 1983.

Reischauer, Edwin O., *The Japanese*, Belknap Press, Cambridge, Massachusetts, 1977.

Roberts, John G., *Mitsui: Three Centuries of Japanese Business*, Weatherhill, New York and Tokyo, 1973.

Sansom, G.B., *Japan, A Short Cultural History*, Cresset Press, London, 1931.

Seidensticker, Edward, *Low City, High City*, Charles E. Tuttle, Tokyo, 1983.

Shibata, Tokue, *Public Finance in Japan*, University of Tokyo Press, Tokyo, 1986.

Smith, T.C., *Political Change and Industrial Development*, Stanford University Press, Stanford, 1955, 1974.

Tsurumi, Yoshi, with Rebecca Tsurumi, *Sogoshosha: Engines of Export-Based Growth*, The Institute for Research on Public Policy, Montreal, 1980.

Vogel, Ezra, *Modern Japanese Organization and Decision Making*, Charles E. Tuttle, Tokyo, 1975.

Waley, Paul, *Tokyo Now & Then*, Weatherhill, New York,

1984.

Wray, William D., *Mitsubishi and the N.Y.K.,* Harvard University Press, Cambridge, Massachusetts, 1984.

Yoshihara, Kunio, *Sogoshosha: The Vanguard of the Japanese Economy*, Oxford University Press, Tokyo, 1982.

Yoshino, M. Y., *Japan's Multinational Enterprises*, Harvard University Press, Cambridge, Massachusetts and London, 1976.

Select Japanese Bibliography

Chiba, Akira, *Nomura's Corporate Division* (*Nomura Shôken Kigyôbu*), Kanki Shuppan, Tokyo, 1984.

Fujii, Sakae, *Flying Through History: 70 Years of Sanyo Securities* (*Rekishi ni Kakeru: Sanyô Shôken 70 Nen Shi*), Matsui Keizai Kenkyusho, Tokyo, 1981.

Hirose, Niki, *Nomura's Founding Spirit* (*Nomura Shôken Sôgyô no Seishin*), Mikasa Shobo, Tokyo, 1987.

Inoue, Kaoru, *The History of Osaka* (*Osaka no Rekishi*), Sôgensha, Osaka, 1986 (first ed., 1979).

Itagaki, Hidenori, *Nomura's Alarming Ambitions* (*Osorubeshi Nomura Shôken no Yabô*), Yell Shukansha, Tokyo, 1986.

Kadogawa, Sōichi, *Why does 'Finance' mean Nomura Securities?* (*Naze 'Kinyu' wa Nomura Shôken nano ka*), Aska Business, Tokyo, 1985.

Kusano, Atsushi, *May 28th 1965 – The Yamaichi Crisis and the Bank of Japan's Special Loan* (*Shôwa 40 Nen 5 Gatsu 28 Nichi – Yamaichi Jiken to Nichigin Tokuyû*), Nihon Keizai Shimbunsha, Tokyo, 1986 (first ed., 1965).

Matsui Economic Research Centre, *Surviving the Rapids: Sixty Years of Nitto Securities* (*Gekiryû ni Ikiru: Nitto Shôken 60 Nen no Ayumi*), Matsui Keizai Kenkyusho, Tokyo, 1970.

Matsumoto, Michihiro, *Merrill Lynch vs Nomura Securities* (*Meriru Rinchi vs Nomura Shôken*), Diamond-sha, Tokyo, 1986.

Matsunaga, Sadaichi, *The Rise and Fall of Kitahama* (*Shin Kitahama Seisuiki*), Toyo Keizai Shimposha, Tokyo, 1977.

Mishima, Yasuo, *The Hanshin Zaibatsu: Nomura, Yamaguchi, Kawasaki – a History of Japanese Zaibatsu Operations* (*Nihon Zaibatsu Keiei Shi*), Nihon Keizai

Shimbunsha, Tokyo, 1984.

Miyamoto, Mataji, *Businessmen and Culture in Osaka (Osaka Keizaijin to Bunka)*, Jikkyo Shuppan, Tokyo, 1983.

Miyamoto, Mataji (ed.), *An Historical Record of Public Offices and Various Enterprises during the Taisho and Showa Periods (Taishôki Zaihan Kankô sho Shokigyo Enkaku Chôsa)*, Osaka City Historical Editorial Centre, Osaka, 1986.

Miyamoto, Mataji, *Notes on Modern Osaka's Development and its Personalities (Kindai Osaka no Tenkai to Jimbutsu Shi)*, Bunken Shuppan, Tokyo, 1986.

Miyazaki, Masahiro, *Nomura New York (Nyûyôku Nomura Shôken)*, IPEC, Tokyo, 1986.

The Nomura 50th Anniversary Editorial Committee, *50 Years of Nomura Securities (Nomura Shôken Kabushiki Kaisha 50 Nen Shi)*, Nomura Securities, Tokyo, 1976.

The Nomura Research Institute 10th Anniversary Editorial Committee, *10 Years of Nomura Research Institute (Nomura Sôgô Kenkyusho 10 Nen Shi)*, Nomura Research Institute, Tokyo, 1976.

The Nomura Securities Editorial Committee, *The History of Nomura Securities 1976-85 (Nomura Shôken Shi 1976-85)*, Nomura Securities, Tokyo, 1986.

Osaka Stock Exchange, *10 Years of the Osaka Stock Exchange (Osaka Shôken Torihikijo Ju Nen Shi)*, Osaka, 1964.

Osaka Techo Sha, *An Osaka Miscellany (Zuihitsu Osaka Techô)*, Osaka, 1965.

Saito, Tsusumu, *Nomura's Expanding Ambitions (Nomura Shôken no Oki naru Yabô)*, Keizaikai (Ryū Selection), Tokyo, 1986.

Segawa, Minoru, *My Life in Securities during the Showa Era (Watakushi no Shôken Showa Shi)*, Tôyô Keizai Shimposha, Tokyo, 1986.

Segawa, Minoru [and others], *My Personal History* vol.13: *Businessmen (Watakushi no Rirekisho)*, Nihon Keizai Shimbunsha, Tokyo, 1983 (reprint, first ed. 1980).

Tokyo Stock Exchange, *Kabutochô,* 100th Anniversary [Edition], Tokyo, 1978.

Ubukata, Yukio, *Nomura Securities vs Sumitomo Bank (Nomura Shôken vs Sumitomo Ginko),* Goma Shobo, Tokyo, 1985.

Yūki, Rentaro, *The Tale of Nomura's Cruelty (Nomura Shôken Zankoku Monogatari),* Yell Shuppansha, Tokyo, 1984.

Other References

The Financial World Research Centre, *Nomura's Giant Information Strategy (Nomura Shôken no Kyôdai Jôho Senryaku),* Chûkei Shuppan, Tokyo, 1984.

Yoshida, Kozen, *Economic Analysis Report (Keizai Bunseki Shûhô),* Keizai Bunseki Kenkyusho, Tokyo.

Matsumoto, Seicho, *Dissecting the Yamaichi Case (Yamaichi Jiken wo Kiru),* Bungei Shunju, Tokyo, August 1960.

The Asahi Newspaper, 'The Yamaichi Crisis', May 1965.

Nomura Family Source Material

Note: Japanese readers may like to consult Tokushichi Nomura II's copious and, at times, tedious autobiography written between 1939 and 1943. Called the *Tsutakatsura*, it is a collection of stories, pictures, facts and anecdotes. The twenty-four photocopied volumes were provided to me by Nomura Securities. Many of the quotes are from here and I considered this primary source material.

Nomura Securities presented me with *Nomura Tokuan* , a three-volume reprinted history of Tokushichi and the Nomura group published in 1951. Since much of this book came from the *Tsutakatsura*, I considered this secondary source material.

Ikezaki, Chuko, *Nomura Tokuan*: Official Biography, vols I and II*, The Nomura Tokuan Editorial Committee, Kobe, 1951.
Nomura, Kozo, and Iwamoto, Yoshichika (Ed.), *Jingaian Ki***, The Jingai-in Memorial Editorial Committee, 1946.

* The artistic pseudonym of Tokushichi Nomura.
** The pseudonym of Yoshitaro Nomura, the elder son of Tokushichi Nomura II.

Acknowledgements

The House of Nomura really fell into place for me when Robert White introduced me to the Nomura family. It was to be my big break. Tomohide Nomura, the second eldest grandson of the founder of Nomura Securities, sometimes spent as much as six hours at a stretch helping me with his family history. Another great source of help was Kozo Nomura, the founder's nephew, who talked to me for hours on end about pre-war life in one of Japan's richest families. Kozo had been destined to be one of the kingpins of the Nomura empire until the war broke it into pieces. Despite losing everything, however, he maintained his nobility and started again. I must also thank the Nomura wives – especially Hisako, Masumi and Sae Nomura (the wife of Yoshitaro Nomura, the founder's son) – and Fumihide Nomura, the eldest grandson of Tokushichi Nomura. (I must stress, however, that although *The House of Nomura* is an authorized family history, the family had very little involvement in the unauthorized post-war story of Nomura Securities.)

There are many other people who deserve a special mention. Whenever I needed encouragement, I would ring up or drop in on Professor Robert Ballon at Sophia University in Tokyo. The 'professor', as I called him, would sit back, light his pipe and listen to my problems. After a few puffy moments of silence he would give me a thoughtful answer, reach over into his floor-to-ceiling library and send me off with three or four volumes.

Of the six research assistants that I employed at different times, three of them worked for Nomura-related firms. One of these was John Doyle, who was translating financial material from Japanese to English when I first met him. He had spent his entire life in Japan except for the years he

332

took off to earn a degree from MIT in astrophysics. I needed a lightning-quick, Japanese-thinking mind like his to sift through reams of Japanese newspapers, journals and dozens of books, translating relevant passages and, in some cases, entire books. Soon after I met him, John went to work for Kokusai Securities as a dealer, sitting in their main trading room. He later joined me at James Capel.

After graduating from Sophia University, and before joining Salomon Brothers as an analyst, Kazumi Watanabe was extremely helpful in translating articles and acting as my interpreter. Munetaka Umehara proved very helpful in the early stages of the book, while David Semaya of Sanyo Securities helped in the later stages. Toake Endo assisted me in her summer off from college and was courageous enough to research underworld aspects of the *machki*, or finance houses. My sixth and final assistant must, however, remain anonymous since she is at present employed in one of Nomura's most sensitive departments.

The most helpful partner on the project was my wife, Anne, who worked for Yoichi Tsuchiya (president of Sanyo Securities) for five years, setting up Sanyo's international marketing department. Before we were married, I discovered Anne was an expert in detecting speculative stock price movements in the Japanese market, and on the pretext of discussing the market, asked her out to dinner. We were married in the summer of the next year – on 8 August 1988 – the luckiest day of the century to the Chinese.

Researching *The House of Nomura* was one thing, writing it was another. At about the time of the Great Crash, with thousands of pages of notes in semi-literary form, I began writing. Fortunately, I stumbled upon the man who would become my unofficial editor, Stephen Barber of INVESCO MIM, who had just moved to Tokyo to run their office. Brilliant in finance, versed in Japan and a man of letters, Stephen slashed my texts and sent me back for rewrites. I am also indebted to Francis Pike – a colleague of Stephen's, who introduced me to Bloomsbury Publishing

Limited; and I would like to thank Nigel Newton, David Reynolds and Penny Phillips of Bloomsbury. I would also like to thank Anne McDermid of Curtis Brown, Jim Levi and Stephen Aris. Finally, I should like to thank Brother Richard Devine of Sophia University, who was kind enough to read through the Meiji chapters for historical accuracy – any mistakes that remain are those I failed to correct.

The following individuals and organizations have also proved invaluable: *Nomura Research Institute (NRI):* Kiichi Saeki, ex-Chairman and Senior Adviser; Jiro Tokuyama of Mitsui Research Institute, founder Nomura School of Management, now Senior Adviser; Mitsuaki Muneoka, Director; Yoshinobu Hirayama, Senior Researcher; Haru Nakayama, Senior Analyst. *Nomura Computer Systems, Co. (now merged into NRI):* Teiichi Aruga, General Manager. *Nomura Investment Management Co. Ltd (NIMCO):* Yukio Aida, ex-Chairman and Senior Adviser. *Nomura Real Estate Development Co. Ltd:* Norio Wakabayashi, ex-Chairman and Statutory Auditor. *Nomura Tourist Bureau Inc. (NTB):* Masao Nagasawa, ex-Chairman Nomura Investment Trust and Adviser to NTB Board of Directors. *JAFCO. Nomura International Ltd (Nomura's European operations):* John Howland-Jackson, Senior Executive Adviser; John-Paul Kernot; Andrew Jacobs. *Nomura Thailand:* Kazufumi Ozaki, Chief Representative. *Kokusai Securities:* Shoshi Kawashima, Chairman; Masao Kumon, Executive Managing Director; Shuzo Nagata, President and Managing Director, Kokusai Europe; Hiruharu Matsumoto, Director; anonymous traders and salesmen. *Sanyo Securities:* Yozaburo Tsuchiya, Chairman; Yoichi Tsuchiya, President; Anne Cabot, ex-Senior Marketing Manager; Shigeru Yoshida, Manager, International Department.

Nomura Securities: Tetsuo Okumura, ex-General Manager, Global Trading Department; Shinichi Sakai, Assistant Manager, Trading Department; Nobuo Nakazawa, Director, ex-General Manager, International Department; Mr Kurita, Deputy General Manager, International Department; Katsuhiko Sori, General Manager, Legal Department; Mikio Yamashita, Manager, Legal Department; Dr Hirohisa Saito, General Manager, Corporate Services and Strategy; Michio Katsumata, Deputy General Manager, Public Relations Department; Hiroshi Okamoto, Technical Analysis; Mr Koyama, Salesman; anonymous salesmen, traders and office workers. *International Department:* Yoshio Terasawa, ex-Chairman, NSI; Hisashi Moriya, ex-Director, Vice-Chairman, Merrill Lynch, Tokyo; Akira Shimizu, Executive Managing Director, Nomura Securities Investment Trust, ex-President, NSI; Katsuya Takanashi, President, NSI; Akio Mikuni, ex-International Research, President, Mikuni & Co.; Robin Koskinen, ex-Senior Vice President, NSI US Treasuries; Norm Ohtaka, ex-NSI Trading Manager; Hitoshi Imuta, Senior Vice President, NSI Investment Banking; Keisuke Egashira, ex-President, NSI, Director; John Ferree; Robert Starbuck; Richard Meinick; John Kleinheinz; Paul Smith; Steve Brunner; John Quinn; J. Whitney Halloran. *Daiwa Bank:* Hirashi Ohfuji, Director, International Department; Hiroshi Yamanaka, Archives. *Ministry of Finance:* Rintaro Tamaki, Deputy Director, Securities Company Division. *Scholars on Japan:* Professor Robert Ballon, Sophia University; Brother Richard J. Devine, Sophia University; Dr Yashuo Mishima, Professor of Economic History, Konan University, Kobe. *Journalists (positions held when interviewed):* Cindy Babski, *60 Minutes*, CBS, London; Christopher Chipello, ex-Tokyo Bureau Chief, *Asian Wall Street Journal*; Karl Schoenberger, ex-Tokyo Bureau Chief, *Asian Wall Street Journal*; Kenji Nagano, Yoshifumi Kimura, Katsumi Fujimori, correspondents for the *Nihon Keizai Shimbun*; Marcus Brauchli, *Wall Street Journal*; Doug Tsurouka, AP-Dow Jones, Tokyo; Greg Davis, freelance photographer; Henny Sender, *Institutional Investor*; Haruhito Sakurai, Hakko Publishing; Andrew Tanzar, Tokyo Bureau Chief, *Forbes* magazine; David Lewis, Studio Proteus; Richard Hanson, Publisher, *Tokyo Financial Letter*; Kenji Ino, author.

The other people I would like to thank are, in no particular order: Kim Barber; Louis Cabot; Hidemi Moue; Kouzi Suzuki; Takaaki Yoda of Daiwa Securities; Yasunami Ohtake, Chief Counsel, Tokyo Stock Exchange; Fujio Kodama, ex-Chairman, Wako Securities; Masayoshi Katsuta, President, Kleinwort Benson Investment Management; Stephen Cohen and Peter Johnson; J. Brian Waterhouse, Nayoya Ozawa, John Wilson, Tokumatsu Iida, Graham McDonald, Jessica 'Stardust' Khine, Charles Edmund, Christopher Rampton, David Heron, Nicholas Wilcockson, Kenneth Lucas, Adrian Hope, John Charleton-Jones, Philip Whalley, Hiriko Nakazawa and Shigeru Nakano of James Capel, Tokyo; Perry Gary and Mark Lerner; John Fitzgerald of Merrill Lynch; Kazuyoshi Ishizaka, ex-Bank of Japan, Chairman Trio Kenwood; David Keller; Kevin Murphy; Bruce Holcolm of Lexis; Brian Kelly of Morgan Stanley; Steven Leist; Brian Milton, adventurer, author, journalist; Andy Willner; Iwajiro Noda (RIP), ex-Chairman, Holding Company Liquidation Committee and Chairman Emeritus, Hotel Okura; Kozen Yoshida, Chairman, Economic Analysis Institute; Mitsuo Yoshida, Senior Managing Director, Economic Analysis Institute; Mas Saito, President, Toyo Securities; Mac Nakata, Toyo Securities; Edmund Rothschild; Tatsuhiko Yagashita, Associated Japanese Bank; Martin Gordon.

Index

INDEX

INDEX

INDEX

INDEX

INDEX